VIOLENCE IN CANADA

List of Contributors

Mary Lorenz Dietz
University of Waterloo

Mary Alice Beyer Gammon
Queen's University

Richard J. Gelles
University of Rhode Island

John Hagan
University of Toronto

Martha D. Huggins
University of New Hampshire

Reneé Goldsmith Kasinsky
University of Utah and *Operon Research Associates*

Peter H. Lindsay
Ontario Institute for Studies in Education

Marshall McLuhan
University of Toronto

Maureen McTeer

Robert C. Prus
University of Waterloo

Paul Reed, Teresa Bleszynski and Robert Gaucher
Statistics Canada

Michael D. Smith
York University

Murray A. Straus
University of New Hampshire

J. C. Thatcher
Queen's Printer for Ontario

Sharon Thomas
Lyndhurst Hospital

Peggy Ann Walpole
Street Haven at the Crossroads

Barbara Warme
York University

Dr. James Wilkes
Scarborough General Hospital

VIOLENCE IN CANADA

Mary Alice Beyer Gammon

METHUEN

Toronto New York London Sydney

Copyright © 1978 by Methuen Publications
A division of the Carswell Company Limited

Canadian Cataloguing in Publication Data

Main entry under title:

Violence in Canada

Includes index.
ISBN 0-458-93170-5

1. Violence—Canada—Addresses, essays,
lectures. 1. Gammon, Mary Alice Beyer, 1938-

HN110.Z9V58   301.6′33′0971   C78-001075-2

29,822

Printed and bound in Canada
1 2 3 4 5   81 80 79 78

To Ted and Geoffrey

CONTENTS

ACKNOWLEDGEMENTS

Many good friends and colleagues have contributed substantially during the development of this book. It is impossible to thank them all. A special expression of gratitude is extended to Barbara Warme and Robert Whitehurst, to whom I attribute the strengths of this text and absolve completely of its weaknesses. My thanks as well to my favourite historian, Harold Averill.

To a gentleman equally at home in his demanding business endeavours and as my short order cook, maid, secretary and complaint department during the final stages of this manuscript, to my husband Ted my deepest respect and appreciation.

INTRODUCTION

Basically, there are two ways of approaching a study of violence. One is to limit the study to a specific type of violence. The other approach examines many types of violence from different perspectives. There are many recent efforts at the former. The broader approach, which attempts to bring together some of the research on various types of violence, is rarely attempted.

Universities have been in need of a text on violence for some time, yet only a few specified books, useful in a single course and without Canadian application are available. The problem has perhaps been that while violence is a word we hear every day, it is rarely clearly defined, and the listener quickly learns to associate the word "violence" with the word "bad." While cultural and socioeconomic class differences tell us something about the nature of crime, what is perceived as violence is frequently a matter of interpretation. From this perspective violence is in the eye of the beholder.

This book will identify a number of dimensions of violence providing a taxonomic base for urgently needed research in the field.

Violence in Canada is examined from the following perspectives:

1. Violence as a statistical trend
2. Violence as a qualitative act
3. Violence as a sex-role stereotyped behaviour
4. Violence as originating from many causes
5. Violence as subcultural behaviour
6. Violence as a function of mass media influence

It is widely agreed that one of the major differences between Canada and the United States is that Canadian society evolved relatively peacefully, unlike the American tradition of revolution and civil war. Canadian historian Kenneth McNaught has challenged this point of view in recent years. Canada, according to McNaught, has a history of violence enacted through legitimate institutions, in contrast to a pattern of individual and group violence in the United States. In the past few years, Canadians have demanded a redefinition of the concept of violence, which has until now been clearly based on American criteria.

Contrary to reality, the media portrays violence outside family relationships. In the major cities of Canada, it is still assumed that a man's home is his castle. Witness the importance of this old adage as millions of Canadians crowd every means of transportation available in an impatient rush-hour chaos to get home. The facts stand in sharp contrast to the notion of home as a refuge for family fun, love and understanding: forty percent of Canadian murder suspects are related to the victim by either marriage or blood, and common-law relationships account for a sizeable increase in Canadian murders.

A study of murder can begin by an analysis of Canadian statistics, such as the following report of Statistics Canada. It points out here that murder is actually a rare phenomenon. During the last fourteen years, large numbers of Canadians died of cancer, automobile accidents and suicide. In numerical terms, murder is a minor problem. But by its nature, it is a considerable social problem. The stability of murder rates is surprising. One would have expected that during this period of Canadian history there would be variation in the stresses experienced by different segments of the population. Such is not the case. Murder in Canada over the past fourteen years has risen only from 1.1 to 1.5 victims per 100,000 population.

It is obviously not murder alone which has prompted an upswing in Canadian violence research but, rather, a variety of behaviours viewed as an aberration from the norm. Our contributors have taken a wide range of approaches to the notion of violence in Canadian society. Some of these are largely theoretical, others are descriptive, informative and analytical. Keep in mind that the words "violence" and "deviance" are used interchangeably. This is not to imply that a violent act is always considered to be deviant, for a great deal of violence is construed as normal, acceptable behaviour. However, when violence is defined as a social problem, it is generally researched within the theoretical constructs of the sociology of deviance.

The newcomer to the field of sociology will find useful the following brief discussions utilizing the variety of theoretical approaches either applied or referred to in this text. A wide variety of books exist discussing each approach and what is presented here is only a skeletal introduction to theories which can be applied to violent behaviour.

STRUCTURAL FUNCTIONALISM

This approach originally emanated from the work of an anthropologist known as Radcliffe-Brown. It is concerned with the interrelationships of the elements of a social system. It asks how they are structured and what they do. It assumes that all societies have norms which govern conduct and that although societies differ in the manner in which conduct is controlled, such controls are always related to a hierarchy of dominant values in a society relating to its persistence and change. In other words, there is always an acceptable manner of reaching out for a societal goal. That which meets social goals is "functional" and that which does not is "dysfunctional."

In North America, Parsons and Merton, among others, can be identified with this framework. Its use has been less frequent than formerly in modern sociology; however, it has provided the basis for new theoretical approaches. It is still identified as a major approach by many sociologists.

Merton tells us that in some instances a goal can become far more important than the manner in which that goal is achieved. Soon, the procedure which is most effective becomes the preferred over prescribed conduct and as this process continues, a society becomes unstable and develops what Durkheim refers to as anomie (Merton, 1968).

> Thus, in competitive athletics, when the aim of victory is shorn of its institutional trappings and success becomes construed as "winning the game" rather than "winning under the rules of the game," a premium is implicitly set upon the use of illegitimate but technically efficient means. The star of the opposing football team is surreptitiously slugged; the wrestler incapacitates his opponent through ingenious but illicit techniques; university alumni covertly subsidize "students" whose talents are confined to the athletic field.

We refer the reader here to Chapter 15, where Smith, analyzing the effect on viewers of professional hockey, stresses the overwhelming concern with winning the game.

The functionalist framework has been criticized for emphasizing that which is static and failing to cope with processes of change. While it could predict which areas of the social structure would have high rates of deviant behaviour, it could not account for the fact that some persons within these areas engaged in deviant behaviour, yet others did not. Systems theory, an offshoot of the traditional, functionalist approach, incorporates a measure of change into the functionalist framework.

SUBCULTURAL THEORIES

A variety of subcultural theories exist, all of which can be said to be cultural transmission theories, which means that deviant or violent behaviour is taken on in the same way as is nondeviant and nonviolent behaviour. It is in interactions with others that such behaviours are learned.

Like functionalist theory, subcultural theories maintained the affinity between poverty and pathology. Unlike functionalist theory, violent behaviour was not viewed as a means to an end, as a way of acquiring something valued by society. The violent subculture assumes the existence of a group smaller than a total society which emulates values different from that of the dominant culture. Specific ethnic groups, social classes and youthful gangs entertain different attitudes toward the use of violence. While functionalist theory failed to explain why some people within the same area of the social structure committed deviant acts yet others did not, Sutherland explained this on the basis that deviance is learned (Sutherland and Cressey, 1970). His theory of

"differential association" suggested the element of choice for the individual. One becomes a deviant because of "an excess of definitions
favourable to violation of the law" (Merton and Nisbet, 1971). How
effective the learning experience is depends on its relevance to the kind
of self one chooses to maintain. One limitation of Sutherland's theory is
that it does not take into consideration that what one learns is not
entirely deviant. Individuals move between deviant and conventional
realms (Matza, 1969).

Cohen, as well, undertook an explanation of violent behaviour within
a theory of cultural transmission and arrived at his theory of a delinquent subculture. Cohen's delinquents are boys in a situation of anomie
who have come together and formed a subculture which rejects middle-
class values. By way of demonstration, Cohen explains the existence of a
subculture within a culture. As children, we learned to play jacks and
marbles. As adults, we have already forgotten the rules of the game. Yet
our children, whom we have not taught the roles, belong to a subculture
of children and have learned within that subculture. What becomes
valued are the norms of the gang, which may or may not run counter to
societal norms.

It appears that functionalists laid the foundation for subcultural
theories. The notion that social pathology existed within certain
geographical pockets persisted and became somewhat modified. Dietz,
Chapter 1, presents subcultural theory tempered by the dynamics of
symbolic interactionism which we will shortly discuss. Wolfgang and
Ferracuti's notion of the subculture of violence is the basis of this work
(Wolfgang and Ferracuti, 1967). Dietz demonstrates that an act of
violence grows out of an interaction between actors which comes to be
defined as a situation requiring a violent response.

SYMBOLIC INTERACTIONISM

It is commonly agreed that the father of the symbolic interactionist
perspective is George Herbert Mead. Advocates of this approach reject
theories of violent behaviour based on biological determinism. Human
beings are not born with a self. The self is acquired through interaction
with others (Gordon and Gergen, 1968). Interaction is a mode of
communication which is uniquely human and is symbolic in nature.
Language, for example, is one mode of symbolic communication. When
one speaks of a dog, we all immediately possess a similar mental image
which we are able to share in discussion without the presence of an
actual dog. Such symbolic communication is not possessed by other
beings. Symbolism is not confined solely to language. It may take the
form of a gesture or a facial expression. Symbols are vehicles which
make it possible for us to influence others and in turn to be influenced

by others. The unit of analysis for the symbolic interactionist is the attri-bution of meaning to behaviours as well as objects. As a child grows, he learns through interaction with others and develops a sense of self-iden-tity. Part of this developmental process is the evolution of the individual who has learned to reflect on his own behaviour. Taking this one step further, the socialized self is the individual who is able to reflect upon what the reaction of an audience would be to his behaviour, if, in fact, he performed such behaviour. In more concrete terms, if one were to contemplate the assault of another person, he would be capable at the same moment of interpreting the reaction of that person to the blow, not only the physical reaction, but the feeling of that person toward him. In Chapter 3 it is stressed that while persons agree that it is wrong to kill another, they learn that under certain conditions, one has that right.

An underlying principle should now be evident to the reader. There is a notion that there is some agreement among people as to the meaning of acts, and this very point is objectionable to critics of the symbolic interactionist approach (Wilson, 1970). To the phenomenologist the meaning of an act is totally subjective and individual. No two assaults by the same person would have the same meaning for that person. Thus the symbolic interactionist approach objectifies a presumed shared view of a social order of rules, norms and meanings. At the other extreme, the symbolic interactionist approach is concerned as well with one-to-one behaviour and has neglected the relationship of individuals within the context of a larger institutional framework (Ishwarin, 1976). Symbolic interactionist theory, however, may be seen as bearing on conflict theory and violence insofar as we know that shared meanings between intimates is variable, problematic and potentially conflictual. Thus, when people "share" meanings, these are subject to influence, power, personal vested interests and in other ways can be seen as generating violence and conflict. Our standard assumption in this culture that *communication* helps solve problems is often off the mark. Communica-tions can also be seen as causing problems due to a range of difficulties in value discrepancies, as well as inability to communicate adequately.

BIOLOGICAL THEORIES

Early in the history of sociology, violence was defined as a quality inher-ent in an individual. "Scientific" study of "the born criminal" was begun in 1876 by the Italian army doctor Cesare Lombroso. Influenced by the "still controversial Darwinian theory of evolution and its corol-lary, that contemporary man had antecedents in various forms of primi-tive man" (Clinard, 1974), Lombroso studied the anatomy of criminals and concluded that criminals could be characterized by specific atavistic physical features, such as a long lower jaw, a flattened nose, and a sparse beard. Lindsay and Walpole in Chapter 2 note that despite the fact that Lombroso's findings were largely discredited, such research shifted study of the criminal from a legal to a scientific study of criminal behaviour. In 1877 Richard Dugdale (Dugdale, 1877) wrote the first of many books to follow detailing family histories of degeneracy in an attempt to relate violence to biological phenomena. It is stated: "All these theories have been unconvincing to sociologists and biologists alike" (Cohen and Short, 1971); but as we shall see, such theorizing continued.

Bernard Glueck in 1916 tells us that the results of his research of 608 prison inmates in New York confirm that "it is now universally recognized that the pauper, the prostitute, and the criminal classes are primarily the product of mental defect and degeneracy and as such must come within the purview of mental medicine" (Glueck, 1916).

A German psychiatrist by the name of Kretschmer proposed a body-type theory in relation to mental illness. An outgrowth of Kretschmer's work and one which became more widely used was that of Sheldon in 1942, known as somatotype theory. According to Sheldon's classification three basic body types could be identified with corresponding personality types: endomorphy, a tendency toward roundness and softness, mesomorphy, a predominance of muscle and bone, and ectomorphy, fragility and linearity in body build. The temperament of the mesomorph was likely to lead him, more so than other types, to violent behaviour.

Toward the mid-1900s biological theories of violent behaviour reverted to the basically violent nature of mankind in relation to those social controls which would prohibit such behaviour. To name a few, Montagu, Lorenz and Ardrey (Montagu, 1968, Lorenz, 1969, Ardrey, 1961) attribute violence to man's natural, inherited animal instinct, referred to by Montagu as "inner depravity." Reaction to such theorizing is related to the implications of accepting this thesis. To explain man's aggression in these terms is to relieve him of the responsibility for his own aggression, and to justify and "sometimes encourage" violent behaviour (Chan, 1977). Yet the Canadian media still engages in this justification:

> The chimpanzee has a very human heart.
> There's love in it, affection—and a bent for murder too.
> *The Globe and Mail,* September 24, 1977

In 1969 American educator Arthur Jenson brought back an old theory, i.e., I.Q. is largely inherited and is related to social class. Since blacks have a lower I.Q. than whites and since blacks have a higher reproduction rate, he postulated that the number of Americans with low I.Q.'s would mushroom, widening the gap between the blacks and the whites (Ritzer, 1974).

The front page of the *New York Times* recently reviewed *Sociobiology*, the latest synthesis of animal and human behaviour, and subsequent discussions of this monograph were received with extremes of reaction (Blute, 1976). Wilson concludes: "If we wish to reduce our own aggressive behaviour . . . we should design our population densities and social systems in such a way as to make aggression inappropriate in most conceivable daily circumstances" (Wilson, 1975). Sokol, discussing the activity of rats in close quarters, as did Wilson, applied such theorizing to humans in suggesting that it would be reasonable to assume that the abuse of children would occur in homes where parents and children live in close quarters (Sokol, 1976).

Biological theories, however unreasonable one might consider them to be, still persist and according to Pierre Van den Berghe, "Books like Wilson's will make further resistance to biological concepts not only difficult but patently silly" (Van den Berghe, 1976). Obviously, very few sociologists share this view.

LABELLING THEORY

The conceptual framework underlying this approach is that of Howard Becker and is as recent a perspective as the 1960s. While Becker is known as a labelling theorist, he regrets that his work has been called labelling theory and for that matter, never intended that his research be considered theory. In the future, says Becker, he will refer to his work as an interactionist theory of deviance (Becker, 1966). Becker's central position is that deviance is created by society. Deviance in the Durkheimian sense implied an infraction of an agreed-upon rule. Thus those who have broken a rule, in that they have committed the same deviant act, constitute a homogeneous category. From Becker's point of view, however, deviance has nothing to do with the quality of an act. It is the result of others applying rules and sanctions to particular people and labelling them as outsiders. If deviants did constitute a homogeneous group, all deviants would have broken a rule and this is not the case. Similarly, if the category were homogeneous one could expect to find common factors among the deviants and thereby include all cases which rightfully belong in the category. A behaviour may be considered an infraction of a rule at one time, yet not at another time, an infraction of a rule when committed by one person, but not when committed by another. Since the category "deviance" is neither sufficient nor exhaustive of what is considered to be the rule-breaking population, it can hardly account for the supposed deviance. What deviants have in common is the label and the experience of being labelled. How other people respond to an act determines whether it is considered deviant or not. Crucial to Becker's argument is the point that the response of other people is regarded as problematic.

One can readily notice the shift from Durkheim's position emphasizing society to the much more subjective perspective of Becker, which emphasizes the viewpoint of the individual. Labelling theory asks the question—what is the process by which one comes to be known as deviant? It is crucial to Becker's argument to remember that the deviant act is external to the actor, since it is considered deviant only when so labelled.

In many instances, deviance becomes a master status. That is, people are considered first in terms of their deviance, particularly when the stigma is difficult to conceal, such as colour or when the issue is sensitive, such as homosexuality. The powerless in particular are the least likely to avoid or resist negative labelling.

Some of the major differences between functionalism and labelling theory are in need of further clarification, namely, the issue of rules. Durkheim would have us believe that rules exist at the societal level, that rules are independent of individual action, and that breaking these rules constitutes deviance. Labelling theorists insist that deviance can only arise in interaction, since a change in interaction can produce a change in behaviour. Labelling theorists pay attention to the role of the nondeviant as well as the role of the deviant. Functionalists have frequently made use of official statistics, which use is more than problematical to the labelling theorist. Statistics reflect such inaccuracies as to yield them useless, given this conception of deviance.

THE PHENOMENOLOGICAL PERSPECTIVE

Phenomenology, in the broadest sense of the word, embraces the works of ethnomethodologists and those in the field of what is known as the Sociology of Knowledge.

In our discussion of functionalism and of labelling theory, we spoke in terms of cause and effect. Of functionalism, for example, we spoke of the relationship between aberrant behaviour and society. Of labelling theory, we pointed out that what is examined is the effect of society on the production of aberrant behaviours. The flow of causality is juxtaposed in the two instances, as demonstrated below.

Functionalist Theory	Aberrant behaviour ⟶ Effect on Society
Labelling Theory	Effect of Society ⟶ Production of Aberrant Behaviour

Phenomenologists, it should be noted, reject the entire notion of causality. Functionalism and labelling theory embrace deductive logic. Phenomenology utilizes inductive logic. Deduction is "the logical process of drawing specific conclusions from general propositions or observations." Induction is "the logical process of moving to general principles or conclusions from specific observations" (Douglas, 1973). Like labelling theorists, phenomenologists contend that the categories into which official statistics are placed are merely socially-created categories. These categories reflect the commonsense meaning which specialists under pressure create so as to make a "standardized, meaningful whole of phenomena" (Douglas, 1973).

One of the problems that the newcomer to the realm of phenomenology must contend with is the use of a particular vocabulary which is not consistent with that found in the *Concise Oxford Dictionary*. A knowledge of such terms and their meanings is crucial to understanding the manner in which phenomenologists view their world. The word "indexicality" is one such term. Garfinkel (Garfinkel, 1967) adopted the term from Bar Hillel (Bar Hillel, 1954). According to Bar Hillel, an indexical expression depends for its meaning on the context in which it is produced. An indexical particular includes nonlinguistic expressions as well, such as behaviours which are dependent for meaning upon the context in which they are produced. Thus, an explanation of suicide, for example, must take into consideration the meaning of the act for the person, and the context in which he finds himself. Of concern to the phenomenologist is the manner in which people organize their activities to produce rational accounts of aberrant behaviour. As Kasinsky tells us in Chapter 9, a rape trial is merely the "official version" of a rape incident. Activities are necessarily indexical and "reflexive," which brings us to a second word which cannot be overlooked. For the phenomenologist, all activities are reflexive, which means that all behaviour is accounted for or reproduced by a process of introspection, of thought directed back upon itself. And thought directed back can only be an "account" of action and nothing more.

Virtually no theoretical approach goes without criticism or overlap with other points of view. You will notice that some authors in this text have combined several theoretical approaches. Quite intentionally a few chapters have not presented explicit theoretical viewpoints. Currently, linkages between theory and violence in our society are weak, and we must work from a theoretical base which is not always clear.

The variety of empirical and conceptual works herein should supply the reader with a broad range of intellectual application.

REFERENCES

Ardrey, Robert
    1961   *African Genesis*. New York: Dell Publishing Co.
Bar-Hillel, Yehoshua
    1954   "Indexical Expressions," *Mind*. pp. 359-379.
Becker, Howard
    1966   *Outsiders: Studies in the Sociology of Deviance*. Toronto: Free Press.

Blute, Marion
1976   Review Symposia, *Contemporary Sociology*. Vol. 5, No. 6, Nov. on Wilson, Edward O., *Sociobiology: The New Synthesis*. Cambridge: Belknap Press of Harvard University.
Chan, Kowk Bun
1977   "Intra Familial Violence: Myth-Making Versus Theory Building." Paper presented at the Canadian Sociology and Anthropology Association meetings, Fredericton, New Brunswick, June.
Clinard, Marshall B.
1974   *Sociology of Deviant Behaviour*. Fourth Edition. New York: Holt, Rinehart and Winston.
Cohen, Albert K. and James F. Short, Jr.
1971   "Crime and Juvenile Delinquency," in *Contemporary Social Problems*. Third Edition. New York: Harcourt Brace Jovanovich, Inc.

———
1955   *Delinquent Boys*. New York: The Free Press.
Douglas, Jack D.
1973   *The Social Meanings of Suicide*. Princeton: Princeton University Press.
Dugdale, Richard
1877   *The Jukes, A Study in Crime, Pauperism, Disease and Heredity*. New York: Putnam.
Garfinkel, Harold
1967   *Studies in Ethnomethodology*. Englewood Cliffs, New Jersey: Prentice-Hall, Inc.
Glueck, Bernard
1916   *Studies in Forensic Psychiatry*. Boston: Little Brown.
Gordon, Chad and Kenneth J. Gergen (Eds.)
1968   *The Self in Social Interaction*. New York: John Wiley & Sons, Inc.
Ishwarin, K.
1976   *The Canadian Family*. Toronto: Holt, Rinehart and Winston.
Lorenz, Konrad
1969   *On Aggression*. Translated by Marjorie Kerr Wilson. New York: Bantam Books.
Matza, David
1969   *Becoming Deviant*. Englewood Cliffs, New Jersey: Prentice-Hall.
Merton, Robert K. and Robert Nisbet
1971   *Contemporary Social Problems*. Third Edition. New York: Harcourt Brace Jovanovich.

———
1968   *Social Theory and Social Structure*. New York: The Free Press.
Montagu, Ashley
1968   *Man and Aggression*. New York: Oxford University Press.
Ritzer, George (Ed.)
1974   *Issues, Debates and Controversies: An Introduction to Sociology*. Boston: Allyn and Bacon, Inc.
Sokol, Robert
1976   "Some Factors Associated with Child Abuse Potential." Paper presented at the American Sociological Association Meetings, New York.
Sutherland, Edwin and Donald R. Cressey
1970   *Criminology*. 8th ed. Philadelphia: J. B. Lippincott Co.
Van den Berghe, Pierre
1976   "Review Symposia," *Contemporary Sociology*. Vol. 5, No. 7.
Wilson, Thomas P.
1975   "Normative and Interpretive Paradigms in Sociology." *Understanding Everyday Life*, Jack D. Douglas, Ed., Aldine Publishing Company.
Wolfgang, Marvin E. and Franco Ferracuti
1967   *The Subculture of Violence*. New York: Tavistock.

PART ONE

IN THE BEGINNING THERE WAS MAN: A THEORETICAL OVERVIEW OF THE ORIGINS OF VIOLENCE

Chapter 1

THE VIOLENT SUBCULTURE:
THE GENESIS OF VIOLENCE

Mary Lorenz Dietz

In the general introduction we discussed briefly the theoretical assumptions of subcultural theory. In this chapter Dietz applies this perspective to a specific geographic area widely considered to be a violent and potentially difficult location in which to conduct research. Her presentation of data is descriptive in nature. This particular type of research presupposes considerable knowledge of the problem to be investigated. Unlike explanatory subcultural studies, descriptive research establishes a relationship between variables but does not offer the "why." In other words, it makes no causal inferences. Unstructured observational data of this nature is necessarily beset with some problems. For example, (1) those observations recorded may not be representative of the broader population, and (2) extra precautions must be taken to minimize bias and maximize reliability.

Unobtrusive measures have been employed by Dietz in order to illuminate rich data, available only when the observed are unaware that they are subjects of research. The possibility of the researcher influencing the responses of the respondent is removed.

Dietz's research probes deeply into the issues behind a culture in which violence is not only accepted, but condoned. Violent conduct is determined to be both rational and controllable, a notion which Prus pursues further in Chapter 3.

INTRODUCTION

Interpersonal violence is a form of conduct that occurs frequently among certain groups in our society. This conduct, sometimes culminating in felonious assault or murder, involves a complex process of selection and training as well as special situational factors. Most of the studies concerned with interpersonal violence have regarded those who engage in it as mentally unbalanced, criminally deviant or both (Hartung, 1965). They conceive of a violent act as impulsive and uncontrollable and often as symptomatic of some underlying psychic maladjustment (Berkowitz,

* This work is a revision of a section of the author's unpublished doctoral dissertation entitled Violence and Control: A Study of Some Aspects of Violence and Control in the Violent Subculture, Wayne State University, Detroit, 1968.

1962). From this viewpoint violence can only be regarded as unpredictable and uncontrollable, which in turn makes necessary such procedures as psychotherapeutic intervention and treatment and/or institutionalization for those who have demonstrated such violent capacities.

Sociologists have maintained that interpersonal conduct, lawful and unlawful, is learned through a process of association, identification and interaction. They contend that criminal conduct is learned in the same manner as other forms of human conduct, through symbolic interaction and principally in small, intimate groups. Further, motivations must be learned for this conduct and a self-concept developed that allows the individual to engage in the conduct without damage to his self-esteem (Hartung, 1953). Human conduct cannot be studied in isolation from the symbolic environment in which it occurs. Violence will be dealt with here as learned conduct, occurring in a symbolic environment, taking into account the self and others, and resulting from a conscious and deliberate evaluation of the situation and a decision to act.

Wolfgang and Ferracuti have stated that "overt use of force or violence either in interpersonal relationships or in group interaction is generally viewed as a reflection of basic values that stand apart from the dominant, the central, or the parent culture." They hypothesize that the overt (and often illicit) expression of violence is part of a subcultural normative system (1967, p. 158). Implicit in this theoretical approach is the conceptualization of violence as a conduct pattern and not as a manifestation of pathology. The overall disapproval of the use of violence in interpersonal interactions in the dominant culture has resulted in viewing violations of nonviolent norms as irrational conduct. Violence is not approved in interpersonal conduct in the middle-class culture. Even as self-defense the norms relating to the use of physical force provide only for self-protection and control of the other and not for revenge or punishment by individuals. Nor is violence approved when used by or toward women or children or the aged or handicapped. Violence is generally approved in North American culture only when used by specifically designated functionaries and only as a protective measure. There is limited approval of violence by social control agents as a means of controlling lawbreakers, but even in this situation it is designated as a method of last resort. This is not necessarily the attitude of the enforcement agents themselves, but is recognized by them as that of the larger culture. Since violent conduct is not approved in the basic cultural norms, when it does occur some explanation must be sought. Early explanations of violent behavior tended to center on possession by the devil or inherent human evil, but these have been replaced now by the concept of mental illness. A mental health organization recently repeatedly announced on television that "temper explosions" or irritability and violent outbursts should be sympathized with as they were signs of emotional problems. When violence occurs as identifiable group behavior, the group itself may be labeled sociopathic or atavistic (Thompson, 1966:78). Thus the explanation for violence generally held by members of the middle class has changed radically: interpersonal violence is now perceived to be psychiatrically pathological, rather than as morally or theologically pathological.

In a theory that conceives of violent conduct as essentially acceptable, approved behavior within a violent subculture, it becomes important to examine the conditions in which violence is required. We need to learn when a violent response is preferred, when it is tolerated and if there are situations under which it is not acceptable, even in a violent subculture. If the structural components can be delineated, including the general normative limitations, it will then be possible to determine what personal and situational conditions lead to the decision to use nonviolent alternatives or to control violence once it has been initiated.

Wolfgang and Ferracuti have raised the question of situationally produced violence:

> Some ideas, attitudes, means, goals or conduct may be situationally induced, not simply normatively induced. If the situation changes, in these circumstances presumably values and behavior change, thus indicating no real and enduring normative allegiance. This is not an entirely satisfactory distinction. If it were, the issue would then be how permanent the situation has been or might be or, particularly, whether attitude or behavior is unsituational, i.e., whether there is only a single situation that induces a typically common response. The statistical rather than the subculture norm is more likely to be used in analysis of behavioral response to a specific situation. For a response to be normatively induced, it seems that we must resort to such a phrase as "style of life" in order to indicate the pervasiveness involved in the normative character of action. But again, what this means quantitatively and empirically is that the action at least must be multisituational. If we were to use permanence of a social response as a criterion of normativeness, any modification of the norm would require our classifying it ex post facto as situational. But if values change when situations change, it is also likely that situations change when values change, or that varied adherence to the values causes a differential choice of situations on the part of the individual.
>
> We are suggesting, then, that a given conduct norm or set of values must function to govern the conduct in a variety of situations in order to classify that norm or value-set as a (sub)culturally expected or required response and not merely a statistical modal reaction (1967:105).

The cultural variations that overlap and support the violent subculture can be divided into three general categories. These are: social class based values and conditions conducive to violence; conduct norms specific to the violent subculture; and variations in degree of experience and commitment to norms by groups in the violent subculture context. These areas will be treated separately, although they are observed more as a process of selection moving from a general condition that is favorable to the development of violent conduct patterns, to specific training in violent conduct, and finally to the groups committed to violence as a preferred means of interpersonal conduct.

CLASS-BASED VALUES AND CONDITIONS
CONDUCIVE TO VIOLENCE

Much research has been conducted in the past few years on the life styles of the lower classes under the several headings of poverty and cultural deprivation. Some of the more salient features that seem to be related to the development of violent subcultures within these groups are a unique cognitive and linguistic style; age-graded single-sex peer groups; a cyclical pattern of seeking action or excitement; physical or motor-oriented styles of action; and specific differences in child rearing techniques (Reissman, Cohen, and Pearl, 1964).

Cognitive Style

The aspects of the cognitive style that seem to be common and most important to violence are:
Physical and visual rather than aural
Content-centered rather than form-centered
Externally oriented rather than introspective
Problem-centered rather than abstract-centered
Inductive rather than deductive
Spatial rather than temporal
Games and action versus test-oriented
Expressive rather than instrumental oriented
One-track thinking and unorthodox learning rather than other-directed, flexibility
Words used in relation to action rather than word-bound orientation (inventive word power and "hip" language)
(Reissman *et al.*, 1964; 116)

Nettler (1975:231-32) discusses the effect of perceptual/cognitive style on predisposition toward criminality. He uses a dichotomy of "expanders" and "reducers" developed by Petrie (1967) and quotes a number of studies supporting the relationship of the "reducer" style to excitement seeking and insensitivity to pain which he considers criminogenie.

The particular importance of this style for our purposes is that it leads to certain approaches to life situations and interpersonal relationships that are conducive to violence.

First, these elements lead to a pattern of direct confrontation on the basis of overt conduct and verbal response rather than indirection and analysis of underlying motives (Gough:1947). There is a tendency to behave as if an act or statement has had the same underlying motives for everyone as it has had for the actor making the evaluation. The fact that there is little consideration of motives limits the awareness of casual relationships, as well as developing a lack of concern with the other's feelings or emotions. Situations are often approached in terms of effect rather than cause. A simple example of this can be seen in the response of many lower-class parents to the breaking of a window. The parent usually responds to the fact that the window has been broken and is rarely concerned with *why* it was broken. If the parent sees children playing or any of their equipment near, he will probably confront the most likely culprit, not in terms of "if she broke it, why?" or "was it an accident?" but simply to make sure that the real culprit will be punished. If there is evidence, however, the investigation usually ends at that point and the presumed guilty child is often swooped down on without warning. Since this is a common response, whether to a child or an adult, it leads to a pattern of immediate and overt causal sequence, and a tendency to be unaware of motive except as it is projected. Lower-class people are likely to relate to others not in terms of seeking to understand the conduct of others relative to the other's own particular personalities or circumstances, but rather in terms of the actors' own personality, conduct, motives or circumstances. "The restriction on the use of adjectives, uncommon adjectives, uncommon adverbs, the simplicity of the verbal form, and the low proportion of subordinations supports the thesis that the working class subjects . . . do not explicate intent verbally" (Bernstein, 1962:234).

Age-Graded Single-Sex Peer Groups

A second important related class condition is the age-graded, single-sex peer group which is the focal point of many youth and activities. This pattern is rarely disrupted to any great extent even by marriage and family relationships. This is particularly significant in terms of the situational control aspects of violent encounters as well as the likely significance others present at violent encounters. Same age, same sex peers are likely to be present during violent encounters and also likely to influence conduct. Male streetcorner life in the lower classes has been well documented and demonstrates the constant presence and importance of the peer group. This is of even greater consequence in the violent subculture where the group represents not only social activity but also safety and protection. Many social workers and counselors have been dismayed to find that the youth they are working with bring friends with them to probation sessions, job interviews, and other (in the worker's opinion) inappropriate situations. It is almost as if they are unable to cope with these situations alone. Thompson said of the Hell's Angels, "There is something pathetic about a bunch of men gathering every night in the same bar, taking themselves very seriously in their ratty uniforms, with nothing to look forward to but a chance of a fight or a round of head jobs with some drunken charwoman" (1966:119).

Cyclical Pattern of Seeking Action or Excitement

Many social class studies deal with the phenomena of action or the seeking of excitement as a part of the working/lower-class life style. Gans emphasizes this as a difference between the working and the lower classes, although it seems to be more of a variation than a difference (Gans, 1964). A regular payday and the weekend off structures the time for excitement seeking in the working class, thus following a more regular pattern, with shorter periods between, and shorter periods of excitement seeking. The sporadically employed or the unemployed worker usually waits for a monthly check (someone's) or works for several weeks or months and then lays off so that his/her periods of inaction are longer, as are his/her periods of action. A further difference between the steadily employed blue-collar worker and the sporadically or unemployed worker is the necessity of getting up in the morning and the possibility of physical fatigue if he/she is working at a job that requires much physical exertion. This is particularly noticeable in the pattern of the working-class male who ends his career in delinquency and his commitment to violence, or drastically limits them in his early twenties. The unemployed male or the one who works part-time or irregularly has a chance to rest for subsequent periods of action, but a one- or two-day drunk on the weekend is usually enough for the older or more steady worker.

Child-Rearing Techniques, Bodily Contact and the Introduction to Violence

The final class-based pattern deals with the number and kind of experiences with physical contact which may be partially related to the more motor-based responses common in the lower classes. The use of physical punishment is one of the experiences which may have important consequences in providing a climate for violence (Kohn, 1964; Goode, 1971).

First, lower-class child disciplining teaches the child to evaluate an act in terms of the likelihood of being caught and punished. Middle-class parents usually punish by withdrawing privileges or scolding, or imposing some kind of activity for a specific time period (very much like society's punishment of criminals). They also remind the child that the punishment was brought on by his/her own actions. The middle-class parent relates punishment to feelings and relationships that tend to produce guilt, which is a very effective method for the control of conduct. This difference in training procedures causes the middle-class child to calculate whether or not an act will be worthwhile in terms of conscience, effect on others and potential punishment. The lower-class child, in contrast, learns more commonly to evaluate the act in relation to the probability of being caught and punished (Straus, 1971).

A second consideration is the tendency of middle-class people to associate physical violence with hatred, loss of love or both. They usually are afraid of violence because they have had little direct experience with it, and have no scale by which to judge how physically harmful various acts may be. Many lower-class children are not spanked in a calm and deliberate manner, but instead are hit with hands, objects and fists, kicked, jerked off their feet, and thrown across the room. Since this kind of punishment is imposed on the spur of the moment and often when the parent is angry, many of these acts are accompanied by yelling and swearing. Lower-class children are often exposed to loud quarrels between others that have no visible results, and which may be forgotten in a short time without any effect on the interpersonal relationships of the persons quarreling. This difference is important because the familiarity with violent physical contact diminishes the unknown aspect for lower-class children and allows them to perceive violence as a part of normal interactions. The controlled behavior of most middle-class parents results in their children believing that raised voices and violence are not only unusual, but also that when they do occur, are an indication of a serious breakdown in the relationship of the persons involved.

Third, and perhaps most important, is that physical punishment helps to teach a disregard for the sanctity of the person. This is not to say that physical punishment is not used by middle-class parents, but the way in which it is used, the frequency and duration are different. The stress on privacy and the great care accorded the body in the middle classes hardly exists among the lower classes. This difference exists from the very earliest weeks of the child's life. It is partly due to the difference in physical environment created by financial conditions and partly due to the fact that the middle-class household tends to be child-centered and more concerned with the child's comfort and development. A major consequence of physical punishment and how it is perceived can be observed in variations in subcultural response to pain. If a middle-class child is hurt or ill he is likely to be regarded with concern and sympathy. In contrast, lower-class children may be rewarded with approval when they do not complain or cry, and often irritate the parent when they do complain. Children in the lower class receive care and concern but are rarely catered to when ill. The lower-class parent tends to allow the child to fall or bump his/her head rather than trying to prevent it. When the child is picked up after falling there is rarely evidence of panic or overt concern on the part of the parent unless the injury is severe. The parent often laughs at the child's struggles. The same treatment is given for whining and crying. Even when the child is being punished she/he is expected not to cry or make a great show of emotion. The child learns very early to swallow his/her tears or other outburst when she/he hears the common phrase, "You'd better shut up or I'll really give you something to cry about."

THE VIOLENT SUBCULTURE

The child in the working or lower classes is thus prepared for violence. The subculture of violence is created by approval, encouragement and expectations relative to the use of violence toward others as both instrumental and defensive conduct between peers and beyond childhood. Although violent punishment of the child is more common to the lower, and to some extent the working classes, norms and conduct that deal with the use of violence toward others, in equal as well as subordinate positions, are the ones that create the violent subculture. Both boys and girls in the lower classes are expected to fight for their siblings or property. In later childhood and preadolesence girls withdraw from physical violence. The age at which the influence increases for the girl to cease fighting varies by class and race. The white working-class girl is the first and the lower-class low status nonwhite girl is usually the last to stop fighting. In fact, the rate of interpersonal violence for the lower-class nonwhite woman continues for a longer time and at a higher rate (Beattie and Kenny, 1966; Wolfgang, 1967; Silverman and Teevan, 1975). The education of the girl in violence, however, is never emphasized as it is with the boy. Her failure to fight is usually accepted with tolerance, as are her tears and overt responses to pain. Boys and girls are fairly evenly matched physically until adolescence; in fact many girls have a slight edge in size and agility. Even in our society, however, where girls participate in athletics and are encouraged to be somewhat competitive in preadolescent years, boys still have more freedom and are more likely to engage in hard, physical, muscle-building types of activities. The real education in violence, however, occurs for boys in a violent subculture in the beginning school days. The earlier a boy achieves the freedom of the streets and thus can roam beyond the immediate home area, the earlier he begins to participate in the peer culture.

The following examples illustrate some variations in support of education in violence theory in the home.

Working-class family in a changing neighborhood

Eight-year-old Paul came home from school one day without his hat. When his mother questioned him he said that it had been taken from his locker. She said, "Have you seen any boys with hats like yours?" He replied that he hadn't. She told him, "Now tomorrow when you get to school you look for the boy who is wearing your hat and when you find him you get your hat back." "But what if he won't give it to me?" "Then you'll have to take it from him." "But you told me never to start a fight and what if he's bigger than me?" "Nobody in the school is that much bigger than you. Anyhow some of those kids don't know any better than to take someone else's things and if you don't let them know right away that they can't mess with your stuff, you won't be able to keep anything. Just don't come home tomorrow without that hat."

The following day when Paul returned from school he was wearing his hat. "Who had your hat?" said his mother. He told her the boy's name and then went on to say that when he saw the hat he had gone over and taken it off the boy's head. He said the boy chased him and when he caught up with him he had turned and punched the boy as hard as he could, saying, "this is *my* hat." Paul said after he had been punched the boy no longer wanted to fight. His mother nodded in approval, saying "That's the boy! They'll think twice before they take anything from you again."

A lower-working class marginal family
The father of a six-year-old boy called his sister one afternoon and asked her to come over and bring her nine-year-old son. When she arrived he explained that his son had been outside playing with one of his toys with a child from the next block. The boy wanted to take the toy home and they began to fight; just then the neighbor child's older brother came along and took the toy and went home. He said that his son had tried to fight with the older boy but he just wasn't big enough. He said he would go down there himself but he didn't know what to do if the child wouldn't give him the toy and he didn't want to get mad and end up with both families fighting. He then turned to his son and said, "Joey, you go and get your truck from that kid now. Jim will go with you to take care of his brother. You don't have to start right in fighting; just tell him you want your truck and if he don't give it to you kick him in the balls." The two boys marched down the street with about equally divided feelings of fear and excitement. They returned with the truck in short order, feeling very proud and brave, and sure that the sight of the two of them had scared the fight right out of the brothers. The father, much relieved that he did not have to cope with the situation himself, praised both boys and told everyone nearby greatly exaggerated stories of their courage.

Maria Campbell—*Halfbreed*[1]
School wasn't too bad—Heaven compared to the Residential School. We had a lot of fights with the white kids, but finally, after beating them soundly, we were left alone. There were many remarks made but we learned to ignore or accept them as time went on (1973:46).

Cheechum was sitting on her pallet listening through all this and when Dad said nothing, she got up and led me outside. She didn't speak for the longest time, just walked. When we were about half a mile from the house she told me to get her a long willow stick and bring it to her. Then she told me to sit beside her and listen. Many years ago, she said, when she was only a little girl, the Halfbreeds came west. They left good homes behind in their search for a place where they could live as they wished. Later a leader arose from these people who said that if they worked hard and fought for what they believed in they would win against all odds. Despite the hardships, they gave all they had for this one desperate chance of being free, but because some of them said, "I want good clothes and horses and you no-good Halfbreeds are ruining it for me," they lost their dream. She continued: "They fought each other just as you are fighting your mother and father today. The white man saw that that was a more powerful weapon than anything else with which to beat the Halfbreeds, and he used it and still does today. Already they are using it on you. They try to make you hate your people." She stood up then and said, "I will beat you each time I hear you talk as you did. If you don't like what you have, then stop fighting your parents and do something about it yourself." With that, she beat me until my legs and arms were swollen with welts. After she was finished she sat with me till I had stopped crying, and then we walked home. Nothing more was ever said about clothes or food. My first real lesson had been learnt. I always tried to keep my head up and defend my friends and cousins in front of those white kids, even when I knew we were wrong (1973:47).

The violent subculture provides a continuing socialization in the norms governing violence. This socialization begins and is reinforced in the home and is continued and refined in the street.

Common Uses for Violence Approved in the Violent Subculture

Punishment. Usually violence as punishment is reserved for members of the family, subordinates, or occasionally for others when a strongly sanctioned value has been violated. Punishment is not only reserved for children but may extend to any affiliated females in the violent subculture or to persons of either sex who violate important parts of the code of their clique.

The following examples illustrate the belief and acceptance of physical punishment of adults. Husbands and wives can be heard commenting that some friend or relative might manage his wife or girlfriend more effectively if he gave her a good beating.

Jackson Toby—"Violence and the Masculine Ideal"

Dr. Toby: . . . Since he couldn't work with a hurt arm, he lost his job. He and his wife had to live in the car. It was very rough. He finally left the state, came to New Jersey, got into trouble here, and was put in jail. While he was gone, his wife shacked up with another guy. When he learned about this he was furious. He wanted to kill this other guy.

James: Why the other guy?

Dr. Toby: What would *you* have done?

James: Cut her face, cut her all open. Slashed her face.

Dr. Toby: That's interesting that you say that. Do you think she did something so bad?

James: In my opinion?

Dr. Toby: Yes.

James: Because, because if she's a good girl, she stays with you no matter what. I don't say she should wait if you get locked up for fifteen years or twenty years. But if you're only doing a year bit or a two-year bit, it's like going in the service (1965:19).

Claude Brown—*Manchild in a Promised Land*

When one of Johnny's girls messed up on him—tried to hold back some money or gave somebody some pants and didn't get any money—he sure was hard on them. It was good to be around when that happened. Sometimes Johnny would beat their ass and throw them out and not listen to anything. He would say, "Git outta my sight, bitch, and don't ever come back."

She must have really made him mad, because he'd beat her ass, and Johnny didn't beat chicks unless they'd done something really bad or made him mad (1965:112).

Maria Campbell—*Halfbreed*

He was also a very jealous man and was sure his wife was having affairs with all the Halfbreeds in the area. So when the Rebellion broke out and he had to attend meetings away from home he would take his wife with him. She in turn passed on all the information she heard at these meetings to the rebels and also stole ammunition and supplies for them from his store. When he found out he became very angry and decided the best way to deal with her was by public flogging. So he stripped the clothes from her back and beat her so cruelly she was scarred for life (1973:14).

Everything was all right for the first couple of months, but then Darrel began to drink. Soon he lost his job and had to find another. I was pushed around the first few times he was drunk, but then he started to beat me whenever the mood hit him. The children were frightened and Robbie would try to protect me. I became pregnant in the spring and was so sick I could hardly move. Dad knew by then that I had lied about being pregnant before, but he didn't know about the beatings.

One night he was staying with us when Darrel came home drunk and in an ugly mood. He slapped me and I fell down the stairs. I was taken to the hospital because the doctor was afraid I would lose the baby. However, I was okay except for a sprained ankle and a broken wrist. When I got home Daddy had beaten Darrel up, and he didn't hit me again for a long time. The rest of the year was grim. Darrel would be gone for days at a time and when he came home he would jeer at me and call me a fat squaw. The children were unhappy and confused, and did badly in school (Campbell, 1973:106).

In each of the cases, the physical punishment was accepted as the necessary way to punish. The final lines in both examples indicated the acceptance of the idea that this type of beating is not the result of any sadistic tendencies but a necessary punishment that the person had brought on him/herself.

Retribution. This is a use for violence extensively practiced in the violent subculture, but that is also accepted in the larger culture. The code of retribution is basically comparable to the earlier codes of punishment that demanded an eye for an eye. The code goes beyond equal payment or payment in kind. The expectation is that the person seeking retribution will go beyond the degree of injury that was suffered and exact further suffering commensurate with the indignity that was suffered. Usually when violence is punishment, companions will either not participate or will simply assist by holding the victim. When the action is in retaliation as retribution, however, the family and friends are usually expected to participate.

Excerpt from a defendant's statement in an assault case

I swore vengeance on Clarence before he left Ionia because he swore vengeance on me for snitching on him at the time of the robbery. I used this as an instrument of vengeance to get the guys one by one. I beat up about twelve before the officials in Ionia became aware of what I was doing. These guys were mad at me because I hit a guy in the head with a horseshoe because he wanted to make a sissy out of me, and also because my rap partner lied on me and told everyone that I was a snitch and I hate to be called a snitch. Then they sent me to Jackson where I was put under close supervision. Now, in Jackson, I never received any violations but, while I never did anything wrong, I had friends and associates who took out vengeance on these guys for me.

Excerpt from a police report

The police received a call on a big fight at an east side park. When they arrived they found two brothers on the ground with injuries to their heads and bodies. They told the police that their brothers had a fight with the brother of one of the men who had attacked them earlier. About an hour and a half later two car loads of men pulled up and beat them with jack handles and tire irons. The defendant corroborated the statement although he maintained two brothers had beaten up his brother.

Control. Violence as a means of controlling the conduct of others is conceived by the actor not only as a means of preventing others from taking a given action but also as a means of forcing others to comply with the actor's bidding against their will. This type of violence may be intended to protect the other from his own bad judgment, as in the case of the parent who beats a small child for running into the street or a teenage daughter for staying out too late. The object, in any case, is to impose the will of the actor on the victim.

Claude Brown—*Manchild in a Promised Land*

After I was wide awake, Danny slapped me again, real hard. I wanted to hit that nigger then—I didn't go for that big brother thing any more. But I knew I couldn't beat him yet—Danny was more than six feet tall—so I just took it. And after he hit me, he held my collar real tight, and he said, "Sonny, if I ever again, as long as I live, hear about you usin' drugs, I'm gon kill you. I'm gon git my gun, and I'm gon beat you wit my gun in your head, nigger, until you go in the hospital. Cause I'd rather see you there than see you on shit" (1966:267).

Frank Elli—*The Riot*

"Lay off!" Bugsy yelled as Duke Trusdale, crawling stealthily toward the onlookers was slammed flat on his back by a rib-cracking kick from the con wearing the catcher's chest protector. "Get screwed!" the con shrieked, and began kicking insanely at Trusdale, who was writhing on the floor, his knees drawn up to his chin, both hands protecting his crotch. "No convict tells me what to do!" He was aiming a kick at Trusdale's unprotected head when Cully grabbed him from behind and slung him to the floor. As the con scrabbled out of reach, Cully glanced about (1966:166).

Maria Campbell—*Halfbreed*

Dad got home Sunday afternoon and called me to his room. He warned me that if I ever saw Smoky again he would beat me until I couldn't walk. He said Smoky was only trouble and I was too young to get mixed up with a grown man, especially one with such a reputation. He said if he ever came around again he'd break his goddamn back. When I tried to interrupt, I was told to shut up. He said that I had acted like a common whore. "Your mother never did anything like that in her life, and as long as you're under my roof you'll act like a lady." Finally I got angry and shouted that if he could go to such places, then why couldn't I; that if Smoky was good enough to be his best friend why wasn't he good enough for me? I told him I was a Campbell, not a Dubuque and if Mom was a lady then why did she run off with him? I had never talked back before, much less yelled at him. He slapped my face and knocked me over a chair, and when he went to slap me again, I said, "You're not so hot. You're living with that woman when you should be married to her, so don't tell me what's right and wrong." He got a hurt look on his face and walked out (1973:101).

Prestige or Position. To engage in interpersonal violence and come out victorious is the measure of position in the violent subculture. The literature on juvenile gangs and prison life is filled with cases of boys and men gaining a reputation through the use of violence. Prestige is accorded to winning fighters by gang members as well as others in the community. This also extends to the person who does not emerge the winner in a violent encounter as long as he gives a good account of himself. Status is achieved not only in exclusively young male circles but throughout age and sex groups of the nonparticipant members of the violent subculture. Claude Brown emphasizes the general acceptance of success with violence as a mark of status:

A man was respected on the basis of his reputation. The people in the neighborhood whom everybody looked up to were the cats who'd killed somebody. The little boys in the neighborhood whom the adults respected were those little boys who didn't let anybody mess with them . . . (Brown, 1965:267).

Following is an excerpt of an interview between a probation officer and a youth convicted of aggravated assault in a stabbing.

> The defendant in a very earnest fashion expressed remorse. He said
> . . . he normally got along well with people in his neighborhood but
> since he was smaller than most of the boys his age he tended to be
> picked on by bully types. With some show of pride he said now he
> was held in greater respect.

Release of Tension. Violence as tension released is no different from any other physically violent conduct, such as hard physical labor or competitive body-contact sports. The other person exists as an object, and the person committing the violent act is not responding to the victim personally but to his own internal state. The difference between this use of violence and socially acceptable combatives is that the victim is an unwilling participant. Bettleheim has suggested that the growing number of assaultive acts may be the result of the increasingly limited socially acceptable situations in which violent actions can be released. He suggests that the availability of inanimate objects in forms such as rocks, trees and animals, and involvement in vigilante actions probably served this purpose in the past (1966:50-59). Many records show defendants attempting to explain their acts in terms of having nothing to do. This does not mean that there is in fact nothing to do, but that often there is no acceptable outlet for physical energies.

Maria Campbell—*Halfbreed*
> I remember one party he had in particular. We all came—Campbells
> and Vandals together from our area, as well as Arcands from the
> other area and the Sandy Lake Indians too. As we arrived Mom said,
> "There's going to be a fight for sure with those Sandy Lake people
> here," but I paid little attention because there was never a good
> dance unless there was a good fight. Yes—Sant's cabin was a very
> long one-room log house with a big stove and heater, and four beds
> on one side. He had dragged all the furniture outside so there was
> plenty of room to dance. He was also the proud owner of the largest
> cellar in the country with a huge trapdoor on the floor.
>   Everybody was enjoying themselves dancing and eating when
> suddenly a fight broke out. The mothers chased all the little kids
> under the beds and we big ones climbed up to the beams to watch.
> Soon everyone was fighting and no one knew who was hitting
> who—Dad even punched out his brother. The heater pipes were
> knocked over and there was smoke everywhere; then the kitchen
> stove pipes went down. Dad finally made it to the door and threw it
> open. Whenever someone came near the door Daddy would slug
> him and he would go sliding head first or backwards down the slip-
> pery hill to the lake. The lights went out and it was pitch black
> inside, mothers were yelling, kids screaming—a total mass of confu-
> sion! (1973:51).

What is suggested in this discussion is that most violence is instrumental, goal-directed conduct. That this conduct may serve hedonistic values, as Hartung (1965) suggests, in no way detracts from this fact. It does, however, deny Cohen's (1966) approach to violence as a part of the "nonutilitarian" conduct of juveniles. Violence is in fact often effective and goal directed.

Education in Control. It has been proposed that in the contest of a violent subculture, violence is an acceptable form of conduct for achieving a variety of objectives. One might ask, since violence seems to be both acceptable and effective, why is there not even more violence? There are two major reasons for the limiting of violent conduct. First, most acts of interpersonal violence are against the law and may result in jail sentences. Second, and at least equally important, not everyone is able to utilize violence effectively enough to make the benefits outweigh the liabilities.

Yablonsky (1963) implies that the reason the groups he observed used violence to attain general societal goals such as money, power, or prestige is that violence requires little skill or training. That is not true. Violence does, in fact, require both. Violence is much like any other activity: success depends on the number, skill and training of the competition as well as the scarcity of that for which the competition exists. One of the first lessons learned in the violent subculture, and one that is repeatedly reinforced, is that to be on the receiving end of violent interpersonal action is unpleasant and painful and is to be avoided whenever possible. The majority of persons in the violent subculture learn that lesson early and well. For the most part they receive their first lesson in violence and in the control of their own conduct at the same time. They learn that when a person is in a position of authority (that is, when she/he makes demands and has sufficient force to insure compliance) one had better cooperate, and control any thoughts of resisting or reciprocating. This type of authority is rarely challenged once it has been recognized.

Maria Campbell—*Halfbreed*

The men would get happy-drunk at first and as the evening progressed white men would come by. They all danced and sang together, then all too soon one of the white men would bother the women. Our men would become angry, but instead of fighting the white men, they beat their wives. They ripped clothes off the women, hit them with fists or whips, knocked them down and kicked them until they were senseless.

When that was over, they fought each other in the same way. Meanwhile, the white men stood together in a group, laughing and drinking, sometimes dragging a woman away. How I hated them! They were always gone when the sun came up. Our men would be sick and hung over and ugly-mean, the mothers black and blue and swollen. The men would go into the beer parlour every day until the money ran out and every evening the fighting would start again. After two or three days, we all left, usually at the request of the R.C.M.P. (1973:37).

When authority is challenged it is usually under one of the three following conditions: the force is evaluated as inadequate against one's own counterforce in the specific situation; a stronger value demands action in spite of the expected penalty; or the ultimate result of control has more potentially negative aspects than the possibility of failure as negative consequences in the present situation. Although tolerance of pain can be developed, especially as familiarity diminishes the intensifying effect of fear, even the toughest, most experienced person seeks to avoid being the recipient of violence whenever possible. Particularly in any situation in which violent actions are evaluated as having minimal rewards and high chance for punishment. Through observation and experience in the violent subculture, one learns that punishment at the hands of persons in authority may be avoided: if one is not caught violating rules where punishment is mandatory; if one accepts and does not question the right of the authority when caught; and if one takes the punishment "like a man."

Control training begins with parent-child and child-sibling relationships and continues throughout adolescence and in some cases into the adult years. For the most part education in control is not conducted deliberately except in specifically subordinate-superordinate roles, but there are usually admonitions during punishments that announce expectations of control.

Following are examples of deliberate control training by others than parents.

Claude Brown—*Manchild in a Promised Land*

He said, "Look, I'm gon hit you in you face. I'm just gon slap you with my hand, and I'm not gon tell you when, and I'm not gon tell you how many times. If you cry, I'm gon walk away, and I'm gon forget about it. And if you get mad, it's like the whole thing is just lost, and we gotta start all over again."

I had to go along with it. He hit me. He hit me in my face ten times, and each time was harder than the time before. He just slapped me on one side and I didn't even know which hand was going to come. He said, "Remember, don't get excited. Don't get excited." When he slapped me the fifth time, I was ready to cry. But there was no sense in me even thinking about hitting this nigger, because I knew there was nothing in this world, even with God on my side, that could have helped me kick his ass.

I just held it back and fought it. After hitting me ten times, each time harder than the time before, he stopped. He said, "You mad at me, man?"

"No, man, I'm not mad at you. I think it's a whole lotta bullshit, and if you wanted to hit me in the face, you coulda told me."

He said, "Uh-huh."

So we sat down, and he started telling me things about bitches and things I like to hear (1965:265-6).

   This type of training in control of violence is a part of the life of the child in the violent subculture. Whether the person(s) doing the teaching are friends, relatives or enemies, lack of control is punished in a variety of ways. If the younger boy cannot take it, he is excluded from the company of older boys and ridiculed by his peers. Education in control of violence results in learning the following rules for control.
1. Defiance of persons with a stronger force usually results in severe punishment.
2. Persons in the violent subculture admire the ability to take as well as inflict pain or, in other words, the ability to suppress futile raging and crying. The expressed value can be seen in such statements as "Be a man, don't be a baby."

OBLIGATIONS RELATED TO THE USE OF VIOLENCE ATTACHED TO THE MALE ROLE IN VIOLENT SUBCULTURES

The violent subculture provides a specific value orientation toward violent acts both as offensive, instrumental acts and as defensive, controlling acts. The norms governing the latter, however, also receive some support from the dominant culture (Parsons, 1947:167). Tradition in western society has always been supportive of the violent defense of country, home and family. Although the "fighting man" is held in high esteem when he acts in this type of defense, the nonviolent culture has always regarded violent action as acceptable only if other alternatives have (apparently) been exhausted. The enlisted army man and the policeman do not have high status positions in western society. They are often recruited from groups that support norms conducive to the use of violence. In the violent subculture the protection of home and family is much less impersonal than in the larger culture and cannot easily be delegated to legitimate social control agents, particularly if the others are hired and have no personal commitment to insure punishment or retribution. The traditional approach to the family still operative in the lower classes gives the family the aspect of property, the members of which are an extension of the head of the household (Reisman, 1962). This belief makes any attack, theft or "use" of the family members or property without the "owner's" permission an attack on the owner. The male in the violent subculture regards any conduct that takes on the aspect of a personal insult as an indication that his manhood is deemed insufficient to provide a protective aura over what is his.
   As his possessions are often few he is especially vulnerable with regard to them. The masculine sexual association in connection with "nerve" or courage can be emphasized in many colloquial expressions of admiration, for example, "That took a lotta balls."

The general norms readily recognized in the violent subculture as demanding violent action can be seen in the following:

Claude Brown—*Manchild in a Promised Land*

I remember they used to say on the streets, "Don't mess with a mon's money, his woman, or his manhood." This was the thing when I was about twelve or thirteen. This was what the gang fights were all about. If somebody messed with your brother, you could just punch him in his mouth, and that was all right. If somebody messed with your sister, you really had to fuck him up—break his leg or stab him in the eye with an ice pick, something vicious.

I suppose the main things were the women in the family and the money. This was something we learned very early. If you went to the store and lost some money or if you let somebody gorilla it out of you you gon get your ass beaten when you came back home. You couldn't go upstairs and say, "Well, Daddy, that big boy down there took the money that you gave me to buy some cigars." "Shit you don't have any business letting anybody take your money."

You were supposed to go to war about your money. Maybe this was why the cats on the corner were killing each other over a two dollar crap game or petty debt. People were always shooting, cutting, or killing somebody over three dollars.

It wasn't the value of the money. It couldn't have been. It was just that these things symbolized a man's manhood or principles (1965:265-66).

Hunter Thompson—*The Hell's Angels*

Their claim that they don't start trouble is probably true more often than not, but their idea of provocation is dangerously broad, and one of their main difficulties is that almost nobody seems to understand it. Yet they have a very simple rule of thumb: in any argument a fellow Angel is always *right*. To disagree . . . is to be *wrong*—and to persist in being wrong is an open challenge (1966:95).

Maria Campbell—*Halfbreed*

Smoky tried to make me leave about eleven o'clock, but I coaxed him to stay till midnight as I knew Bob and Ellen would not leave without us. About eleven-thirty people started coming in from the bar—white people as well—and you could almost cut the tension with a knife. When a Frenchman came over and grabbed me for a waltz, Smoky told him to leave me alone. Everything happened so fast: it seemed that one minute Smoky was leading me away and the next everyone was shouting and fighting, and he was gone. Karen came over and pulled me back. Smoky and the Frenchman were fighting, and because Smoky was winning, a whole group of French guys started to kick and beat him. I couldn't stand watching so I grabbed a stove poker and waded right in. I ended up exchanging blows with a white woman and then saw Dad and a couple of men coming to Smoky's rescue. When the fight was over, Daddy saw me and went purple with rage. He looked at Smoky and said, "She's my daughter, what the hell are you doing here with her? I'll settle with you later," and with that he dragged me over to the truck where Ellen and Bob were waiting. They took Karen and me straight home. I was worried sick wondering what Daddy would do with Smoky and what was going to happen to me when he got home (1973:100).

It is evident that there are many reasons for instigating or responding to violence, or for expecting to have it used against you in the violent subculture. However, it is only in defense of family or property or when one's manhood is challenged, that violence is required. The distinct set of values in the violent subculture require conformity in these situations. One can expect in the ordinary behavioral setting that others will also conform to these norms:

> As I saw it in my childhood, most of the cats I swung with were more afraid of not fighting than fighting. This was how it was supposed to be, because that was what we had come up under. The adults in the neighborhood practiced this. They lived by the concept that a man was supposed to fight. When two little boys got into a fight in the neighborhood, the men around would encourage them and egg them on. They'd never even think of stopping the fight (Brown, 1965:112).

The necessity for fighting and the knowledge that even when one wins it is likely to be painful represents another aspect of the education in cognitive control. Using violence when one would rather not is as much an exercise in control as *not* using it when one would like to. For some reason this aspect of control and control education has not been explored. Many cases were observed of individuals taking violent action as a result of group influences and expectations of the violent group. This action can be conceived as a very difficult exercise in self-control.

The punishment for nonviolence in the violent subculture can be as psychologically and physically painful as the results of the violence itself. The norms of the violent subculture do not provide for the observation of rules of fairness in violent encounters nor for the matching of opponents in size as in boxing matches. In the violent subculture experience teaches that the opponent is most likely to initiate violence not when the odds are evenly matched, but when they are in his favor. Thus someone is usually at a disadvantage, and relatives and friends will step in to prevent a severe injury when it seems as if their affiliate is losing. However, if they have to interfere because their friend or relative is not fighting hard or is simply defensive, the loss of prestige is also shared. In this case the punishment may be taken over by the rescuer.

Racially mixed low-income housing project

Ten-year-old Jerry shot a BB gun out of the door of his house and the ricochet caused one boy in a group playing across the street to receive a cut. The boys came to the house to revenge themselves and Jerry's mother told them he was being punished so he couldn't go out that day but that it was a dumb trick and he deserved whatever he got. For the next four days the boy went to school by a roundabout way and managed to avoid the group. Finally on the fifth day one of his sisters came running home and told the mother that a bunch of boys were beating Jerry up. She walked down to make sure he wasn't being too badly hurt. When she got there she saw him standing there letting the boys pound him without fighting back. She grabbed a stick herself and beat him all the way home in front of the group of boys, all his friends and siblings. As she hit she said, "When you do something you have to pay for it. You can't go through life with your mama watching over you. Don't ever let me hear of you standing there and letting anyone beat on you. No matter how many there are or how big they are or what you've done. Let them know they've been in a fight. You shouldn't have shot the gun in the first place, that was your first mistake. But letting them beat on you was even worse, because then you'll be a target. When you're wrong you have to try to apologize, but after that if they start it, it's up to you to make them think twice before refusing your apology again."

In spite of the fact that it is difficult to avoid violent encounters within the violent subculture, there are a number of persons, even in such violent groups, who would prefer to use nonviolent means. To begin with, the violent actions are generally restricted to adolescent boys and young male adults, although in the most violent areas some of the older adult and adolescent females are also frequently involved. There are a number of tactics that are commonly used by persons in the violent subculture who wish to avoid the results of the violent encounter without suffering the loss of prestige that accompanies backing down. These should not be confused with the tactics used to postpone violence when the situational factors are interpreted as detrimental for success. The following tactics are used by individuals who want the protection and approval of the violent group, but do not have the ability or character to engage in violence themselves.

TACTICS FOR AVOIDANCE OF VIOLENT ENCOUNTERS IN THE VIOLENT SUBCULTURE

Pretense. The actor in this case pretends to be drunk or asleep or in some other way prevented, through no fault of his own, from being aware of any situation or insult that requires the initiation of violence on his part. In drug-using areas drugs can be used. The function of obvious drunkenness is to allow the group to change their expectations by rationalizing that the actor was too drunk to know what was going on.

Faking Out. This technique is very dangerous and is usually only used after the actor has evaluated the situation and has decided that the potential antagonists do not want to engage in violence themselves. The behavior involved is called "jumping in the other guy's face" or "sounding" and involves threats and swearing designed to indicate that if the other makes the wrong move, it will be his last. If the actor's judgment is incorrect in using this technique, it often has worse results than simply attacking outright would have.

> On the Angel scale of values the only thing worse than a fink with a loose frightened mouth is a loud antagonist who can't follow through. People like this get the full measure of retribution—the natural attack on any human obstacle, plus the hyped-up-heel-grinding contempt for a man who tries and fails to deal with them on their own terms (Thompson, 1966:112).

Verbal Battle. The exchange of insults and threats is common among all lower-class male groups. It is partly to test how willing the opponent is to fight. That is, if he is willing to accept and exchange insults, he is probably not very eager to fight. This is a common tactic used by those freely engaged in violence when they are confronted by someone who is also reputed to be tough and willing to fight. Both parties know that they are likely to be badly hurt no matter who is considered the winner. This tactic is usually used, however, by someone who has superior verbal skills. He sets up the situation so that he can make the opponent look bad and then can move out of range quickly. He also stays away from the kind of insult that has demand characteristics.

Passing to Another. This tactic involves verbal and sometimes physical maneuvering to set up an antagonist for a friend who is a readier fighter. Sometimes it is accomplished by simply saying, "Did you hear what that punk said to *us*?" or "Did you see how he looked at *us*?" Other times it is a matter of being one step behind a ready fighter when the actual action is initiated. This tactic is of necessity always used when a group is present and, occasionally, the tactic user will move in when someone is down and "put the boots to him." He usually maneuvers completely away from the action until it is over. Then he steps back and gently reprimands his friend for not letting him handle his own "beef."

Diversion. This tactic involves drawing the attention of the onlookers away from the preaction situation, and the timing is especially important. If the stage has been reached where the onlookers expect action, they are not easily diverted and distraction usually has to be achieved by interaction with someone not involved in the original encounter. By starting an argument, for example, the tension can be broken; some nonviolent members of these groups become quite adept at avoiding the actual encounter.

Even though persons of this type are sometimes tolerated, in the violent subculture they never are really in a very high status in the group. Most of these tactics are developed where expectations for violent action are high, and pressure is constantly on men to engage in violence. In places where there is real commitment to violence, however, these tactics are, for the most part, ineffective. The benefits of participating in violence, at least with the group, are sufficient to induce most of the young men and boys to develop skills in using violence.

Specific Norms for Violent Encounters in the Violent Subculture

The norms governing violent conduct in the violent subculture are not simply general expectations; they also involve specific techniques that are learned within violent groups. The general norms concerning defensive violence are not only known to members of the violent subculture but the larger culture as well. Knowledge of the more specific techniques and of ways of successfully using violence instrumentally rather than simply defensively indicate deep involvement in the violent subculture.

Learning specific norms of violence is subtle and often a matter of identification and association. Physical preparedness is a part of this education. Thompson's comment on the Hell's Angels could be made of most men and boys in the violent subculture.

> There is not a Hell's Angel riding who hasn't made the emergency-ward scene, and one of the results is that their fear of accidents is well tempered by a cavalier kind of disdain for physical injury. Outsiders might call it madness or other more esoteric names . . . but the Angels inhabit a world in which violence is as common as spilled beer, and they live with it as easily as ski-bums live with the risk of broken legs. This casual acceptance of bloodletting is the key to the terror they inspire in the squares. Even a small, inept street fighter has a tremendous advantage over the average middle-class American, who hasn't had a fight since puberty. It is a simple matter of accumulated experience, of having been hit or stomped often enough to forget the ugly panic that nice people associate with a serious fight. A man who has had his nose smashed three times in brawls will risk it again with hardly a thought. No amount of instruction in any lethal art can teach this—not unless the instructor is a sadist, and even then it would be difficult because the student's experience would be artificially warped and limited (1966:128).

Thompson's observations can be confirmed in the boxing world, where the best trained fighters from the colleges and middle-class suburbs are rarely able to compete with the fighter who has had his earliest training in the violent subculture.

The range of activities that require or tolerate the initiation of violence, the characteristics and potential objects of violence, and the norms that govern actions once violence is initiated are the subjects of common and extensive discussions within the violent groups. The norms are of particular importance when it comes to prediction of the potential for violence under certain conditions: a man must be able to predict the point in the violent sequence at which specific types of control, internal or external, may be expected. Most persons who engage in interpersonal violence are well aware of the pain involved in the violent encounters, as they have themselves frequently been objects of violence. Experience as the victim is a constant part of the discussion in the violent subculture; it generally confirms the fact that the perpetrator of violence has also been a victim. Recent victim studies, by Koenig (1975), for example, reaffirm that the actual incidence of crime is rarely reflected in crime statistics, even in the section dealing with crimes known to the police. Statistical evidence indicates an actual increase in assaultive crimes; however, experts are unable to estimate how much of the increase is due to an actual increase in crime, how much is due to better emergency treatment in cases that might have resulted in death in earlier times, and how much is due to better crime reporting techniques.

The potential for success in violence depends on a number of variables related to the individual and his life experience. The success of early experiences in violent encounters is one. In observing beginning classes in boxing, the effect of winning can be seen in the differences in the developing self-concepts of the boys. Initial successes allow them to see themselves as winners and as successful fighters. The boys who do not develop this self-concept are likely to drop out of the program or to refrain from participating in actual boxing and concentrate on exercises. Another factor that leads to success in violence is the development of expectations of violence on the part of others. This type of expectation makes the individual ready to respond to the cues of others more quickly. The individual who is expecting violence is responsive and perceives cues that might pass unnoticed by others. The more experience he has had with violence in a variety of situations, the more likely he is to have this type of expectation. In bars where fights occur frequently, the scraping of a chair, which precedes many fights, will cause everyone to be ready to move quickly. When a chair is pushed back in a classroom most people are not alerted and prepared for a fight, even when the sound follows an argument. A further result of early and extensive experience in violence is that it tends to reduce the tendency to search for alternative forms of conduct. Within the violent group the alternative means of goal-achievement are often limited and inefficient and they recede more and more from the individual's range of possibilities. This, in turn, widens the range of situations in which violence has been used effectively, as well as increasing the ability to use violent techniques.

The following rules are a part of the education of members of violent subcultures who are the actual users of violence toward others. These rules are not usually part of the general knowledge of the violent subculture, but are often learned prior to actual serious violent encounters by hearing stories recounted by others. Often fathers and brothers discuss their violent encounters, although the majority of male children are with their peer groups and witness violent encounters themselves at a very early age. Even when the family does stress nonviolent norms, the subcultural influences are very strong.

RULES FOR THE SUCCESSFUL USE OF
VIOLENCE IN THE VIOLENT SUBCULTURE

Be first: Get your opponent before he gets you. Do not let him know
your intentions.

Be fast: Hit as quickly, as hard and as often before he knows what's
happening. This will not only discourage him but is likely to hurt
him so that he won't be so effective.

Be final: Get him off his feet and make sure he hasn't the ability or the
inclination to attempt to come back at you. Kick him when he's
down. If you haven't hit him hard enough and you don't at least
temporarily put him out of commission, he is likely to get up mad
and really be dangerous.

The object of these rules is to make sure that he is not eager to come at
you again, but not to hurt him so badly that he will feel obligated to
return with a bunch of his friends.

Thompson has pointed out in *Hell's Angels*, "In this league, sports-
manship is for old liberals and young fools." He contends that the
majority of people that actually start trouble with the Angels do not
understand the rules of the violent subculture.

> Many of their "assault victims" are people who have seen too many
> western movies; they are victims of a John Wayne complex which
> causes them to start to swing the moment they sense any insult. This
> is relatively safe in some areas of society, but in saloons frequented
> by outlaw motorcyclists it is the worst kind of folly (Thompson,
> 1966:95).

The last comment in that quotation can be added not only for motorcy-
clists but for any group deeply committed to the norms of the violent
subculture. Even those who might be willing to operate by less dangerous rules can have no assurance that the other person will. Thompson
amplifies the differences between these rules and the defensive rules of
the nonviolent culture in the following comments:

> Many (from the nonviolent culture) . . . would have lost their taste
> for the fight the moment that they realized that their opponents
> meant to inflict serious injury on anybody they could reach.
>
> Red-blooded American boys don't normally fight this way. Nor do
> they swing heavy chains on people whose backs are turned . . . and
> when they find themselves in a brawl where things like this are
> happening, they have good reason to feel at a disadvantage. It is one
> thing to get punched in the nose, and quite another to have your eye
> sprung or your teeth shattered with a wrench (Thompson,
> 1966:184).

The final and most important rule in a subculture where the above
rules are the expectation is:

Be careful: Keep the *odds* in your favor. Stay in your own territory. Don't get caught off guard. Keep your back to the wall. In strange places locate the exits. Don't "run your mouth" when you're in somebody else's neighborhood.

The odds are manipulated largely by the use of companions and weapons. If the object of the attack is not a participant in the violent subculture, the speed and viciousness of the attack will often outbalance differences in size and weight. For the opponent with the same rules, however, this is not in itself sufficient to prevent one from being badly hurt. Many middle-class observers of the violent scene have regarded such techniques as group attack and punching and kicking the man when he is down as indications of cowardice. Those more familiar with street violence do not think this is true. As Thompson says of the Hell's Angels," . . . despite everything psychiatrists . . . have to say about the Angels, they are tough, mean and potentially dangerous" (1966:110). Even under the most carefully contrived circumstances, the victim of any assault may be dangerous. If he realizes that he is going to be hurt anyhow, he is likely to be even more dangerous. There is no intention here to justify the rules that govern the violent encounter but only to identify them in the context of the situation in which they occur most often.

SUMMARY

The general conditions that set the scene for violence can be readily recognized as having their origins in cultural patterns that are supported by the characteristic milieu existing in the lower classes. The development of a violent subculture within this climate occurs primarily in the youthful male groups. The extent to which this subculture of violence is inclusive for all or most of the adolescent and adult males in the group is dependent on a number of factors. Some of these are the extent to which nonviolent forces may reach and influence the group; the relative frequency of opportunities for violent encounters; the tradition of violence in the community; the quality and quantity of law enforcement; and perhaps of other temporary conditions, such as unemployment. The violent subculture provides not only general values regarding violence, but also a specific set of rules of conduct of a more technical nature that serve to structure and intensify the incidence of violence. In spite of all of the education in violence that occurs in the violent subculture, there is evidence indicating that education in cognitive control occurs simultaneously for most, if not all, members of the violent subculture. The observational materials suggest that violent conduct is rational and controllable and has, for the most part, its origins in a subculture in which violence is an approved form of conduct.

NOTES

[1] This excerpt and those on following pages are from *Halfbreed*, by Maria Campbell, reprinted by permission of the Canadian Publishers, McClelland & Stewart Ltd., Toronto.

REFERENCES

Beattie, Ronald M., and Kenny, John P.
1966   "Aggressive Crimes." *Patterns of Violence*, Special Edition, The Annals of the American Academy of Political and Social Science. Philadelphia.
Bernstein, B. B.
1965   "Social Class, Linguistic Codes and Grammatical Elements." *Language and Speech*. Vol. 5, 221-40.
Bettleheim, Bruno
1966   "Violence, a Neglected Mode of Behavior," in Marvin Wolfgang, ed., *Patterns of Violence*, The Annals. Philadelphia.
Brown, Claude
1966   *Manchild in the Promised Land*. New York: Signet.
Campbell, Maria
1973   *Halfbreed*. Toronto: McClelland and Stewart.
Cohen, Albert K.
1966   *Deviance and Control*. Englewood Cliffs, New Jersey: Prentice-Hall, Inc.
Curtis, Lynn A.
1974   *Criminal Violence*. Lexington, Mass.: D. C. Heath and Co.
Elli, Frank.
1968   *The Riot*. Avon Books.
Ferracuti, Franco, and Wolfgang, Marvin E.
1964   "The Prediction of Violent Behavior." *Corrective Psychiatry and Journal of Social Therapy*. X, 289-300.
Gans, Herbert
1964   "A Survey of Working Class and Lower Class Studies," in Reissman, Frank.; Cohen, Jerome; and Pearl, Arthur., eds. *Mental Health of the Poor*, Part II, "Low Income Behavior and Cognitive Style." New York: The Free Press, 119-126.

———
1964   "Routine-Seekers and Action-Seekers," in Reissman, Frank; Cohen, Jerome; and Pearl, Arthur., eds. *Mental Health of the Poor*, Part II, "Low Income Behavior and Cognitive Style." New York: The Free Press, 155-158.
Goldstein, Bernard
1967   *Low Income Youth in Urban Areas: A Critical Review of the Literature*. New York: Holt, Rinehart and Winston, Inc.
Goode, William J.
1971   "Force and Violence in the Family" *Journal of Marriage and the Family* 33, Nov. 1971: 624-636.
Gough, Harrison G.
1947-8   "A Sociological Theory of Psychopathy." American Journal of Sociology, LIII, 359-366.
Hartung, Frank E.
1965   *Crime Law and Society*. Detroit: Wayne State University Press.

———
1963   "Manhattan Madness: The Social Movement of Mental Health." *Sociological Quarterly*, LXIII, 261-272.
Koenig, Daniel J.,
1975   "Police Perceptions of Public Respect and Extra-Legal Use of Force: a Reconsideration of Folk Wisdom and Pluralistic Ignorance," in *Canadian Journal of Sociology* I:313-24

Kohn, Melvin L.
    1964   "Social-Class and Parent Child Relationship: An Interpretation," in Reissman, Frank; Cohen, Jerome.; and Pearl, Arthur., eds. *Mental Health of the Poor*. New York: The Free Press, 159-169.

Parsons, Talcott.
    1947   "Certain Primary Sources and Patterns of Aggression in the Social Structure of the Western World." *Psychiatry*, X, 167-181.

Reissman, Frank.
    1962   *The Culturally Deprived Child*. New York: Harper and Row.

Strauss, Murray A.
    1971   "Some Social Antecedents of Physical Punishment: A Linkage Theory Interpretation", *Journal of Marriage and the Family* 33 Nov., 658-663.

Thompson, Hunter S.
    1966   *The Hell's Angels*. New York: Ballantine.

Toby, Jackson.
    1966   "Violence and the Masculine Ideal: Some Qualitative Data," in Wolfgang, Marvin, ed. *Patterns of Violence*, The Annals, Special Edition.

Wolfgang, M. E. and Ferracuti,F.
    1967(a)   *The Subculture of Violence*. New York: Barnes and Noble.

—————.
    1967(b)   "A Sociological Analysis of Criminal Homicide, M. Wolfgang, ed., *Studies in Homicide*. New York: Harper and Row.

—————.
    1966   "A Preface to Violence," in M. Wolfgang, ed. *Patterns of Violence*, The Annals, Special Edition, March.

Yablonsky, Louis.
    1963   *The Violent Gang*. New York: Macmillan.

Chapter 2

CRIMES OF VIOLENCE
AND THE FEMALE OFFENDER

Peter H. Lindsay and Peggy Ann Walpole

The literature on violence rarely talks about women, except as undeserving victims. This chapter, however, deals solely with female criminality or that which is perceived as such.

Statistics on female crime immediately bring to mind the issue of actual as opposed to reported statistics, a contradiction which is pursued further. In addition to the findings of Lindsay and Walpole, this chapter presents a number of interesting possibilities for the adoption of a labelling-theory perspective by the sociologist. Labelling theory embraces the notion that a specific segment of the population is selected as criminal on the basis of labels, screening out a portion of persons who in fact do commit crimes. The manner in which this process is achieved here is related to sexual stereotypes which may well favour females, at least in the area of apprehension. Research on violent females whether based on notions of innate tendencies or learned behaviours leads to the conclusion that women are domestic, gentle and above all "clean" and that males, particularly youthful males, involve themselves more readily in antisocial behaviour. Examples of the exchange of sexual favours for freedom from apprehension and of the "misguided chivalry" of courts and police, exemplify the interactive process of labelling theory. The labelling theorist, however, would not be interested in the use of official statistics to explain these differences.

Lindsay and Walpole bring to light a significant change in the nature of acts committed by women. It appears that, as the relationship between male and female becomes more egalitarian, so do their crimes.

INTRODUCTION

A frequently cited phenomenon in the literature on crime and criminal violence is the fact that women seem to be very much under-represented in criminal statistics. The data on arrests for Criminal Code offences in Canada during 1974, for example, show that of the some 250,000 arrests made only one in seven involved a female. Females accounted for less than one in thirteen arrests for crimes of violence against a person (e.g., murder, manslaughter, wounding, assault) and less than one in twenty arrests for crimes of violence involving property (e.g., robbery, extortion, breaking and entering).

---

* An original article written for this volume.

These figures raise some interesting and important questions about the causes and prevention of violence. The first question is the most obvious one: Why should female involvement in crime, particularly violent crime, be so low? Is there something about a woman's psyche or her upbringing that especially inhibits her from becoming involved in criminal activities, particularly crimes of violence?

The second issue we will consider is the evidence for whether this low incidence of female criminal activity is changing or remaining stable. The last decade or so is of particular interest since it is during this period that there has been a substantial effort mounted towards redefining the role of women in society and expanding her opportunities. Has this larger social movement had any impact on the criminal activities of women? Has the attempt to make opportunities for women more equal to those of men also produced an increased propensity in woman to commit traditionally "male" crimes, including crimes involving aggression and violence?

When considering these issues, we use Canadian data and statistics whenever possible. The problem is that a systematic study of female violence and the female offender is itself a very rare commodity and work based specifically on the Canadian scene is almost non-existent. Thus, we have to rely more than we would have preferred on relevant American data.

SOME THEORETICAL EXPLANATIONS OF FEMALE CRIMINALITY

Theoretical explanations of criminally violent behaviour in men usually encompass a complex and intricately interrelated set of social, biological, economic and psychological factors (Wolfgang, 1958). Theories of the causes of female criminality, by contrast, are incredibly simple, even simplistic. In fact, much of the theoretical writing, such as it is, has not gone much beyond one of the most primitive of questions—the nature/nurture issue: Are the major factors that influence female criminality a matter of inborn physiological characteristics? Or are they a result of learning and the unique socialization process that the female undergoes?

It's in the Nature of Women

> From the predecessors of Lombroso to the followers of Freud and into modern times, the search for causes of female criminality have focused on her biology with scant heed to her sociology (Adler, 1975, p. 53).

The first systematic and still influential attempt to examine criminal violence in females was carried out by Caesar Lombroso, an Italian doctor who began his studies in the middle of the last century.

Lombroso was convinced that our criminal tendencies are almost exclusively a matter of inborn physiological and psychological traits. Thus a "good" (i.e., non-criminal) woman is born with the inherent feminine characteristics of passiveness, chastity and dependency. She also has child-like nature, a "deficient moral sense" and an "underdeveloped intelligence." These rather bovine qualities are biologically pre-ordained by the fact that she is woman, and together they practically eliminate the possibility of her becoming involved in any kind of criminal activity, let alone crimes of violence.

But some women do commit crimes, and they did even in Lombroso's day. According to Lombroso, criminal women are biological anomalies who are unfortunate enough to be born with those masculine qualities that will lead them into crime. Aggression, passion, dominance are the masculine criminogenic traits. But Lombroso went further than this. On the basis of careful measurements carried out during autopsies on the bodies of numerous prostitutes and other female felons, Lombroso claimed he could actually tell from their appearance and physical measurements which individual would be most likely to exhibit criminal behaviour. Criminal women looked more masculine. In comparison to "good" women, they tended to have darker skin, a more "virile cranium" and an excess of body hair.

Lombroso's procedures and to some extent his theories were subsequently discredited, and they seem somewhat bizarre when viewed from a modern perspective. Without the identification of specific criminal traits with specific physical characteristics, of course, Lombroso's whole explanation becomes completely circular: Criminal women show deviant behaviour because they have inherited deviant traits.

Nevertheless, Lombroso's work has had considerable impact on subsequent investigators. It encouraged a more humane treatment of criminals and shifted the concerns of criminologists from a sole concentration on purely legal matters towards the scientific study of criminals and criminal behaviour. Even his stereotype of a woman as a passive, dependent creature has persisted in one form or another to the present day. Moreover, his conviction that these feminine characteristics are inherited biological traits is still with us in a number of modern theories (Konopka, 1966; Vedder and Somerville, 1970; Cowse, Cowse, & Slater, 1968; Klein, 1975). Since the 1930s, however, there has been a gradual but steady shift away from a primary concern with biological factors towards an emphasis on social factors as an explanation of the criminal behaviour of females.

It's a Matter of Social Roles and Stereotypes

In the profoundest evolutionary sense, the social factors create our destiny, and biology must follow where society leads. (Adler, 1975, p. 53).

With the rise to pre-eminence of sociological theories of behaviour, a woman's criminal behaviour was no longer considered to be an immutable part of a woman's biological endowment. Rather, it was proposed that whatever traits she had were a result of a socializing process that begins at birth and continues throughout the child's development into adulthood. Though the exact course and the details of the learning experience can vary from person to person, ultimately most individuals will come to adopt the roles, values and behaviours that are expected of them and take their place as "normal" female members of society.

Note that the socialization theory doesn't say anything about what the content of the stereotype is or should be. The end product could still look very much like the stereotype proposed by Lombroso—a passive, dumb, dependent female. The difference would not be in what she ended up as, but how she got there.

Also similar to Lombroso is the way in which deviance is handled. A violent or criminal female is simply an aberration from the cultural norm which can be expected to occur now and then. Again, however, the root cause is a failure in the socialization process rather than a breakdown in the underlying genetic machinery.

Apart from some general characteristics such as passivity and gentleness, other aspects of the female stereotype can also come into play and effect the probability that the female will become involved in violent crime. One aspect is an expectation common in most Western societies that the woman should stay home to take the primary responsibility for raising the children and managing the house. To the extent that she adopts this role, the woman's opportunity to become involved in certain types of crime outside the home will obviously be reduced. The converse of this is that if she does become involved in criminal violence, it is most likely to be a domestic incident involving a spouse, a lover, a relative, a child or some other member of the household since that is her primary domain.

The relevant statistical evidence on this point is suggestive but not conclusive. Considering both males and females together, it is typical to find that about four out of every ten murders in Canada involve victims who are spouses, lovers, relatives, part of a love triangle or children in the household. When women murderers are considered separately, this figure tends to be higher, in the neighbourhood of 70 per cent or better. This phenomenon seems to be similar throughout North America. In the California Institute for Women, for example, of the 179 females who were incarcerated for homicide between 1963 and 1968, 70 per cent of the victims were members of the murderer's household. One should keep in mind, however, that we are referring here to percentage figures, not absolute numbers. Proportionally speaking, the number of domestic murders committed by men is less than for women. In absolute numbers, of course, men commit a far larger number of murders than women.

Women Are Really No Different
From Men After All

A third prominent explanation of the differences between male and female crime and violence is that there really is nothing to explain because there really is no difference after all. That is, the statistical difference is illusionary and doesn't reflect the facts.

This argument has been put forth most persuasively by Pollak in an influential book, *The Criminality of Women* (Pollak, 1950). Pollak's basic contention is that women in fact commit as much crime as men. The difference is that female crime tends not to show up on statistical reports because it tends to be "hidden crime." The first factor that contributes to this concealment is that females, more than men, tend to commit crimes that are less likely to be detected. Acts such as shoplifting or credit card frauds are predominently female crimes that would fall in this category.

The second factor is that even if the crime is detected, the circumstances may be such that the victim is reluctant to report it to the police. A client who has just been beaten and robbed by a prostitute, for example, may not want to get further involved.

The third factor, according to Pollak, is that the police and courts themselves also contribute to hidden crime by showing undue leniency and a misguided chivalry in their attitudes and actions towards female offenders. This latter factor was cited by Reckless and Kay (1967) as the most important explanation, in their view, for the relatively low incidence of female crime in comparison to men. According to these two authors:

> Police are less willing to make on-the-spot arrests or 'book' and hold a woman for court action. Courts are also easy on women because they are women (Reckless and Kay, 1967, p. 16).

Such biases apply not only to the judicial system but also to the street subculture itself. By and large, when a female on the street gets into trouble, she has a better chance of finding someone in the street community to shelter her than a male does, and therefore has a better chance to avoid getting caught. Frequently, as might be expected, the price for this preferential treatment is her sexual favours or a commitment to future prostitution. Moreover, the street girl will claim that often the police will also look the other way for similar favours.

There can be little doubt that a number of these factors are operating to systematically bias the reported crime rates towards an underestimation in the actual number of crimes in which females get involved. But surely these factors are not sufficient to explain the whole difference between the male and female statistics. To explain the Canadian arrest data for 1974, for example, one would have to assume that over thirty thousand crimes of violence against persons went undetected, were excused or were ignored simply because they were committed by women. A similar number of crimes of violence involving property and over forty thousand nonviolent property crimes would have to be explained on the same basis. Surely these discrepancies are simply too large to be attributed to "hidden crime" factors.

CHANGING PATTERNS IN FEMALE CRIME

> When size and strength between the sexes are discounted by technology . . . social expectations and social roles including criminal roles tend to merge (Adler, 1975, p. 52).

If social stereotypes and expectations play such a prominent role in influencing our potential for criminal behaviour, then any dramatic shifts in these societal expectations should be accompanied by equally significant changes in the observed pattern of criminal activity. This proposition is particularly relevant right now as North American society goes through a period of redefinition and expansion in female roles. The objective is to attempt to provide as wide a range of alternative roles as possible. The question is will this move towards equalizing the opportunities between the sexes also lead to an equalization in their behaviour in less desirable areas such as criminal behaviour? Will the new emphasis on assertive behaviour and militancy spill over into other areas to produce more aggressive illegal behaviour as well?

Most observers would agree that the proposition is at least worth considering. They would also agree that some significant changes do seem to be taking place in the criminal activity of women. What is much less clear is the exact nature and extent of these changes.

INCREASING CRIME RATES:
THE STATISTICAL EVIDENCE

The most careful and extensive study to date on the changing pattern of female crime and its potential relationship to the Women's Movement has been done by Rita Jones Simon (Simon, 1975). Using the Uniform Crime Reports published by the FBI, Simon has examined the changes in criminal activity of women during the two decades between 1953 and 1972. Her data show some interesting trends.

When all arrests are considered together, the proportion of women among those arrests has increased slowly but steadily from 10.8 per cent in 1953 to 15.3 per cent in 1972. Serious crimes (criminal homicide, robbery, aggravated assault, burglary, larceny and auto theft) increased somewhat faster from 9.4 per cent to 19.3 per cent. Larceny (theft) offences rose the fastest of all. They started relatively high at 13.9 per cent in 1953 and by 1972 had risen to the point where almost one in three arrests were female (30.8 per cent), the largest proportion of female arrests for any crime except for prostitution.

For crimes of violence the story is different. The two most serious crimes of violence—criminal homicide and aggravated assault—showed no consistent trends during the period. Female homicide arrests started at 14.1 per cent in 1953, rose to a peak of 17.2 per cent by 1962, then declined again to 15.6 per cent by 1972. The percentage of females arrested for aggravated assault actually decreased from 15.9 per cent to 13.9 per cent during the twenty-year period. In terms of total number of arrests, homicide accounts for about 0.2 per cent of arrests for both males and females and aggravated assault is about ten times as frequent or about 2.0 per cent of all arrests. Both of these rates have hardly fluctuated during the last twenty years.

On the basis of her findings, Simon concluded that there has indeed been a significant increase in both the number and proportion of women arrested over the twenty-year period covered by her study. That increase, however, can be attributed almost exclusively to increases in the frequency of larceny/theft offences. If the present rate of increase continues, these crimes will be the first ones for which the female arrest rate will actually be commensurate with their representation in the population, that is, equal to males.

Violent crimes show quite a different picture. Here the rates for females has not changed, which leads Simon to conclude:

> Contrary to impressions that might be gleaned from the news media, the proportion of female arrests for violent crimes has changed hardly at all over the past two decades. Female arrest rates for homicide has been the most stable of all violent offences (Simon, 1975, p. 46).

The Canadian trends in arrests data seem to follow a very similar pattern. Table 1 shows a tabulation of the Canadian arrest data for the years 1964 and 1974 broken down by sex and the type of crime. The major crimes have been grouped into three basic categories. The first category of crimes, *Against Person with Violence*, includes all crimes directly involving the death or injury of another human being—murder, attempted murder, manslaughter, assault, rape and other sexual assaults, criminal negligence. This category combines both the criminal homicide and aggravated assault cases discussed previously in the American data. Crimes in this category tend to be unpremeditated and often involve irrational uncontrolled behaviour motivated by emotion and passion rather than economic gain. The next category of crimes, *Against Property with Violence*, includes crimes where economic gain is a major motivation but where violence or the threat of violence is also involved. The third category, *Property Crimes, Non-Violent*, is a mixed bag of offences, most of them relatively minor and none of them involving the overt use or threat of violence—theft, fraud, false pretenses, forgery, possession of stolen goods, etc.

Table 1
Number of Charges and Percentages for
Males and Females for Various Offence Categories

		Adult charges—Canada 1964			1974		
		Males	Females	% Females	Males	Females	% Females
Against Person with Violence	No. of arrests	19,481	975		34,181	2,838	
	% Total arrests	14.2%	.7%	4.8%	13.6%	1.1%	7.7%
Against Property with Violence	No. of arrests	15,011	339		30,652	1,225	
	% Total arrests	10.9%	.2%	2.2%	12.2%	.5%	3.8%
Against Property Non-violent	No. of arrests	38,851	5,555		66,937	21,192	
	% Total arrests	26.8%	4.1%	12.5%	26.5%	8.4%	24.1%
Other Criminal Code	No. of arrests	53,332	5,870		85,255	9,820	
	% Total arrests	38.9%	4.3%	9.9%	33.8%	3.9%	10.3%
Total Criminal Code	No. of arrests	124,675	12,689		217,025	35,075	
	% Total arrests	90.7%	9.3%	9.3%	86.1%	13.9%	13.9%
Total		137,364			252,100		

Source: Adapted from data presented in *The Female Offender—Selected Statistics,* 1977 (Tables 1.1 and 1.2, pp. 5 and 8) produced by the Statistics Division, Solicitor General, Canada.

The overall picture shown in Table 1 looks very much like that found in the American research. The relative role played by females in American crime is somewhat larger (15.3 per cent) than that played by their Canadian counterparts (13.9 per cent). Like the Americans, however, Canadian women tend to be least involved in crimes of violence either against a person or against property and most involved, comparatively speaking, in non-violent property offences. Moreover, the only evidence for any substantial increases in the relative involvement of females in any of the crime categories is in the category of *Against Property Non-violent.* As with their American sisters, female crimes of violence are remaining relatively stable while non-violent property crimes are on the increase.

Although one cannot draw unequivocal conclusions from correlational data of this type, the results do seem to make sense when interpreted in the light of the Women's Movement. Much of the change that has come about is related to an increase in the rate of participation of women in the labour force. If we assume that women are by nature no more moral than men, then this increased participation in the labour force brings an increased opportunity for certain types of "commercial" crime—fraud, larceny and embezzlement. This is the most obvious prediction and it has been the most prominent pattern in the observed data to date.

Changes in Violent Crime

Attempts to link the Women's Movement with possible increases in violent crime by females is a much more tenuous endeavour. To the women living in the subculture, these larger social movements are for the most part irrelevant. The need for equal pay for equal work or improved day-care facilities are not the kinds of issues with which the average prostitute or the desperate drug addict are concerned. She certainly becomes involved in situational violence related to her day-to-day attempts to stay alive on the streets. But these tend to be standard altercations that are simply an accepted part of street life, not outbursts that result from pent-up emotions and frustrated goals.

In spite of the lack of any statistical evidence showing significant increases in the incidence of violent crimes by females, a number of prominent investigators still maintain that women are becoming more violent and aggressive. One of the most prominent of these, Freda Adler, acknowledges that homicide rates are remaining stable for females but goes on to cite contradictory anecdotal evidence gathered from her interviews with workers in various aspects of the criminal justice system from right across the United States. Her interviews ranged from the police working in the front lines to prison and after-care workers. Her conclusion from all this information is that women are indeed becoming more violent. One Washington DC patrolman was quite startled to discover women were not quite as nice as he thought they were:

> I have been punched in the mouth, grabbed, kicked in the groin and threatened by women (Adler, 1975, p. 49).

or a Washington police lieutenant:

> . . . I mean girls were throwing bricks just as hard as boys, and their language was just as rough. They would throw the trashcans and rock the buses and cars just like the males. No, toward the end there we had to change our thinking, I guess (Adler, 1975, p. 103).

And finally, there is the opinion of a New York City youth worker with twenty-five years of experience behind her:

> It's difficult to put a finger on exactly what is happening but something quite drastic has taken place out there. . . . Through the 50s, we would get the occasional girl for shoplifting . . . mostly a spur of

the moment thing. . . . Girls we're seeing now are involved in a whole range of new activities . . . like extortion. A group of girls ganging up on another girl and shaking her down for money. I mean that was simply unheard of a few years ago. Now you don't get the name calling, hair pulling that used to go on between girls . . . *you get vicious physical assault* (Adler, 1975, p. 97).

Adler is particularly concerned about indications of the emergence of female gangs in both the United States and Great Britain (i.e., "granny bashers"). Rather than being an adjunct to a male gang as was the case in the past, these gangs are operating independently. More and more they are becoming indistinguishable from their male counterparts who terrorized the streets of North America during the '50s and '60s. In the colourful language of *Time*, October 16 edition, 1972:

Sometimes silently, sometimes shrieking, they swoop down in groups on unsuspecting victims in dark streets, at lonely bus stops, and in deserted toilets, kicking, biting, scratching, punching, they reduce the victim—usually another female—to hysteria and then disappear, stealing perhaps a few pence.

What is the motivation for their crime—the few pennies they steal or the thrill of attack? Such behaviour is unquestionably disturbing, but how do we interpret it? Are we witnessing here a temporary aberration of some juvenile girls who will eventually grow out of their violent ways? Or are we seeing the beginnings of a fundamental change in female behaviour, a change that will have to be confronted in tomorrow's female offender.

REFERENCES

Adler, F.
1975   *Sisters in Crime*. New York: McGraw-Hill.
Cowie, J. Cowie, V., and Slater, E.
1968   *Delinquency in Girls*. London: William Heineman.
Crites, L.
1976   "Women offenders: myth vs. reality" in *The Female Offender*, L. Crites (ed.). Lexington: D. C. Heath.
Crites, L. (ed.)
1976   *The Female Offender*. Lexington: D. C. Heath.
Klein, D.
1976   "The etiology of female crime: a review of the literature," in *The Female Offender*, L. Crites (ed.). Lexington: D. C. Heath.
Konopka, G.
1966   *Adolescent Girls in Conflict*. Englewood Cliffs, N.J.: Prentice-Hall.
Lombroso, C.
1958   *The Female Offender*. New York: Wisdom Library. (Originally published 1899.)

Pollak, O.
1950   *The Criminality of Women.* Philadelphia: University of Pennsylvania Press.
Reckless, W. C. & Kay, B. A.
1967   *The Female Offenders.* President's Commission on Law Enforcement and Administration of Justice.
Simon, R. J.
1975   *Women and Crime.* Toronto: D. C. Heath.
Solicitor General, Canada
1977   *The Female Offender—Selected Statistics.* Statistics Division, Canadian Penitentiary Service.

1977   *Report on the National Advisory Committee on the Female Offender.* Public Affairs Division, Canadian Penitentiary Service.
Vedder, C.,
1970   *The Delinquent Girl.* Springfield: Charles C. Thomas.
Ward, R., Jackson, M.,
1968   *Crimes of Violence by Women.* Crimes of Violence 13, Appendix 17; President's Commission on Law Enforcement and Administration of Justice.
Wolfgang, M. E.
1958   *Patterns of Criminal Homicide.* New York: John Wiley & Sons, Inc.

Chapter 3

FROM BARROOMS TO BEDROOMS: TOWARDS A THEORY OF INTERPERSONAL VIOLENCE

Robert C. Prus

Unlike most research on violence, this chapter makes the basic assumption that violence is an inevitable feature of social life. It is neither anti-social nor individualistic. It is when rules become ambiguous that people must "negotiate" responses, only some of which are violent. The dynamics which result in non-violent as well as violent behaviour are of concern to Prus. From this interactionist point of view, violence cannot be understood in terms of consequences but, rather, in terms of the motivation of the participants.

Although Prus presents a very convincing case theoretically, some methodological qualifications are in order. First, data was elicited from some 740 "free citizens" in order to avoid the use of official crime statistics. This data was admittedly not representative of any particular population and most of it was acquired by asking an individual to reconstruct a potentially violent situation. Retrospective data is necessarily problematic in nature. Secondly, of the large sample interviewed, only a very small percentage were used to support conclusions of the author. Perhaps all the data would do so. However, some demonstration of the results as a whole would seem reasonable. Given these constraints, Prus presents a valuable contribution, sensitive to the ongoing interaction and self-reflectivity of social behaviour.

INTRODUCTION

This paper presents an interactionist statement on interpersonal confrontations. Working towards a theory designed to explicate the conditions under which anger and violence are likely to occur, interpersonal confrontations are examined as social phenomena, with particular emphasis on the definitions of situations by involved persons and the processes by which these definitions are articulated.

In developing this paper, a number of seemingly popular notions of anger and violence are challenged. In contrast to the notion that anger

---

* This paper was presented at the Canadian Sociology and Anthropology Meetings in conjunction with the Learned Societies, Fredericton, N.B., 1977.

** The author would like to thank Steve Vassilakopoulos, Nancy Suits and Abe Birnbaum for comments on earlier drafts of this chapter.

and violence are anti-social and individualistic phenomena, it is suggested herein that these are basic and inevitable features of social life. While anger and violence are often conceptualized as impulsive, instinctive and irrational responses, the position developed in this paper is that these are socially based and negotiable responses, reflecting self-reflectivity and ongoing interaction. Whereas persons becoming angry and violent are frequently thought different from others, it proposes that anyone (with values) may become angered and that the emergence of violence is in every case problematic.

In part, these challenges are predicated on the way in which the study of violence was approached. First, while many researchers focus on "violent" outcomes, the scope of this study included both these and "nonviolent" outcomes, asking when any given encounter was likely to move in one or other direction. Second, in contrast to the tendency to limit conceptions of violence to behaviours having extremely harmful consequences, frequently of an illegal nature, it was decided to establish a more encompassing definition of violence, one which would allow us to consider a wider variety of situations. Third, while much of the explanational attention is commonly focused on precipitating events, the emphasis here is on the processes by which interaction sequences develop. Thus, instead of attempting to locate the cause of anger in a single unit or set of factors, with the assumption that there is a disruptive act and/or actor, the approach taken was to suspend judgment on elements of the encounter, except as the actors themselves indicate that particular aspects of an association affected them in one way or other ways. Fifth, while many discussions of violence utilize official crime data, the data for this study was gathered from "free citizens" and reflects their accounts of events.

THE LITERATURE

A library search for explicitly sociological statements explaining when and how violence was likely to occur provided relatively little assistance. Although confrontation seems a basic feature of social order (Simmel, 1955), it may be the case as Goode (1972) suggests, that sociologists are not fond of considering the role of force (and violence) in society.

One of the most frequently cited works in the area is Wolfgang and Ferracuti's (1967) discussion of violent subcultures. Assuming a multiple-factors approach, their "integrated conceptualization" concludes with seven propositions:

1. No subculture can be totally different from or totally in conflict with the society of which it is a part.
2. To establish the existence of a subculture of violence does not require

that the actors sharing in this basic value element express violence in all situations.

3. The potential resort or willingness to resort to violence in a variety of situations emphasizes the penetrating and diffusive nature of this culture theme.

4. The subcultural ethos of violence may be shared by all ages in a subsociety but this ethos is most prominent in a limited age group ranging from late adolescence to middle age.

5. The counter-norm is nonviolence.

6. The development of favourable attitudes toward, and the use of, violence in this subculture involve learned behaviour and a process of differential learning, association, or identification.

7. The use of violence in a subculture is not necessarily viewed as illicit conduct, and the users therefore do not have to deal with feelings of guilt about their aggression (Wolfgang and Ferracuti, 1967:314).

This statement tells us little about when and how incidents occur. And, if violence in violent subcultures is of the sporadic and infrequent nature suggested by Matza (1964) and Miller (1966), this statement is strikingly inadequate. Discussing this and similar studies of violence relying on official statistics, Hepburn (1972) thus seems justified in asking "what have criminologists accomplished in the last three decades?" Although attempts to explain violence through the use of official crime statistics may be useful in some senses, they tell us very little about how people work out their lives on a day-to-day basis.[1]

Only a small number of studies focus on the ongoing processes by which violence occurs. Thus, of published works, we refer the reader to Wolfgang's (1957) analysis of victim-precipitated homicide; Gelles's (1972) discussion of interpersonal violence in families; Horowitz and Schwartz's (1974) examination of the role of honour and normative ambiguity within violent subcultural contexts; and Athens's (1974) analysis of the role of self in emergent confrontations. An insightful discussion of the mechanics of violent encounters, within violent subcultures (Dietz, 1968) is, unfortunately, unpublished. Also useful is another group of research, which while discussing violence in a peripheral sense, nevertheless develops some important themes. See, for example, Lemert (1962), Matza (1964), Parnas (1967), Couch (1968), Conklin (1972:102-122), Letkemann (1973: 90-116), Prus and Sharper (1977:107-123). Taken together, these studies suggest that human violence has both a self-reflective and an interactive quality. While persons' cultural backgrounds influence their responses, private assessments of the situation by involved actors and the joint and ongoing contributions of involved parties appear critical to understanding the emergence of violence.

THE DATA

In seeking material that would lend itself to an interactionist perspective, two somewhat different sources of data were utilized. Although this material was gathered neither with the intention of being exhaustive nor representative, nevertheless it had considerable range and was therefore extremely useful, not only in assessing existing notions of violence, but also in suggesting revisions of these conceptualizations grounded in the perceptions and sequenced interaction of the participants.

One source of data was some sixty accounts of disruptive behaviour taking place in hotel settings. These were compiled with the assistance of one male and two females working at three different, but "rough," hotels. These incidents denoted some of the more physical aspects of violence.

In an attempt to provide a more general basis on which to examine violence, another 680 accounts of incidents were gathered from a variety of people (n = 85), nearly all of whom had some university contact. These people were asked to describe situations in which they found themselves upset with others, telling: who was involved; what happened and how it took place; whether or not other persons were present and what effect if any they had; whether or not the incident had a history; and if they thought the incident could have been (a) more and (b) less intense, and how that might have happened. While only about 10 per cent of the reported incidents involved physical violence, it was in many ways richer than the hotel material; the participants generally provided more information than the observers could typically gather. This material was also instructive in some other ways as well. First, it provided numerous instances of situations in which persons chose to avoid confrontations or to deliberately limit their involvements. It also indicated a number of alternatives to physical violence, which, nevertheless, could be used to do violence to another. Third, it provided further indications of the complexity of violence. While these accounts enable one to get closer to the situation, it became increasingly apparent that there were typically two confrontations going on, the one A was having with B and the one B was having with A (in some instances B might not be aware that anything was amiss between A and himself). It also became clear that any violent exchanges were best seen in the context of careers of confrontations, such that subsequent events were best understood in the context of preceding ones.

CONCEPTUALIZING VIOLENCE

For the purposes of this paper, "violence" refers to any activity (thought, word or deed) in which persons engage, anticipating that this activity will cause some degree of harm or discomfort (physically or socially, temporarily or permanently, directly or indirectly) to a target(s). This is distinguished from "violent consequences" and "attributions of violence," each of which may be at variance with the intended activity, and neither of which may be helpful in accounting for the activity.

Violent Consequences

Although popular attention may be focused on those behaviours having more extensively harmful consequences, it seems extremely useful to consider these outcomes in a broader and more complete context, to step back and ask when and how persons are likely to act upon their violent thoughts. While intensifying the drama, the issue of "violent consequences" adds little to the understanding of the careers of interpersonal confrontations. Although violent consequences may represent a basis on which individuals may be singled out as being "violent persons," so many fortuitous and attributional considerations come into play that a consideration of consequences seems an unreliable basis on which to make inferences regarding the emergence, intensification, or dissipation of violent encounters.

Not only are consequences "after the fact" phenomena, but conceptions of (violent) consequences are often limited to physical personal or property damages and tend to promote highly simplified notions of humans as being physical or not acting. The more social and subtle aspects of doing others harm are omitted. Direct physical harm represents only one of a number of methods of harming others and may occur before or after or in combination with other behaviours intended to harm others, as well as exclusively. It should not be assumed, either, that physical harm is a more effective or injurious form of violence.

Attributions of Violence

So far as possible, the focus on the present study will be limited to violence as defined by the participants rather than by outsiders witnessing any exchanges. Although there may be some correspondence between the interpretations of witnesses and the intentions and definitions of participants, it is also possible that witnesses may have quite different perceptions of situations than those of the participants. Thus, for example, an unintended injury might be perceived as "extremely malicious" by an observer. Additionally, while consequences may be specifically defined, participants may have only had vague intentions ("I only wanted to hurt him, not to hurt him like that"). As with violent consequences, attributions of violence may be more instrumental in selecting out certain persons as violent (after the fact) than in explaining the emergence of violent behaviour.

Anger et Hoc Genus Omne*

Although one can be angry without being violent and violent without being angry, the two are so frequently related that any discussion of violence would seem to require a discussion of anger as well.

Rather than view anger as a psychological entity or emotion, it is suggested that anger is most productively seen in the terms of moral indignation. Moral indignation refers to a situation in which one judges that some aspect of his experience has been (unjustly) transgressed or offended by some act or quality of another. Offended persons may, but need not, associate a sense of threat or urgency in conjunction with the feelings of indignation. When these other elements do occur, however, the event becomes more problematic and imposing and is more likely to become a reference point for action.

Once one perceives moral indignation as the basis of anger, it becomes apparent that persons do not become angry for "bad reasons," but rather become angry in the context of values generally proclaimed desirable in their social groupings. In contrast to the view that "evil or maladjusted persons desire to harm others," it is suggested that in providing persons with moral standards, social groupings provide persons not only with the guidelines for their own behaviour, but also with a basis on which to assess and react to the behaviours of others.

Consistent with the material on face-work (Goffman, 1955; Ho, 1976), the data gathered suggests that moral indignation reflects what might be termed "trust violations" of a group and individual nature.[2] Thus, norm violators, persons who neglected their duty, broke their word, were found lying or spreading rumours, making improper advances, or taking uninvited advantage of others, were frequent targets of anger; as were persons who in one way or another were seen as responsible for denigrating one's integrity by raising questions about one's competence, desirability and rights, or by otherwise slighting or making one feel insignificant. Our data also suggests that persons may become angered in reference to just about anything and that one cannot infer reactions from the locus of the anger.

CONFRONTATION CONTINGENCIES

In what follows, it is suggested that confrontations represent a "normal" aspect of ongoing association. Intended as a general statement applicable to anyone, the emphasis is on examining careers of incidents rather than the careers of persons reputed to be violent. Perceiving every encounter as problematic, it is posited that in each case so-called "violent persons" would be subject to the same concerns as "anyone

---

* Translates anger "and all things of that sort."

else." In this respect, it is useful to distinguish "careers of confrontations," referring to the processes by which confrontations take place over a time period, from "careers of violent persons," referring to the processes by which persons become involved in violent encounters on a more regularized basis (what Lemert, 1967, terms "secondary deviance").[3] Our concern, here, is with the former.

In discussing the careers of confrontations a number of themes become important: (1) the differential receptivity of persons to various forms of violence; (2) the problematic and negotiable quality of interaction; (3) drift or temporary release from moral restraints; (4) situational closure, committing participants to particular lines of action; and (5) disentanglement options, allowing persons to become disinvolved from confrontations.

Reflecting basic notions of differential association (Sutherland, 1955) and symbolic interactionism (Mead, 1934; Blumer, 1969), it is suggested that persons not only learn both positive and negative definitions of behaviours, but also acquire notions of when particular behaviours might be most appropriate. For example, persons might learn that it is wrong to kill, but also learn that one has the right to protect himself from the attempts of another to take his or her life. Depending upon the particular communities with which persons associate, one may expect to find: varying levels of acceptance of particular forms of violent behaviour; and differential notions of conditions exempting persons from blame for particular activities. In this respect, the persons researching subcultural violence make some valid points, although it seems that support for violence (especially exemption from blame) may be much more widespread across social groups than they infer. Additionally, insofar as they rely on physical violence resulting in more extreme physical consequences as their data base, they miss much of the complexity of violence. Although it makes sense to speak of persons entering encounters with differential dispositions to varying forms of violence, to stop here would be extremely misleading. The greater relative acceptance of a particular form of violence does not explain its appearance.

Although persons act toward the world as they know it and themselves, it is important to stress the problematic and negotiable aspects of ongoing interaction. While existing rules of thumb will enable people to handle routine matters, any time persons find these inconsistent, ambiguous, or otherwise inadequate, they have to "ad hoc" or work things out on their way through the situation (Garfinkel, 1967). At this point, experiencing what Horowitz and Schwartz (1974:243-244) term "normative ambiguity," persons are more likely to find themselves open to personally more atypical solutions. And it is under conditions of the rule inconsistency that persons become particularly sensitive to cues from immediate-situated others (Prus and Sharper, 1977:165). Further, where persons experience a sense of threat and urgency in a situation of uncertainty, they seem more likely to select options that provide immediate, although possibly only short term, solutions.

DRIFT AND CLOSURE

To this point, we have suggested that persons may enter associations with somewhat different orientations vis-a-vis the appropriateness of particular forms of violence in particular situations, and that under conditions of uncertainty people would be more open to suggestions from others, particularly those seen to help them handle their immediate situations. Although helpful, this is still insufficient to account for the emergence of violence on the part of anyone who does not consider violent behaviour the preferred mode of association. It is in this context that the concepts of "drift" and "closure" seem strikingly relevant.

Matza (1964) introduced the notion of "drift" to account for the delinquent involvements of young people. Seeing these activities as occasional, temporal and sporadic, rather than systematic in nature, and positing that the value systems of the youth were not so different from those of other people, Matza argued that some sort of neutralization had taken place, so that the normally effective moral rules could be bypassed. He therefore uses the term "drift" to refer to situations in which persons feel released from normally operative moral restraints.

Somewhat related to Matza's concept of drift is Lemert's (1953) depiction of "situational closure." Discussing naive cheque forgers, Lemert notes that persons proffering particular images of self may find themselves engaging in behaviours, which while apparently relevant to immediate situational pressures, may be quite at variance from those which they had earlier intended and may be quite different from those with which they later feel comfortable. Intentionally or otherwise, persons may find themselves having made commitments to particular lines of action and, rather than a call a costly and/or embarrassing retreat, attempt to see the event to its conclusion. Although closure is by no means limited to persons becoming angered, as persons become more indignant, they may feel freer to say or do things which may commit them to more extreme lines of action.

Drift

Assuming that persons encounter some definitions of violence as undesirable, it becomes important to ask, as Matza does, how they overcome these reservations. To this end, an attempt was made to codify the forms which these "releases from the moral responsibility of not injuring others" assume, recognizing that where persons are less committed to this norm, concerns with drift are less consequential. Allowing "conventional citizens" to maintain personal integrity while engaging in deviant activities, four basic forms of release seem operative: community control concerns, situational conduciveness; favourable targets; and personal justifications.

Community Control Concerns

Release from propriety via control concerns takes three forms (morals enforcement, reformation, and community priorities). While related, these reflect somewhat different control themes. First, those persons defined by community (or self-appointed) as "morals enforcers" perceive a legal and/or moral responsibility to punish violators, to show those who have transgressed group standards that they cannot do so with impunity:[4]

> This drunk came in and was creating a disturbance with some of the people at one of the tables. The bouncer approached him and asked him to leave. The man said he would stay if he wanted to. The bouncer then grabbed the man by the jacket, took him to the exit and sort of kicked him out the door saying, "You keep your ass out of here."

The second form of control involves "reformation," wherein specific instances of violence are excused on the grounds that they promote conformity, cooperation or education, ways of gaining control over persons whose activities are seen as detrimental to the effective community. With an emphasis on shaping subsequent behaviour, one may consider as examples the attempts of parents and teachers to educate those in their charge through discipline,[5] and the attempts of rehabilitating agencies to reform their clientele. Perceiving a social obligation and/or assuming that their own perspectives are superior, these persons may feel genuinely benign in knowingly imposing discomfort upon others when they perceive them requiring their instruction or assistance. However, not all uses of violence to promote community order are benign:

> I will always ask the guy to leave first. Give him a chance to back down and leave. There are just a lot of people who just don't listen to reason and you have to beat the hell out of them. That's the only way to deal with them.

"Community priorities" represent a third basis on which groups and their representatives may claim exemption from the moral restraints opposing violence. This exemption rests on the inevitability of harm to some, given the desirability or necessity of certain goals for the community. Thus, any discomfort or injury may be viewed as an "unfortunate side effect," or, perhaps, "only temporary." Defining themselves as having an ennobling mission or crusade, or possibly just a necessary task, groups may in this way disqualify the culpability normally associated with activities causing harm to otherwise innocent persons.

Situational Conduciveness

A number of features of situations in which persons find themselves may also serve to exempt persons from otherwise effective moral restraints. First, persons may jointly agree to bypass normal concerns with violence. The formal roles of competitive events may require that any participants of the event normally subject themselves to various discomforts as other participants attempt to realize their goals. Although more informal, a similar exemption from moral responsibility is operative when two persons agree to "step outside" to settle a dispute. Within parameters of "fair play" then, violence may be a demanded feature of the event.

A second, but somewhat related, notion of situational conduciveness pertains to groups in which ongoing participation in some forms of violence is seen as a requisite for membership. Although acceptable targets may be limited, one may find groups in which certain "normal" concerns of violence are suspended. While one might think, here, of street gangs, there are other groupings in which certain other forms of violence (e.g., overt expressions of contempt for specific targets or exhibiting a capacity for being "catty," "ruthless," or "open" with other people) are requisites for "members in good standing:"

> At _____, where I worked as a youth worker, the rule was to express anger. That was the norm—you told people whatever you thought of them when you got angry. That was encouraged, there was to be no holding back . . . physical hitting, though, was forbidden.[6]

A third way in which situations may "free up" persons from moral restraints is by providing indications that the interaction parameters are more open than is the case in other places. Thus, an assessment that "fights happen here, a lot" may not only lead persons to become more suspicious of the motives of others, but is also suggestive of ways in which to relate to others. Similarly, witnessing one's associates as engaging in unchallenged violence in a particular setting (regardless of the underlying reasons) may be used as a reference point in developing one's own line of action. While persons need not respond in like manner, any tolerated violence suggests that tight moral restraints may be situationally inoperative; violence becomes a more viable resource in handling one's relations with others.

The last form of situational conduciveness to be mentioned here is the "nonserious" definition of harm. Although one may know that the behaviour will likely cause the recipient discomfort in one or other ways, to the extent that the activity is defined more totally in other terms (e.g., humour, respect, toughness), persons are less apt to be concerned with moral restraints opposing violence. Where target discomfort is not in any way anticipated, regardless of the consequences, an activity involving the target would not be classified as a violent one by our definition. For example, although the following incident resulted in considerable discomfort to the subject, whether or not the act of "spiking her drink" was a violent activity depends not on the consequences, but rather upon the definitions of the actor at the time he did this:

> I had gone to a party with two girlfriends. They were the only ones at the party who weren't doing any dope. One of the guys at the party apparently dropped some acid into a drink that he had made me. And only after one drink, I found that I could barely walk. I made it to the washroom and the people who had the party eventually came and helped me to the bedroom. I had been so sick that I ended up vomiting blood and was literally immobile for two and a half hours. While I was throwing up and seeing four of everything, I could not even talk or attempt to walk for several hours. I remember a fight between the fellow who had doped my drink and some other people. A few hours later my girlfriends and a couple of guys drove me home and carried me to bed. Three days later, this fellow who had spiked my drink called to see how I was. I all but hung up in his ear. He thought the whole thing was pretty funny. I was furious but felt unable to do anything that would in any way correct or help the situation.

Feasible Targets

Another basis on which one may negate norms prohibiting violence involves the denigration of targets. Persons thought "social discounts" (e.g., "punks," "suckers," "no-accounts," "drunks," etc.), insofar as they are not viewed as "conventional citizens" release those with whom they associate from the usual norms of propriety. Although they do not, in themselves, invoke violence, disaffiliated or otherwise "inconsequential" persons are frequently seen as persons with whom one can be more irresponsible and, to this extent, represent more favourable targets for violence:

> These two men were grappling at the bar and the bartender asked what the trouble was. One of the men, who was drunk, said something nobody could understand. The bartender told the man to get lost. The man then said, "You hit my brother last week. You can't get away with that." The bartender then went up to the guy and gave him a shot in the face, saying, "There, now I've hit you too." The man then did something very unusual, he started crying, like a baby. Everyone was kind of taken back. Some of the guys helped console the man and then led him out of the bar. Everybody had a good laugh afterwards.

Personal Justifications

In addition to the somewhat external features serving to reduce moral culpability over the use of violence, people may exempt themselves from typically appropriate behaviour on a more personal basis.

Somewhat parallel to community-control concerns, one pair of personal concerns reflects: personal rights enforcement, and gaining personal control over troublesome others. In the first instance, persons judging their personal dignity to have been offended may endeavour to show the parties responsible that this is not accomplished without penalty. While notions of personal rights are integrally linked to perceived group values, in the absence of community indignation offended parties may feel sufficiently justified in protecting their own rights to overcome usual restraints against violence. Further, in as far as the targets have become at least temporarily personally disvalued, they are less likely to be seen meriting polite attention:

> I had been dating Pete for about three months and we had become quite intimate. I cared for him a lot but I grew to hate him more than anyone I knew. I thought our relationship was a private affair but he felt obliged to share the details with others—his family and his friends who I didn't know, fellow workers and people we both knew. When I found out, I was furious, my self-esteem was reduced to zero and I felt betrayed. I called off our relationship although he badgered me for about another month or so. Finally I wrote him a very insulting but true letter and refused to communicate any further with him. He called a few times, being very confused and upset. His mother even called and insisted that no negative opinions of me had been made, but at this point my pride had been damaged beyond repair. Finally, he left me alone.

> I was clerking the other day and a lady and her son were my next customers. The lady started putting her order on the counter and I started ringing it through. Her son was about four years old and he was helping me, or so he thought. He was putting an item or two over the bar for every item I had rung. Thus, it was difficult for me to tell what I had rung through and what I had not. I had to stop and check the sales slip twice. I asked him to stop helping, but I said that it was nice that he wanted to. He did stop for a minute but then he began doing it again. His mother was watching him all the while, but she simply smiled and said nothing. I finally asked him again to stop but this time he said he would do it if he wanted to. The mother again said nothing. I decided that I was losing the battle and said nothing more. I finished the order. But when I packed it I put the apples on top of the eggs, hoping that they might break.

The second control-based justification, that of managing troublesome persons, allows for violence as a means of promoting personally desired objectives and/or avoiding undesired situations. Where a particular form of violence is seen as a more expedient and, particularly, a more exclusive route to a desired end, persons may perceive themselves pressured into selecting this otherwise undesirable option.[7]

> My roommate always used to leave his underwear on the floor. I resented this because when I brought my girlfriend over to the room it was kind of embarrassing. I said that if he ever did it again I would throw the underwear out the window. The next time he did it I did throw it out the window. I explained to him that my girlfriend had come over to the room and she should not be subjected to this sight. He seems to have learned from that experience.

> Some drunk guy got into an argument with the doorman and the doorman told him to leave. The guy turned to him and said, "Do you know what you are, you're a fucking pimp!" The doorman hit him and knocked him out cold, saying he didn't have to take that from anybody.

The third form of personal justification for engaging in violent behaviour may be termed the "default" justification. Disavowing responsibility, by virtue of their situations (e.g., illness, fatigue, injury, confusion), persons may conclude that they do not care; that they are exempt from typical moral constraints by virtue of these extenuating circumstances. Occasionally, one finds persons so overwhelmed by moral indignation that they find themselves unable to handle the situation in any collected sense:

> Following my brother's wedding, Fred was too drunk to drive, my younger sister and I left to go home—I drove. Karen sat in between Fred and I. He had put his arm around her and started playing with her hair. When I pulled up in front of our house, he made a pass at her. I went off the deep end and just screeched, "Get the fuck out of this car!" Eventually we all went inside but he was just too drunk to discuss it.

Drift as Problematic

To this point, a number of ways in which persons may feel free from moral restraints regarding the use of violence have been articulated. However, while drift has a number of dimensions, in any given case these may become mixed (initially or as interaction sequences develop). Further, although any number of these "releases" may be operating simultaneously, the extent to which persons feel released from usual moral obligations is variable over time. Any ongoing interaction can free persons from, or constrain persons to, conditions of "polite interaction." Thus, if we were to plot the degree of drift persons experienced during an encounter, we may expect considerable variation as the interaction sequence unfolds. Although the same persons may interact in the same situations, there may be certain points in time at which one or both persons feel more extensively freed from their obligations to associate in a nonharmful manner. Our next task, then, is to examine the interactional features that seem critical in affecting the amount of drift interacting parties experience.

Closure

The concept of closure (Lemert, 1953) implies that certain of one's present activities may be instrumental in shaping one's choice of options. In an interactional context, any activities (and any inferences thereof) could theoretically operate in this direction. In actuality, however, whether a theme is pursued or not depends on the assessment of the activity by the involved persons and the perceived implications of the activity for subsequent relations.

Although any theme, depending on the responses of the other, may be effective in structuring one's subsequent opportunities, the more vigorously and/or persistently presented themes appear more likely to evoke attention and response from others. Thus, while some aspects of closure may be inadvertent and reflect the interests of others, individuals can, through what Goffman (1959) terms "impression management," attempt to promote closure in a desired direction (closure is by no means limited to confrontations or unpleasant associations).

To appreciate the implications of closure for violence, it is necessary to examine some features of confrontations. First, in contrast to the "it takes two to tango" version of confrontations, it is suggested that one person may be totally instrumental in defining the initial theme(s) and pursuing the confrontation. Should the disenchanted party decide not to confront the other, as is often the case, the issue may go entirely unnoticed by the other. Further, while the involved parties may find themselves mutually displeased at the same point in an encounter, this condition is neither necessary nor sufficient for a confrontation to occur. It is also the case that while persons may anticipate impending confrontations, as through the distancing behaviours of offended persons or demands on the target's attention (e.g., "I want to talk to you, now!"), confrontations often come as complete surprises to the targets. In any event, once a disclosure is made, both the style of the approach and the subsequent responses can, in turn, be critical in defining the ongoing relationship between the involved parties:

> Two men were sitting in a hotel beverage room at the same table, but they were unacquainted. One man had struck a match but it went out. He tossed it in the other man's direction. The second man said, "Hey, watch where you're throwing your garbage." The first man said, "I'll throw things where I damn well please." The second man said, "Not at me you don't." And at that point he attacked the first and they started wrestling, knocking over some tables and chairs. The attacker tried to hit the fellow with the table while he was down. He missed and broke the table. Both separated and there were some heated words. They left the hotel separately.

While any actual (or perceived) confrontation may result in the target becoming indignant, regardless of style, it appears that more obvious and more extensive accusations (condemnations) are more likely to shape the subsequent relationship. First, to the extent the confronter has been more overt in expressing negative target assessments, he commits himself personally and publicly not only to an image of the target, but also by implication to anti-target behaviour. Second, as the target perceives greater social distance between himself and the other (the other disvalues him) and finds himself devaluing the other, the degree of drift the target experiences vis-a-vis violence increases; the target feels less constrained to be civil to the other. In those cases in which the confrontation has been initiated by some expression of violence, the target is likely to experience further release of restraint from continuing "normal association" as this act clearly suggests that the relationship is not bounded by usual considerations.

The following account illustrates a common feature of closure. Where involved parties see themselves as having obligations, rights, or investments in a situation, neither may feel justified in giving in to avoid a possible confrontation:

> These two guys had taken two hookers into their room and a little while later one of the bouncers and I heard some loud noises coming from the room. About twenty minutes later the switchboard lit up, but by this time this one bouncer I had been talking with earlier had left, so I called downstairs for another bouncer. We went into the room. The hookers were yelling and the guys were yelling and there were clothes and whatnot scattered all over the floor. The hookers had their dresses on and the two guys were naked. One guy was putting on his pants and the other guy was just sitting on the bed. The guy on the bed had one of the hooker's purses, and he wouldn't give it back. The hooker said, "That guy is trying to steal my money from me." The guy said that she was trying to rip him off for the money. Anyway, when the bouncer and I went in these fellows became rather antagonistic. The one guy, sitting on the bed, said, "Like who invited you guys to come in here? Like what the hell are you two guys doing here? We rented the room! We've got the room, not you!" I said, "Just cool it, now, I want to straighten this thing out." He said, "Who the fuck do you think you are?" By this time he had also gotten his pants on and he took a shot at me and hit me in the mouth. At this point, the manager and another fellow came into the room along with another bouncer. The two bouncers held the man down and the manager told me to go back to the desk, which I did.

Disentanglement

Although the target may feel that the other was justified in his displeasure with the target, it needn't be assumed that consensus on this point would alleviate subsequent confrontations (targets may not, for example, appreciate the manner in which they were approached). In this sense, seemingly more important than agreement, vis-a-vis the ensuing confrontation, are the concerns of the target: of maintaining the overall relationship; and of the implications of this confrontation for the relationship with the other. Thus, as targets perceive a relationship more important, overall, they will endeavour to de-escalate any confrontation. However, as the outcomes of a particular confrontation are, at that place and time, perceived more important for their subsequent relations, persons seem more likely to contest the decision, with violence being viewed as a resource.

Whereas some confrontations may dissolve virtually by default, as when targets are so taken by surprise that they are at a loss to organize appropriate responses or when willing "combatants" are involuntarily separated, the manner in which the target responds can neutralize seemingly violent confrontations. Thus, Dietz (1968:62-64) found that the following strategies were effective in avoiding undesired violence in violent subcultural confrontations: pretense (incapacity or lack of awareness of a potential confrontation); faking out (bluffing the other person down); verbal battle (exchanging noncommittal remarks); passing to another (involving a friend who is a more capable fighter); diversion (steering an aggressor away from the conflict).

In addition to these attempts to escape violence, one may find the target offering a variety of accounts (Sykes and Matza, 1958; Lyman and Scott, 1968; and Prus, 1975) intended to neutralize culpability. Although these disclaims may be effective in reshaping the manner in which the challenger approaches the target, the effectiveness of any account depends on its being honoured. And, where accounts are perceived as attempts to avoid justice, then "cover-ups" may arouse greater indignation than that surrounding the initial concern.

In contrast to disavowal strategies, our data suggests that one of the more effective ways of diffusing a confrontation is to assume responsibility for the event, but to do so in the context of penitence.[8] Although the "repentent sinner" role may be implemented with varying degrees of explicitness (ranging from silent sheepishness to a highly elaborated portrayal of event contingencies, former and past views, affirmation of offended values, and appropriate restitution), once it is recognized it redefines the target as a more acceptable person and, thus, reduces the amount of drift the challenger experiences.[9]

Another means by which confrontations are dissipated is through "cool outs." Here, targets need neither disavow nor admit responsibility for events, but reduce drift predominantly by exhibiting continued interest in the agent. One way of doing this is to express support for, or sympathy with, the agent's concerns, possibly offering to lend assistance to overcome the agent's loss. The second means is through altering the perspective from which the agent views the event. This may be accomplished, variously, by allowing the agent: to discount the significance of the issue[10]; to see side benefits of the situation; or to gain new hope. Cool outs are sometimes initiated inadvertently and needn't be sophisticated to be effective, and given the opportunity to "tell others what's bothering them" persons may help cool themselves out:[11]

> We were making deliveries in our brewery truck. It was a hot day in August and I was feeling quite tired. My coworker who had seniority, was giving me orders and got quite upset when I told him to shut up and do some more work by himself. He said that I shouldn't be working if I couldn't handle it and that I should go sit in the truck

while he did it all. I said that was ridiculous and that I didn't mean to say that he is lazy but that I was tired and not used to working when it was so hot. He said that the part he is doing is harder and I was lucky the way things were. I agreed and then I said that I just didn't like being ordered around like a dog. He said, well it is necessary to tell me what to do until I learn the ropes. I agreed and then said that I still resented being like a slave or something and we sort of dropped the matter.

Cool outs may be initiated by targets, but can also be introduced by other parties, who for one reason or another may prefer to avoid a confrontation:

I used to do volunteer work at a nursing home. One of the patients I was visiting was bedridden and had been in the home for six years. Despite his condition, he was friendly and willing to communicate most of the time. As I got to know him I found that he was missing everyday, different kinds of personal effects—cigarettes, plants, money, etc. Eventually I found that a pillow that his daughter had knit for him had also been taken. I was so angry that I wanted to go to the head of administration and complain but this man and his wife pleaded with me not to say anything. They were afraid that if I did, the same thing would happen to him as had happened when his wife complained. Following her complaint, Fred had a terrible time receiving his tranquilizers on time or getting a proper diet or receiving proper care. I was very torn over whether I should complain or adhere to their wishes. I finally gave in to them and said nothing for his sake. About a month later he developed pneumonia and passed away. I never returned to the nursing home.

Finally, in discussing disentanglements, one would be particularly remiss if some attention was not given to the efforts of participants to disengage themselves, either temporarily or permanently, from situations or relationships in which they anticipate subsequent confrontations. Although the other participants may endeavour to maintain contact, and the individuals contemplating departure may have some reservations about leaving, it is often an effective way of avoiding violence:

One day when I went home my landlady said that I had received some mail and it was on the kitchen table. I went to the table but found that the letters had already been opened. I asked the landlady why she had opened my mail. She told me that she thought it was important and she wanted to know what it was about. I told her that she had no right to tamper with my mail and that as long as I was going to live here, I didn't want her to open my mail again. She said that she wouldn't do it again. A couple of days later I found that she had opened my mail and I decided to move out.

Continuities in Confrontations

We have been discussing confrontations largely as though they were one-time events. Clearly, however, many of the confrontations people have are recurrent in the sense that the same persons and/or issues are involved. In general, it appears that the more often two persons engage in disputes over the same issue, the more likely one or both parties will resort to violence. A number of things may be operative here. First, if in the course of a confrontation, targets have been cautioned, reprimanded, etc., but have continued to offend the others in similar ways, these others may feel that their trust has been doubly violated. Not only is the behaviour initially at issue seen offensive, but the lack of significance given the others' concerns compounds the indignity experienced, thus increasing the amount of overall drift.

A second dimension affecting continued confrontations revolves around the proffering of accounts, apologies, and the like. With continued violations by the same target, tactics which may have extricated the target from culpability at earlier times may be seen as insincere or meaningless and, thus, be relatively ineffective in reducing drift in ongoing confrontations. Third, over time, as more and more alternatives have been employed and been defined ineffective, violence may be seen as the last or only means of resolving the confrontation. Further, each increased level of violence suggests new normative parameters and, as persons attempt to "do the other one better," each is likely to experience increased levels of drift.

Thus, unless some outside demand interferes and/or one or both of the parties redefine the significance of the issue at stake, the confrontation is likely to escalate indefinitely. Additionally, with continued confrontations with the same or similar others, one becomes increasingly aware of the strengths and weaknesses of the other and is better prepared to utilize violence in a more efficient manner.[12] Further, as persons find themselves using a particular form of violence more frequently, they will become less sensitive to moral restraints prohibiting that form of violence. One may, in this way, overcome some of the mystique associated with violence: these acts no longer have the same meanings and so may be invoked with less sense or normative guilt.

With continued encounters there is also the possibility that any specific confrontation will be generalized over time to include more and more themes. As this happens, the likelihood of violence increases as persons find one another disvalued in increasingly more respects.

Build-ups and Spillovers
Two other aspects of confrontation contingencies, "build-ups" and "spillovers," deserve some attention. "Build-ups" refer to situations in which initiators of confrontations cite a number of offensive target activities as having been in combination instrumental in their decision to confront the target. Thus, while persons may have found themselves "overlooking" some earlier incidents, as subsequent events unfolded they felt that, taken together, these offenses justified initiating a

confrontation with the target. Thus, while persons might eventually react over a small thing, only in conjunction with preceding events was it too much to tolerate:

> While camping, I ended up doing all the work as if I owned all of the equipment. No one else seemed to care if they ate or if things were kept clean. So one time after I had put the chicken on to cook, I asked one of them to watch it and turn it over when it needed it. They just continued to sit around and so did I, being slightly mad and always tired of doing the work. The chicken started to smell but I stubbornly sat there until one of my friends got up to turn it over. The chicken was burned at dinner and my friends blamed me, but I said that they could have cooked it. I then refused to wash the dishes when they were finished. I think my friends took the hint and did them. After that the work was split more evenly.

"Spillovers" refer to situations in which persons find themselves in confrontations which, although "normally unjustified," have taken place as a consequence of other concerns they have cognitively carried into the situation. These persons, so to speak, have not cleared themselves for the present encounter. Although instances of violence pertaining to spillovers are frequently accompanied by apologies, one may also encounter phrases such as, "Don't bother me, I'm busy" or "I've got things on my mind," denoting someone who is not prepared to devote usual attention to the other.[13] The incident following illustrates aspects of both build-ups and spillovers, although experienced by different parties:

> After partying, I arrived at my room with three friends who were staying the weekend with me, at 3 A.M., and attempting to prepare ourselves for bed, we woke up my roommate. He complained to me that we were making too much noise. I was drunk and not in the mood to be lectured. To each of these statements I responded, "Goodnight Joe." In only a few minutes my roommate exploded into a torrent of insults and then rolled over and went to sleep. Joe and I have never been on friendly terms since. The next morning I attempted to apologize to him but he would have none of it. Two of my friends joined in the chorus of "Goodnight Joe," and this is why he got so mad. Apparently, if he had had some clothes on he would have resorted to physical violence, but he was embarrassed at having other people in the room.

CONCLUSIONS

In developing this paper, it has been argued that human violence is a social phenomenon and that the emergence of violence should be studied within the general context of everyday association.

Beginning with a conception of violence that extends beyond physical harm and focuses on processes rather than consequences or observer attributions, it is suggested that the following themes are basic to a sociological statement on violence:

1. Persons are typically exposed to definitions of violence as both favourable and unfavourable activity, with notions of forms of acceptable violence and the conditions of their acceptance somewhat variable across groups.
2. Violence is problematic and negotiable; it is, thus, subject to considerations of self-reflectivity and ongoing interaction. Even when participants are offended by some event, they may decide not to make an issue of it, and even when a confrontation emerges, it may be dissipated by the target (or the initiator).
3. The concept of "drift," release from normally operative moral restraints, is particularly significant in accounting for violence, as it allows persons to maintain self-images as "respectable persons" while engaging in normatively disvalued behaviour.
4. Notions of "closure" and "disentanglement" are important for understanding the careers of confrontations, as persons both commit themselves and others to violent lines of action and extricate themselves and others from potential violence.

Although violence is a difficult phenomenon to thoroughly assess, so are a number of other areas in which privacy and respectability are problematic. While we can only speak of these other areas, "sex, religion, politics, *et al.*", by inference, our data suggests that it is essential in the study of violence that we move beyond official statistics (or other behavioural measures) and the search for background correlates. Much of human behaviour entails "behind the scenes" activity as persons assess situations, anticipate and experience outcomes, and work out lines of action. While not suggesting that the search for behavioural correlates be abandoned, it is becoming increasingly clear that unless we utilize procedures (more) sensitive to the perspectives of the participants and the ongoing interaction sequences, our understanding of "social structure," if by this term we mean the ways in which people work out their lives in association with others, will be severely limited.

NOTES

[1] Another difficulty with the subcultural approach is that of establishing the parameters of "violent subcultures." Research by Erlanger (1971) and Ball-Rokeach (1973) has not shown evidence of a subculture based on broad categories of age, sex, race or class in which violence is a preferred way of life. This type of data should not, however, be taken to indicate that groups of interacting persons do not differentially support particular forms of violence.

[2] Please see Cressey (1953) and Jacobs (1967, 1970) for further discussion of trust violation.

[3] Our conception of career contingencies is also influenced by Becker (1963). For a statement on the career contingencies of deviants, see Prus and Sharper (1977:159-168).

[4] This release from constraint theme derives largely from Becker's (1963:147-163) depiction of moral entrepreneurs and rules enforcers. Readers may also refer to Gusfield (1963), Klapp (1969) and Zurcher *et al.* (1971) who develop somewhat similar notions in depicting the righteous indignation accompanying crusades.

[5] See Martin (1975) for a consideration of a number of negotiating tactics employed by school teachers in an attempt to control students from both community and personal concern perspectives.

[6] Blumensteil (1970) notes that this form of disclosure is standard practice in many "T groups."

[7] Similar themes seem operative in instances of self-directed harm. See Jacobs's (1967, 1970) and Henslin's (1970) discussions of suicide.

[8] This seems a particularly effective strategy for the target to implement when dealing with a morally indignant other who may not want to trouble himself with the complexities of the event.

[9] Although apologies are frequently highly effective means of restoring social order, it is surprising, as Goffman (1971:113-114) notes, that they have been so neglected by sociologists.

[10] It is in this respect that humour, by putting the situation in another frame of reference, may operate as a means of cooling persons out.

[11] For more extended discussions of the problematics and procedures of "cooling persons out", see Goffman (1952; 1971:108-118) and Prus and Sharper (1977:107-114).

[12] Gelles (1972:165) suggests that this is commonplace in marital disputes.

[13] In an extreme case of spillover, persons may subject anyone who is handy to rather intense harm. In part, this may reflect a general cultural inability to handle anger. While we frequently tell people not to get angry, or to calm down, the ways in which they handle anger is left largely to their own devices. Lacking institutionalized measures of handling anger, persons seem more susceptible to situational pressures and to cues from immediate-situated others.

REFERENCES

Athens, Lonnie H.
1974   "The Self and the Violent Criminal Act." Urban Life and Culture 3:98-112.
Ball-Rokeach, Sandra
1973   "Violence and Values: A Test of the Subculture of Violence Thesis." American Sociological Review 38:736-749.
Becker, Howard J.
1963   *Outsiders.* New York: The Free Press.
Blumensteil, Alexander D.
1970   "An Ethos of Intimacy: Constructing and Using a Situational Morality." pp. 435-453 in J. D. Douglas (ed.), *Deviance and Respectability.* New York: Basic Books.
Blumer, Herbert
1969   *Symbolic Interactionism.* Englewood Cliffs, N.J.: Prentice-Hall.

Conklin, John
1972   *Robbery.* Philadelphia: J. B. Lippincott.
Couch, Carl J.
1968   "Collective Behavior: An Examination of Some Stereotypes." Social Problems 15:310-322.
Cressey, Donald R.
1953   *Other Peoples' Money.* Glencoe, Ill.: Free Press.
Dietz, Mary Lorenz
1968   "Violence and Control: A Study of Some Relationships of the Violent Subculture to the Control of Interpersonal Violence." Ph.D. Dissertation. Wayne State University.
Erlanger, Howard S.
1971   An Anatomy of Violence: An Empirical Investigation of Sociological Theories of Interpersonal Aggression. Unpublished Ph.D. Dissertation. University of California, Berkley.
Garfinkel, Harold
1967   *Studies in Ethnomethodology.* Englewood Cliffs. N.J.: Prentice-Hall.
Gelles, Richard J.
1972   *The Violent Home.* Beverly Hills, Calif.: Sage Publications Inc.
Goffman, Irving
1952   "On Cooling Out the Mark." Psychiatry 15:451-463.

1959   *The Presentation of Self in Everyday Life.* New York, N.Y.: Anchor.

1971   *Relations in Public.* New York: Harper & Row.
Goode, William J.
1972   "The Place of Force in Human Society." American Sociological Review 37:507-519.
Gusfield, Joseph R.
1963   *Symbolic Crusade.* Urbana, Ill.: University of Illinois Press.
Henslin, James
1970   "Guilt and Guilt Neutralization: Response and Adjustment to Suicide." pp. 192-228 in J. D. Douglas (ed.), *Deviance and Respectability.* New York: Basic Books.
Hepburn, John
1971   "Subcultures, Violence, and the Subculture of Violence: An Old Rut or a New Road." Criminology 9:87-97.
Ho, David Yau-fai
1976   "On the Concept of Face." American Journal of Sociology 81: 867-884.
Horowitz, Ruth and Garry Schwartz
1974   "Honor, Normative Ambiguity and Group Violence." American Sociological Review 39:238-251.
Jacobs, Jerry
1967   "A Phenomenological Study of Suicide Notes." Social Problems 15:62-72.

1970   "The Use of Religion in Constructing Moral Justification of Suicide." pp. 229-251 in J. D. Douglas (ed.), *Deviance and Respectability.* New York: Basic Books.
Klapp, Orrin E.
1969   *Collective Search for Identity.* Englewood Cliffs, N.J.: Prentice-Hall.
Lemert, Edwin M.
1953   "An Isolation and Closure Theory of Naive Check Forgery." The Journal of Criminal Law, Criminology and Police Science 44:296-307.

1962   "Paranoia and the Dynamics of Exclusion." *Sociometry* 25:2-25.

1967   *Human Deviance, Social Problems and Social Control.* Englewood Cliffs, N.J.: Prentice-Hall.

Letkemann, Peter
1973   *Crime as Work*. Englewood Cliffs, N.J.: Prentice-Hall.
Lyman, Sanford M. and Marvin B. Scott
1968   "Accounts." American Sociological Review 33:46-62.
Martin, Wilfred B.W.
1975   "Teacher-Pupil Interactions." Canadian Review of Sociology and Anthro-
            pology 12:529-540.
Matza, David
1964   *Delinquency and Drift*. Englewood Cliffs, N.J.: Prentice-Hall.
Mead, George H.
1934   *Mind, Self and Society*. Chicago: University of Chicago Press.
Miller, Walter B.
1966   "Violent Crimes in City Gangs." Annals of the American Academy of
            Political and Social Science 364:97-112.
Parnas, Raymond I.
1967   "The Police Response to Domestic Disturbance." Wisconsin Law Review,
            914-960.
Prus, Robert C.
1975   "Resisting Designations: An Extension of Attribution Theory into a Nego-
            tiated Context." Sociological Inquiry 45:3-14.
            and C. R. D. Sharper

1977   *Road Hustler: The Career Contingencies of Professional Card and Dice Hustlers*.
            Lexington, Mass.: D.C. Heath.
Simmel, Georg
1955   *Conflict and the Web of Group-Affiliations*. New York: The Free Press.
Sutherland, Edwin
1955   *Principles of Criminology* (fifth edition). Philadelphia: J. B. Lippincott.
Sykes, Gresham M. and David Matza
1958   "Techniques of Neutralization: A Theory of Delinquency." American
            Journal of Sociology 22:664-670.
Wolfgang, Marvin E.
1957   "Victim-Precipitated Criminal Homicide." Journal of Criminal Law,
            Criminology and Police Science 48:1-11.
            and Franco Ferracuti

1967   *The Subculture of Violence*. New York: Tavistock.
Zurcher, L. A. Jr. and R. G. Kirkpatrick
1971   "The Anti-Pornography Campaign: A Symbolic Crusade." Social Prob-
            lems 19:217-238.

PART TWO

DOMESTIC VIOLENCE

Chapter 4

ABUSED WIVES:
WHY DO THEY STAY?

Richard J. Gelles

More Canadian police officers are killed while responding to domestic dispute calls than by any other single cause. It is little wonder that police reluctantly intervene in husband-wife conflicts. Generally it is the wife who requires assistance and it is difficult to understand why wives remain with husbands who beat them. Studies which examine the historical relationship between husbands and wives, however, point out that husbands have traditionally had the right to use physical force in punishing their wives. In recent years women have achieved higher educational levels, greater autonomy, and as Goode (1974) tells us, more economic power in the family. It appears that when wives view themselves as equal to their husbands, less physical abuse is acceptable and the probability of their leaving the household increases. Gelles has conducted extensive empirical research in this regard, some of which is set forth below. Gelles's findings generally concur with those of Goode, but their implications are much broader. A variety of interacting factors, it is determined, are predictive of whether the family will remain intact, among them, the wife's concern with perpetuating the myth·of her peaceful family life.

The manner in which interspousal violence is experienced and the outcome of such conflict is particularly important in view of the growing body of literature which sees the family as a training ground for societal violence (Steinmetz and Straus, 1975). Whether the family is a more influential "transmission belt" in teaching violence than the peer group, as Dietz explores in Chapter 1, is unknown. There is increasing evidence, however, that the family is the basic unit which instills values favorable to violence of a domestic nature and that the seeds of future generations of families in conflict are sown in the formative years.

Why would a woman who has been physically abused by her husband remain with him? This question is one of the most frequently asked by both professionals and the lay public in the course of discussions of family violence, and one of the more difficult to adequately answer. The question itself derives from the elementary assumption that any reasonable individual, having been beaten and battered by another person,

---

* This paper is reprinted by permission of the *Journal of Marriage and the Family* and appears in Vol. 38, Nov. 1976, pp. 659-67. Copyrighted (1976) by the National Council on Family Relations. Reprinted by permission.

would avoid being victimized again (or at least avoid the attacker). Unfortunately, the answer to why women remain with their abusive husbands is not nearly as simple as the assumption that underlies the question. In the first place, the decision to either stay with an assaultive spouse or to seek intervention or dissolution of a marriage is not related solely to the extent or severity of the physical assault. Some spouses will suffer repeated severe beatings or even stabbings without so much as calling a neighbor, while others call the police after a coercive gesture from their husband. Secondly, the assumption that the victim would flee from a conjugal attacker overlooks the complex subjective meaning of intrafamilial violence, the nature of commitment and entrapment to the family as a social group, and the external constraint which limits a woman's ability to seek outside help. As has been reported elsewhere (Parnas, 1967; Gelles, 1974; Straus, 1974, 1975), violence between spouses is often viewed as normative and, in fact, mandated in family relations. Wives have reported that they believe that it is acceptable for a husband to beat his wife "every once and a while" (Parnas, 1967:952; Gelles, 1974:59-61).

This paper attempts to provide an answer to the question of why victims of conjugal violence stay with their husbands by focusing on various aspects of the family and family experience which distinguish between women who seek intervention or dissolution of a marriage as a response to violence and those women who suffer repeated beatings without seeking outside intervention.[1] We shall specifically analyze how previous experience with family violence affects the decision to seek intervention, and how the extent of violence, educational status, occupational status, number of children, and age of oldest child influence the wife's actions in responding to assaults from her husband. Finally, we shall discuss how external constraints lessen the likelihood of a woman seeking intervention in conjugal assaults.

VICTIMS OF FAMILY VIOLENCE

Although no one has systematically attempted to answer the question of why an abused wife would stay with her husband, there has been some attention focused on women who attempt to seek intervention after being beaten by their husbands. Snell, Rosenwald, and Robey (1964) examined 12 clinical cases to determine why a wife takes her abusive husband to court. They begin by stating that the question answers itself (because he beats her!), but they go on to explain that the decision to seek legal assistance is the result of a change in the wife's behavior, not the husband's, since many wives report a history of marital violence when they did not seek assistance.

Truninger (1971) found that women attempt to dissolve a violent marriage only after a history of conflict and reconciliation. According to this analysis, a wife makes a decision to obtain a divorce from her abusive husband when she can no longer believe her husband's promises of no more violence nor forgive past episodes of violence. Truninger postulates that some of the reasons women *do not* break off relationships with abusive husbands are that: (1) they have negative self-concepts; (2) they believe their husbands will reform; (3) economic hardship; (4) they have children who need a father's economic support; (5) they doubt they can get along alone; (6) they believe divorcees are stigmatized; and (7) it is difficult for women with children to get work. Although this analysis attempts to explain why women remain with abusive husbands, the list does not specify which factors are the most salient in the wife's decision to either stay or seek help.

There are a number of other factors which help explain the wife's decision to stay or get help in cases of violence. Straus (1973) states that self-concept and role expectations of others often influence what is considered to be an intolerable level of violence by family members. Scanzoni's (1972) exchange model of family relations postulates that the ratio of rewards to punishments is defined subjectively by spouses and is the determining factor in deciding whether to stay married or not. The decision of whether or not to seek intervention or dissolution of a marriage may be partly based on the subjective definitions attached to the violence (punishment) and partly on the ratio of this punishment to other marital rewards (security, companionship, etc.).

Additional research on violence between husbands and wives suggests that severity of violence has an influence on the wife's actions (see O'Brien, 1971 and Levinger, 1966, for discussion of petitioners for divorce and their experience with violence). Research on victims of violence sheds little additional light on the actions of abused wives (Straus, 1975).[2]

METHODOLOGY

Data for this study were derived from interviews with members of 80 families. An unstructured informal interview procedure was employed to facilitate data collection on the sensitive topic of intrafamilial violence. Twenty families suspected of using violence were chosen from the files of a private social service agency. Another 20 families were selected by examining a police "blotter" to locate families in which the police had been summoned to break up violent disputes. An additional 40 families were interviewed by selecting one neighboring family for each "agency" or "police" family.[3]

Strengths and Limitations of the Sample

The interviews were carried out in two cities in New Hampshire. The sampling procedure employed enhanced the likelihood of locating families in which violence had occurred, but it also meant that this sample was not representative of any larger populations.

Major limitations of this study are that it is exploratory in nature, the sample is small, and the representativeness of the sample is unknown. The small sample, the unknown representativeness, and the possible biases that enter into the study as a result of the sampling procedure all impinge on the generalizability of the findings presented in this paper.

There are, however, strengths in the study which tend to offset the limitations of sample design and sample size. First, this is a unique study. The area of spousal violence has long suffered from "selective inattention" (Dexter, 1958) on the part of both society and the research community. While some data has been gathered on the topic of family violence, most of the studies focus on one type of population—either petitioners for divorce (O'Brien, 1971; Levinger, 1966), patients of psychiatrists (Snell, Rosenwald, and Robey, 1964), or college students (Straus, 1974; Steinmetz, 1974). This study is one of the few which examines not only those in special circumstances (agency clients or those calling police), but also an equal number of families who had no contact with agencies of social service or control.[4] While the sample is obviously not representative, it is one of the closest yet to a study of violence in a cross section of families.

A second strength of the methodology is that it yielded a population without a working class, lower class, or middle class bias. The sample ranged from families at the lowest regions of socioeconomic status, to middle class families in which one or both spouses had graduated from college and had a combined family income exceeding $25,000. (For a complete discussion of the social characteristics of the respondents and their families, see Gelles, 1974:205-215).

Although the methodology was not designed specifically to address the issue posed in this paper it turned out to be particularly well suited for the proposed analysis. The sampling technique yielded wives who were divorced from violent husbands, wives who called the police, wives who were clients of a social service agency, and wives who had never sought any outside intervention.

The interviews with the 80 family members yielded 41 women who had been physically struck by their husbands during their marriage. Of these, nine women had been divorced or separated from their husbands; 13 had called on the police and were still married; eight sought counseling from a private social service agency (because of violence and other family problems); and 11 had sought no outside intervention.

FINDINGS

We derived some ideas and predictions concerning factors which distinguished between beaten wives who obtained outside intervention and those who did not attempt to bring in outside resources or file for a divorce. These ideas are based on the interviews with the 41 members of violent families and on previous research on family violence. We utilized both quantative and qualitative data obtained from the interviews to assess the effect of: (1) severity and frequency of violence; (2) experience and exposure to violence and one's family of orientation; (3) education and occupation of the wife, number of children, and age of oldest child; and (4) external constraint on the actions of the victimized wife.

Severity and Frequency of Violence

Common sense suggests that if violence is severe enough or frequent enough, a wife will eventually attempt to either flee from her abusive husband or to bring in some mediator to protect her from violence.

In order to analyze whether severity of violence influenced the reactions of the wife, we constructed a 10 point scale of violence severity (0 = no violence; 1 = pushed or shoved; 2 = threw object; 3 = slapped or bit; 4 = punched or kicked; 5 = pushed down; 6 = hit with hard object; 7 = choked; 8 = stabbed; 9 = shot).[5] This scale measured the most severe violence the wife had ever experienced as a victim.

Table 1
Violence Severity by Intervention Mode

Intervention	*Mean Violence Severity*
No Intervention	2.1
Divorced or Separated	5.1
Called Police	4.0
Went to Agency	4.6
Total for all who sought intervention	4.6

F = 5.2 Statistically significant at the .01 level

Table 1 indicates that the more severe the violence, the more likely the wife is to seek outside assistance. An examination of wives' reactions to particular instances of violence reveals even more about the impact of violence severity on the actions of abused wives. Of the eight women who were either shot at (one), choked (six), or hit with a hard object (one), five had obtained divorces, two had called the police, and one had sought counseling from a social service agency. At the other extreme, of the nine women who had been pushed or shoved (eight), or had objects thrown at them (one), one had gotten a divorce, one called the police, and seven had sought no assistance at all.

How frequently a wife is hit also influences her decision whether to remain with her husband, call the police, go to a social worker, or seek dissolution of the marriage. Only 42 percent of the women who had been struck once in the marriage had sought some type of intervention, while 100 percent of the women who had been hit at least once a month and 83 percent of the women who had been struck at least once a week had either obtained a divorce or separation, called the police, or went to a social service agency. Frequency of violence is also related to what type of intervention a wife seeks. Women hit weekly to daily are most likely to call the police, while women hit less often (at least once a month) are more inclined to get a divorce or legal separation.

There are a number of plausible explanations as to why frequency of violence influences mode of intervention. Perhaps the more frequent the violence, the more a wife wants immediate protection, whereas victims of monthly violence gradually see less value in staying married to a husband who explodes occasionally. A possible explanation of the findings might be that women who were divorced or separated were ashamed to admit they tolerated violence as long as they did (for fear of being labeled "sado-masochists"). Also, it may be that victims of frequent violence are afraid of seeking a temporary or permanent separation. Victims of weekly violence may be terrorized by their violent husbands and view police intervention as more tolerable to their husbands than a divorce or separation. Finally, women who are struck frequently might feel that a separation or divorce might produce a radical or possible lethal reaction from an already violent husband.

Experience With Exposure to Violence as a Child

Studies of murderers (Gillen, 1946; Guttmacher, 1960; Leon, 1969; Palmer, 1962; Tanay, 1969), child abusers (Bakan, 1971; Gelles, 1973; Gil, 1971; Kempe et al., 1962; Steele and Pollock, 1974), and violent spouses (Gelles, 1974); Owens and Straus, 1975) support the assumption that the more an individual is exposed to violence as a child (both as an observer and a victim), the more he or she is violent as an adult. The explanation offered for this relationship is that the experience with violence as a victim and observer teaches the individual how to be violent and also to approve of the use of violence. In other words, exposure to violence provides a "role model" for violence (Singer, 1971). If experience with violence can provide a role model for the offender, then perhaps it can also provide a role model for the victim.

Women who observed spousal violence in their family of orientation were more likely to be victims of conjugal violence in their family of procreation. Of the 54 women who never saw their parents fight physically, 46 percent were victims of spousal violence, while 66 percent of the 12 women who observed their parents exchange blows were later victims of violent attacks. In addition, the more frequently a woman was struck by her parents, the more likely she was to grow up and be struck by her husband.[6]

There are two interrelated reasons why women who were exposed to or were victims of intrafamilial violence would be prone to be the victims of family violence as adults. It is possible that the more experience with violence a woman has, the more she is inclined to approve of the use of violence in the family.

She may grow up with the expectation that husbands are "supposed" to hit wives, and this role expectation may in turn become the motivator for her husband to use violence on her. Another explanation of these findings integrates the subculture theory of violence (Wolfgang and Ferracuti, 1967) with the homogamy theory of mate selection (Centers, 1949; Ecklund, 1968; Hollingshead, 1950). Thus, it could be argued that women who grew up in surroundings which included and approved of family violence are more likely to marry a person who is prone to use violence.

Given the fact that being a victim of violence as a child or seeing one's parents physically fight makes a woman more vulnerable to becoming the victim of conjugal violence, does exposure and experience with violence as a child affect *the actions* of a beaten wife? There are two alternative predictions that could be made. First, the less a woman experienced violence in her family of orientation, the more likely she is to view intrafamilial violence as deviant, and thus, the more she is willing to seek intervention or a divorce when hit by her husband. On the other hand, exposure to violence may provide a role model for the woman as to what to do when attacked. Thus, the *more* violence she was exposed to, the more she will know about how to get outside help, and the more she will seek this help.

Table 2
Intervention Mode by Wife's Experience with Violence as a Child

	Type of Intervention			
Type of Experience as Child	Divorced or Separated	Called Police	Went to Agency	Total Seeking Intervention
A. *Parents Violent to Respondent:*				
None (N = 3)	33%	0%	66%	100%
Infrequent [a] (N = 13)	23%	38%	15%	76%
Frequent [b] (N = 17)	24%	35%	18%	77%
B. *Parents Violent to Each Other:*				
None observed (N = 25)	28%	28%	20%	76%
Observed (N = 8)	63%	13%	13%	89%

[a] less than 6 times a year
[b] from monthly to daily

Being a victim of parental violence and frequency of victimization appear to have no bearing on the beaten wife's decision whether or not to seek outside intervention[7] (Table 2). Those women who observed their parents engaged in physical fights were slightly more likely to obtain outside intervention after being hit by their husbands. For those women who did see their parents engage in conjugal violence, the predominant mode of intervention in their own family of procreation was a divorce or separation. There is no predominant mode of intervention chosen by those women who did not witness violence in their families of orientation.

Thus, neither of the alternative predictions is strongly supported by the data on experience and exposure to violence. There is the suggestion that exposure to conjugal violence makes women *less tolerant* of family violence and more desirous of ending a violent marriage. Along these lines, some of the women we interviewed stated that after they saw their parents fight they vowed that they would never stand for their own husbands hitting them. However, the data do not support the claim that this position is widespread among wives who witnessed violence as they grew up.

Table 3
Education, Occupation, Number of Children,
Age of Oldest Child by Intervention Mode

	Mean Education	Percentage Completed High School	Percentage Employed	Mean Number of Children	Mean Age of Oldest Child
No Intervention (N = 11)	11.9	63%	25%	2.5	9.3
Divorced or Separated (N = 9)	11.7	66%	44%*	3.3	9.3
Called Police (N = 13)	11.0	69%	38%	3.0	13.0
Went to Agency (N = 8)	11.1	62%	75%	2.6	13.7
All Intervention	11.3	67%	50%	3.0	12.0

* For those wives who are divorced or separated, some may have found employment *after* the divorce or separation. The data did not allow us to determine *when* the wife found employment.

Education, Occupation, Number of Children, Age of Children

Truninger (1971) has proposed that the stronger the commitment to marriage, the less a wife will seek legal action against a violent husband. We have modified this hypothesis by proposing that the fewer resources a wife has in a marriage, the fewer alternatives she has to her marriage; and the more "entrapped" she is in the marriage, the more reluctant she will be to seek outside intervention. Thus, we hypothesize that unemployed wives with low education will not do anything when beaten. It is difficult to predict what influence number of children and age of children have on the actions of the wife. Snell, Rosenwald and Robey (1964) state that the presence of an older child motivates women to take their husbands to court.

Looking at the relationship between each variable and intervention, we see that the variable which best distinguishes wives who obtain assistance from those who remain with their husbands is holding a job. While only 25 percent of those wives who sought no help worked, 50 percent of the wives who called the police, went to a social service agency, or were separated or divorced from their husbands held jobs. This confirms our hypothesis that the more resources a wife has, the more she is able to support herself and her children, the more she will have a low threshold of violence and call outside agents or agencies to help her. Thus, the less dependent a wife is on her husband, the more likely she is to call for help in instances of violence. In addition to this resource dimension, wives reported that holding a job gave them a view of another world or culture. This new perspective made their own family problems seem less "normal" and more serious than they had felt when they were at home. This point is illustrated in the following excerpt from one of our interviews with a woman who was the client of a social service agency and who had been beaten by her husband when they were first married:

> Until I started being out in the public, to realize what was going on around me, I was so darned stupid and ignorant. I didn't know how the other half of the world lived. And when I started being a waitress I used to love to sit there—when I wasn't busy—and watch the people—the mother and the father with their children—and see how they acted. And I started to feel like I was cheated . . . and it started to trouble me and I started to envy those people. So I said, "you know . . . am I supposed to live the way I'm living?"

Women who called the police or went to an agency often had teenage children. The data confirm the Snell, Rosenwald, and Robey (1964) finding that women who brought their husbands to court had teenage children. In some of our interviews, wives reported that they started calling the police when their son or daughter was old enough to get embroiled in the physical conflicts. In these cases, the wives wanted help to protect their children rather than themselves.

Neither education (measured by mean years of school completed and completed high school) nor number of children distinguishes between abused women seeking help and those staying with their husbands.

Table 4
Step-Wise Regression of Independent Variables
and Intervention and Intervention Modalities

	Multiple R	R^2	Beta
A. Regression of Intervention on:			
Violence Severity	.434 [a]	.189	.365
Completed High School	.488 [a]	.238	.331
Parental Violence to Respondent	.530 [a]	.280	—.260
Frequency of Violence	.559 [a]	.312	.221
Wife's Occupational Status [c]	.570 [a]	.324	—.136
B. Regression of Divorced or Separated on:			
Violence Severity	.281	.080	.211
Wife's Education	.314	.099	.298
Frequency of Violence	.324	.105	.154
Completed High School	.340	.115	—.136
Wife's Occupational Status [c]	.347	.120	.089
Violence Between Parents	.352	.124	—.027
Number of Children	.355	.126	.261
Age of Oldest Child	.373	.140	.231
C. Regression of Called Police on:			
Wife's Occupational Status [c]	.195	.038	—.231
Completed High School	.256	.065	.423
Wife's Education	.314	.099	—.245
Parental Violence to Respondent	.319	.101	—.016
Age of Oldest Child	.324	.105	—.233
Number of Children	.340	.115	.233
D. Regression of Went to Agency on:			
Parental Violence to Respondent	.326 [b]	.106	—.191
Age of Oldest Child	.350	.122	.480
Number of Children	.425 [b]	.180	—.496
Violence Severity	.442	.196	.114

[a] statistically significant at the .01 level
[b] statistically significant at the .05 level
[c] Occupational Status measured using Bureau of Census status score (see Robinson, Athanasiou, and Head, 1969:357).

Combined Effects of Variables on Intervention

Up to this point we have examined the effects of the variables which we believed would be likely determinants of whether or not a wife sought intervention. This analysis, however, does not allow us to assess the effects of all these variables in explaining whether or not a wife would seek outside help in cases of conjugal violence. In order to examine the impact of all the variables together, we employed a step-wise multiple regression procedure which allowed us to see what proportion of the variance of intervention or particular intervention modalities is explained by combinations of the independent variables.[8]

Intervention. Table 4 reveals that the best predictor of whether or not a wife seeks intervention is violence severity in her family of procreation.

Thus, women who seek intervention are strongly influenced by the level of violence in their family. The five variables entered into the regression analysis explain 32 percent of the variance in seeking intervention or not.

Divorced or Separated. The best predictor of whether or not a wife obtains a divorce or separation is the level of violence in her family of procreation. The combined effect of all the variables entered into the equation is the explanation of 14 percent of the variance in the dependent variable; however, the multiple R's are not statistically significant at the .05 level.

Called Police. We are able to explain 11 percent of the variance in this variable, but again, multiple R's are not statistically significant at the .05 level. Unlike separation or divorce, in which cases severity and extent of violence in her family of procreation played major roles in the wife's actions, the calling of police is associated with the wife's occupational status and her education. Women with less occupational status and lower education are likely to call the police for help. This finding is consistent with the popular assumption that the poor man's social worker is the police officer.

Went to Agency. The best predictor of going to a social service agency is how much violence the wife experienced as a child. The less violence, the more likely she is to seek a social worker's help. In contrast to the previous dependent variables, age and number of children play a greater part in influencing a wife's decision to go to a social service agency. Almost 20 percent of the variance in seeking agency assistance is explained by the four variables included in the regression.

External Constraint

The fact that a woman would call the police or seek agency assistance after repeated incidents of conjugal violence does not necessarily mean that she will call the police again or continue going to an agency. One fact remained quite clear at the end of the 80 interviews: most agencies and most legal organizations are quite unprepared and unable to provide meaningful assistance to women who have been beaten by their husbands. With minor exceptions, such as the work done by Bard and his colleagues (1969; 1969; 1971), little formal training has been given to police in how to interdede in conjugal disputes. Truninger (1971) reports that the courts are often mired in mythology about family violence (e.g., "violence fulfills the masochistic need of women victims") and consequently the justice system is ineffective in dealing with marital violence. Field and Field (1973:225) echo these sentiments and state that unless the victim dies, the chances that the court system will deal seriously with the offender are slight. Women who are abused by their husbands must suffer grave injury in order to press legal charges. The California Penal Code states that a wife must be more injured than commonly allowed for battery to press charges against her husband (Calvert, 1974:89). As Field and Field (1973) state, there is an official acceptance of violence between "consenting" adults and the belief that this violence is a private affair. This attitude, held by police, the courts, and the citizenry, constrains many wives from either seeking initial help, or once obtaining help, continuing to use it.

Although social work agencies are not as "indifferent" about marital violence as the courts and police are (Field and Field, 1973:236), they are often unable to provide realistic answers for victims of violence because of the rather limited amount of knowledge in this area. The data on marital violence are so scanty that few policy or intervention strategies have been worked out for the use of social workers. Without a good knowledge of the causes and patterns of marital violence, many social workers have had to rely on stop-gap measures which never address the real problem of marital violence.

A final source of external constraint is the wife's fear that the myth of her peaceful family life will be exploded. Many women we spoke to would never think of calling the police, going to a social work agency, or filing for a divorce because those actions would rupture the carefully nurtured myth of their fine family life. One woman, who had been struck often and hard over a 30 year marriage said she would never call the police because she was afraid it would appear in the papers. Truninger (1971:264) supports these findings by stating that part of the reason why the courts are ineffective in dealing with marital violence is the strong social pressure on individuals to keep marital altercations private.

In summary, even if a woman wants to get help and protection from her husband, she all too frequently finds out that the agents and agencies she calls are ineffective or incapable of providing real assistance. During the course of the interviews, many wives who had sought intervention explained about the futility of such actions. One woman in particular had sought agency help, called the police, and finally filed for a divorce. However, none of these actions actually protected her, and her estranged husband almost strangled her one weekend morning.

The deficiencies of these external agencies and the pressure to cover up family altercations are two powerful forces which keep women with their abusive husbands.

CONCLUSION

The purpose of this paper has been to address the important question of why victims of conjugal violence stay with their husbands. Our analysis of the variables which affect the decision to either stay with an abusive husband or to seek intervention, uncovered three major factors which influence the actions of abused women. First, the less severe and the less frequent the violence, the more a woman will remain with her spouse and not seek outside aid. This finding is almost self-evident in that it posits that women seek intervention when they are severely abused. However, the problem is more complex, since severity and frequency of violence explain only part of the variance in abused wives' behavior. A second factor is how much violence a wife experienced as a child. The more she was struck by her parents, the more inclined she is to stay with her abusive husband. It appears that victimization as a child raises the wife's tolerance for violence as an adult. Lastly, educational and occupational factors are associated with staying with an abusive husband. Wives who do not seek intervention are less likely to have completed high school and more likely to be unemployed. We conclude that the fewer resources a woman has, the less power she has, and the more "entrapped" she is in her marriage, the more she suffers at the hands of her husband without calling for help outside the family.

Another factor which appears to influence the actions of a wife is external constraint in the form of police, agency, and court lack of understanding about marital violence.

Although we have presented some factors which partly explain why abused wives remain with their husbands, we have not provided a complete answer to the question this paper raises. The reason for this is that the factors influencing the reactions of an abused wife are tremendously complex. It is not simply how hard or how often a wife is hit, nor is it how much education or income she has. The decision of whether or not to seek intervention is the result of a complex interrelationship of factors, some of which have been identified in this paper.

Although we have provided tentative answers to the central question of this paper, a main underlying issue of this topic has not been addressed. Even though more than 75 percent of the women who had been struck had tried to get outside help, and end result of this intervention was not totally satisfactory. The outlook for women who are physically beaten and injured by their husbands is not good. For those who have few resources, no job, and no idea of how to get help, the picture is grim. But even the women who have the resources and desire to seek outside help often find this help of little benefit.

NOTES

[1] While we would have liked to answer the same question for men who were struck by their wives, we interviewed too few men who had been hit by their wives to conduct any meaningful data analysis.

[2] Since we are focusing on the reactions of victims of intrafamilial violence, we had hoped that some insight could be gained from the literature on "victimology." "Victimology" is defined by its proponents (see Drapkin and Viano, 1974; Von Hentig, 1948; and Schafer, 1968) as the scientific study of the criminal-victim relationship. However, the current work on these relationships does not focus specifically on factors which lead victims to sever relationships with offenders or to obtain outside intervention. Since victimologists' analyses of marital violence are typically limited to cases of homicide (see Wolfgang, 1957), there are few insights to be gained for the purposes of this paper from the study of the literature on the criminal-victim relationship.

[3] For a complete discussion of the methodology, including an evaluation of the sampling procedure and instrument, see Gelles (1974:36-43).

[4] Another study which examines a cross-section of families is Steinmetz' (1975) multi-method examination of 57 families randomly selected from New Castle County, Delaware. The sample size is small, but it is representative, if only of one county in Delaware.

[5] For the purposes of this analysis, we viewed each higher point on the scale as more severe than the previous category of violence. In addition, we treated the scale as interval data in order to conduct a one-way Analysis of Variance. The scale was treated as an interval measure because this was the only possible way to assess the impact of violence severity on the wives.

[6] Many individuals may find it difficult to label the use of physical force on children as "violence." This is because there are many powerful pro-use-of-physical-force-on-children norms in our society (Straus, 1975). If one defines violence as an act with the intent of physically injuring the victim, then physically punishing a child is violent. Note, a complete tabular presentation of these data is available from the author.

[7] Although this study deals with 41 families in which the wife was a victim of violence, Table 2 presents only 33 such wives. The smaller number occurs because in some of the 41 families, we interviewed the husband and have no data on the wife's experience with violence. Some other women reported that they were brought up in foster homes or by one parent, and thus we have no "exposure to violence data" for these women.

[8] In order to conduct this analysis the dependent variables (Intervention, divorced or Separated, Called Police, and Went to an Agency) were transformed into "dummy variables." Each variable was treated as a dichotomy (e.g., "Sought Intervention" or "Did Not Seek Intervention"). Certain ordinal variables (violence severity, completed high school, violence frequency, parental violence to respondent, and violence between parents) are treated as interval measures.

REFERENCES

Bakan, David
1971   *Slaughter of the Innocents: A Study of the Battered Child Phenomenon.* Boston: Beacon Press.
Bard, Morton
1969   "Family intervention police teams as a community mental health resource." The Journal of Criminal Law, Criminology, and Police Science 60 (June):247-250.
Bard, Morton, and Bernard Berkowitz
1969   "Family disturbance as a police function." In S. Cohen (Ed.), Law Enforcement Science and Technology II. Chicago: I.I.T. Research Institute.
Bard, Morton, and Joseph Zacher
1971   "The prevention of family violence: Dilemmas of community intervention." Journal of Marriage and the Family 33 (November):677-682.

Calvert, Robert
1974   "Criminal and civil liability in husband-wife assaults." Pp. 88-90 in
            Suzanne K. Steinmetz and Murray A. Straus (Eds.), *Violence in the Family.*
            New York: Harper and Row.
Centers, Richard
1949   "Marital selection and occupational strata." American Journal of Sociol-
            ogy 54 (May):530-535.
Dexter, Louis A.
1958   "A note on selective inattention in social science." Social Problems 6
            (Fall):176-182.
Drapkin, Israel, and Emilio Viano (Eds.)
1974   *Victimology.* Lexington, Massachusetts:Lexington Books.
Eckland, Bruce K.
1968   "Theories of mate selection." Eugenics Quarterly 15 (June):71-84.
Field, Martha H., and Henry F. Field
1973   "Marital violence and the criminal process: Neither justice nor peace."
            Social Service Review: 47 (June):221-240.
Gelles, Richard J.
1973   "Child abuse as psychopathology: A sociological critique and reformula-
            tion." American Journal of Orthopsychiatry 43 (July):611-621.

1974   *The Violent Home: A Study of Physical Aggression Between Husbands and
            Wives.* Beverly Hills: Sage Publications, Inc.
Gil, David G.
1971   "Violence against children." Journal of Marriage and the Family 33
            (November):637-648.
Gillen, John Lewis
1946   *The Wisconsin Prisoner: Studies in Crimogenesis.* Madison: University of
            Wisconsin Press.
Goode, William J.
1964   *The Family.* Foundations of Modern Sociology Series. Englewood Cliffs,
            N.J.: Prentice-Hall Inc.
Guttmacher, Manfred
1960   *The Mind of the Murderer.* New York: Farrar, Straus, and Cudahy.
Hollingshead, August B.
1950   "Cultural factors in the selection of mates." American Sociological
            Review 15 (October):619-627.
Kempe, C. Henry, *et al.*
1962   "The battered child syndrome." Journal of the American Medical Associ-
            ation 181 (July 7):17-24.
Leon, C. A.
1969   "Unusual patterns of crime during 'la Violencia' in Columbia." American
            Journal of Psychiatry 125 (May):1564-1575.
Levinger, George
1966   "Sources of marital dissatisfaction among applicants for divorce." Ameri-
            can Journal of Orthopsychiatry 26 (October):803-897. Pp. 126-132 in Paul
            H. Glasser and Louis N. Glasser (Eds.), Families in Crisis. New
            York:Harper and Row.
O'Brien, John E.
1971   "Violence in divorce prone families." Journal of Marriage and the Family
            33 (November):692-698.
Owens, David J., and Murray A. Straus
1975   "Childhood violence and adult approval of violence." Aggressive Behav-
            ior 1 (2):193-211.
Palmer, Stuart
1962   *The Psychology of Murder.* New York: Thomas Y. Crowell Company.
Parnas, Raymond I.
1967   "The police response to domestic disturbance." Wisconsin Law Review
            914 (Fall):914-960.

Robinson, J. P., R. Athanasiou, and K. Head
1969   Measures of Occupational Attitudes and Occupational Characteristics. Ann Arbor, Michigan: Survey Research Center.
Scanzoni, John H.
1972   *Sexual Bargaining.* Englewood Cliffs, N.J.,: Prentice-Hall Inc.
Schafer, Stephen
1968   *The Victim and His Criminal: A Study in Functional Responsibility.* New York: Random House.
Singer, Jerome.
1971   *The Control of Aggression and Violence.* New York: Academic Press.
Snell, John E., Richard J. Rosenwald, and Ames Robey
1964   "The wifebeater's wife: A study of family interaction." Archives of General Psychiatry 11 (August):107-113.
Steele, Brandt F., and Carl B. Pollock
1974   "A psychiatric study of parents who abuse infants and small children." Pp. 89-134 in Ray E. Helfer and C. Henry Kempe (Eds.), *The Battered Child.* Chicago:University of Chicago Press.
Steinmetz, Suzanne K.
1974   "Occupational environment in relation to physical punishment and dogmatism." Pp. 166-172 in Suzanne K. Steinmetz and Murray A. Straus (Eds.), *Violence in the Family.* New York: Harper and Row.

————   1975   "Intra-familial patterns of the conflict resolution: Husband/wife; parent/child; sibling/sibling." Unpublished doctoral dissertion, Case Western Reserve University.
Steinmetz, Suzanne K. and Murray A. Straus (eds.)
1975   *Violence in the Family.* New York:Dodd Mead & Co.
Straus, Murray A.
1973   "A general system theory approach to the development of a theory of violence between family members." Social Science Information 12 (June):105-125.

————   1974   "Leveling, civility, and violence in the family." Journal of Marriage and the Family 36 (February):13-30.

————   1975   "Cultural approval and structural necessity or intrafamily assaults in sexist societies." Paper presented at the International Institute of Victimology, Bellagio, Italy, July.
Tanay, E.
1969   "Psychiatric study of homicide." American Journal of Psychiatry 125 (March):1252-1258.
Truninger, Elizabeth
1971   "Marital violence: The legal solutions." The Hastings Law Journal 23 (November):259-276.
Von Hentig, Hans
1948   *The Criminal and His Victim: Studies in the Sociology of Crime.* New Haven:Yale University Press.
Wolfgang, Marvin E.
1957   "Victim-precipitated criminal homicide." Journal of Criminal Law, Criminology and Police Science 48 (June):1-11.
Wolfgang, Marvin E., and F. Ferracuti
1967   *The Subculture of Violence.* London: Tavistock Publications.

Chapter 5

THE BATTERED BABY SYNDROME: A RECONCEPTUALIZATION OF FAMILY CONFLICT

Mary Alice Beyer Gammon

When listening to discussions about husbands beating wives, it is not unusual to hear the response—she deserved it. This rationalization becomes much more difficult when applied to children. Few of us can comprehend broken bones, slashed throats and bottoms burned on a hot stove in attempt to dry wet diapers. This bleak reality exists in approximately one-third of the families in which interspousal violence is also a common occurrence. This chapter sets forth the extent to which this problem exists in Canada. It presents the shortcomings of research thus far and suggests alternatives encompassing whole family problem-solving therapy.

The creation of a model of child abuse is fraught with some basic problems, the most significant of which is an adequate definition of the phenomenon. Child abuse, as defined by the provinces and territories of Canada, includes a continuum of behaviours ranging from verbal, emotional and sexual abuse to the maiming and killing of children. Ematai Etzioni (1971) has cautioned against the use of terms which indicate technical differences in common usage rather than conceptual distinctions. Etzioni tells us that physical violence cannot be lumped in the same category as economic or psychic coercion. Some will argue that there is no difference between a variety of forms of emotional violence and physical violence. Those who justify physical violence by noting the coercion of others by economic and social means find this view particularly helpful. The difference, however, must be noted. Economic and psychic pressures reduce but do not eliminate the freedom of the individual. The ultimate decision is left to the subject. Once a person has used physical force, and is identified, his choice in the matter has diminished considerably. Regardless of the mode of violence of which we speak, this conceptual distinction is a useful research tool.

The physical abuse of children is not new. What is new is the interest taken in the phenomenon by both the media and academia. It is a recent technological development which has resulted in a restraint of the freedoms formerly taken for granted within the privacy of one's home.

---

* This paper is based on a paper presented at a symposium entitled *Changing Family Dynamics in the 70's: North American Perspectives,* held at the University of Windsor in 1976 and supported by the University of Windsor, The Canada Council and The Vanier Institute of the Family.

Parents have long contended that it is their right, indeed their duty, to use physical punishment to discipline children.

Prior to the development of modern radiological techniques, one could only surmise that the injuries of countless children could be attributed to merciless beatings by their parents. The clarity provided by new x-ray techniques in many instances demonstrates proof beyond a doubt of multiple, unreported injuries inflicted by parents. The radiographic signs of a battered child are astonishingly specific. As one expert tells us, "they speak for the child who is unable or unwilling to speak for himself" (Silverman, 1968, p. 59). On the basis of follow-up studies and interviews with the parents of children exhibiting severe abuse upon radiological examination, Dr. Charles Henry Kempe coined the phrase "The Battered Child Syndrome."

Research was initiated by pediatricians, and subsequently by psychologists, lawyers and social workers. Only recently have sociologists begun looking at social factors as causal (Gil, 1970; Zalba, 1974).

The most extensive and exhaustive research by far has been conducted in the United Kingdom, and the United States has an increasing dearth of literature from which to draw, all of which provokes the question, is child abuse a problem in Canada? The mass media has blown out of proportion any realistic attempt to evaluate what is referred to as an emerging Canadian crisis.[1]

This paper is an attempt to set forth clearly the extent to which child abuse is a problem in Canada. It will outline the state of the research conducted thus far, present the shortcomings of such research, and suggest viable alternatives for further exploration.

The magnitude of the problem is illustrated in a set of sophisticated recording procedures located at the Children's Service Bureau for the Province of Ontario, Queen's Park. Table 1 illustrates the reported incidence of child abuse in Ontario for the past five years.

Table 1
Province of Ontario, Ministry of Social and Community Services: Physical Ill-Treatment of a Child 1972-76

Year	Cases Reported	Charges Laid	Convictions Registered	Offence Repeated
1972	491	60	23	59
1973	598	63	12	74
1974	562	50	1	71
1975	769	85	13	86
1976	746	74	11	50

As demonstrated in Table 1, the reported incidence of physical abuse in Ontario has risen 52.5 per cent over the five-year period 1972 to 1976. Based on the 1975 rate, a modest estimate of Ontario's battered children would stand at 1,142 by 1980, assuming that no rapid escalation occurs. Given the social and legal problems encountered in the definition of child abuse, the recidivism rate adds weight to the magnitude of the problem.

Research in the field has taken a variety of approaches, primarily falling into five basic categories:
historical evaluations
legal problems
psychopathological models
social models
social psychological models
Each of these categories is elaborated below.

HISTORICAL EVALUATIONS

Literature related to the earliest mention of child abuse indicates that the maltreatment of children has always been present in the history of mankind. Child abuse is, was, and always will be (Greenland, 1973). The implication is less than subtle; further research on the topic is unnecessary.

Superstition led Egypt, India and China to infanticide (Helfer, 1968, p. 8). Congenital defects bode evil and astrologers did not recommend survival for ill-omened children. In other countries, such as Greece and Rome, the theory of the survival of the fittest prevailed, and only the fittest could strengthen the race.

As far back as 1633 Christians whipped their children unmercifully on Innocents Day to remind the children of the story of the massacre of the innocents by Herod expressed in the *Bibliotheca Scholastica*. In later times economic stress became the justification for abuse. Children were mutilated in sixteenth century England to enhance their appeal as beggars. They were legally bartered and sold (Gil, 1970). King Henry VI was among the most influential to speak up against the maltreatment of children, himself the unhappy product of regular flogging "even if it did make him a scholar and a gentlemen" (Helfer, 1968, p. 4).

The legal rights of children were established at the turn of the century in the now-famous case of Mary Ellen. A group of New York church workers had learned of the maltreatment of Mary Ellen by her adoptive parents. As a group, the church workers convinced the local authorities to take legal action. Since there were no laws under which an agency could interfere, an appeal was made to the Society for the Prevention of Cruelty to Animals. It was established that Mary Ellen was a member of the animal kingdom and she was removed from the home of her parents under laws against animal cruelty. This incident resulted in the formation of the Society for the Prevention of Cruelty to Children in 1871 in New York; Great Britain followed suit in 1899. The United States, and later Canada, established guidelines for the apprehension and treatment of child abusers.

Within the United States and Canada research became increasingly specialized. Studies were conducted by doctors, psychiatrists and social workers, independently and not in cooperation with each other, or other related professions.[2]

Social workers, in particular, were concerned with organizing improved health and welfare services for children and with providing even more specialization. Hepworth, convinced that child abuse had little to do with the economic status of a family, introduced measures to curb localization of centres to aid families in need of help and pushed for better organization in the public sphere (Hepworth, 1973). Increasing rates of abuse were related to a lack of organizational coordination. Social workers and well-trained nurses specializing in children's problems were hired in greater numbers. Caseloads were decreased and follow-up studies increased. It was during the time of Hepworth's research, with its heavy emphasis on social welfare organization, that the definition of the problem shifted to include a family, in addition to a single abuser, as problematical.

> "When my hon. friend is putting out all this advice and information of which I thoroughly approve, will he stress that it is the child and the child's safety that matters far more than concern over the parents, who are much better able to defend themselves? The important question is the vulnerability and the defence of the child.
>
> In considering the welfare of a child one is by definition involved in considering the well-being of the total family. A child isolated from his family is a child already deprived" (Hepworth, 1973, p. 25).

Turning to the problem of abuse solely within its context as a Canadian problem, I refer the reader to the Nova Scotia research of Frazer[3] for an excellent statistical breakdown of the incidence in that province (Frazer, 1973).

Mary Van Stolk, writing on *The Battered Child in Canada* (Van Stolk, 1972) attempted to justify a position on legal reform by relying on statistics for the whole of Canada. However, the intrusion of United States statistics leaves the reader with a totally unclear picture of national abuse rates.[4]

The Greenland report of 1973 (Greenland, 1973) was until recently the most accurate reporting of child abuse in Ontario.[5] Aside from presenting an authentic picture of the extent of child abuse in Ontario, the errors and omissions in reporting procedures, the work of social agencies to rectify procedures and intervene at the prevention level, Greenland added one new twist to Canadian literature. Greenland moved away from the Hepworth position of increasing specialization and asked that serious consideration be given to a process of professional communication, communication between hospitals, family practice units, children's aid societies, physicians, courts, police and community services. He emphasized a multi-dimensional approach and a sharing of information among professionals.

LEGAL PROBLEMS

The literature discussed hereunder may be considered legal in the sense that its purpose and findings were of a legal nature and intent. It cannot be totally separated from a historical evaluation, since our laws evolved through the historical process.

Legal studies focus not so much on the cause of child abuse as on the development of present legislation, its effectiveness, and the need for change in legislation and preventive measures.

Clarification of the definition of "abuse" has been the overriding concern of Canadian legal authorities. The specific definition of abuse is far too lengthy to incorporate herein and can be found in the Child Welfare Act, 1965, for the Province of Ontario. This lengthy document begins with the power of the administrative levels and continues on with such definitions as "child abuse." Its contents are not concise and clear enough to inform the Canadian just what abuse is, and it is far too lengthy to expect a wide reading of the act. Legal issues centre around the duty of the individual to comply with the act.

Mandatory reporting is the thrust of Van Stolk's legal review (Van Stolk, 1972) wherein she discusses the confusion of the medical doctor over the confidentiality of his records. The Canadian Criminal Code cited below requires physicians to report abuse cases, but does not protect them from civil liability suits.

> Everyone, being a member of the medical profession, who fails to report within a week of his knowledge of the facts to the Attorney General of the province in which he is practising, any bodily injury to a child, which, in his opinion, may have been caused by maltreatment, is guilty of an indictable offence or of an offence punishable on summary conviction and is liable to a fine not exceeding five hundred dollars or to imprisonment for a term not exceeding three months, or to both fine and imprisonment (Bill C-219).

The futility of such a law has been pointed out by a research team directed by F. Murray Frazer, Associate Dean of the Faculty of Law at Dalhousie University (Frazer, 1973) which is probably the most outstanding and probing study conducted thus far in Canada.[6] The study comprised two sections. The first part, the Retrospective Study, was an attempt to research the causes and treatment of abused children in Nova Scotia. A reconstruction of cases was attempted via the documentation of official agencies including a follow-up using the court records. Included in the interpretation of the documentation was an attempt to determine the manner in which the decision that one is a child abuser is made by the professional. The second half of the study indicated that since some professionals were left with the choice of assuming a person to be an abuser, it was necessary to find out (a) what professionals know about abuse and (b) how they make these decisions.

The Frazer report includes many categories of professionals whom it is felt come into contact with and may in part be responsible for decisions as to whether a parent might be considered an abuser.

The Frazer study introduced Canadian researchers to the possibility that not one but many factors may account for child abuse in Canada.

In keeping with the Frazer approach, Jerry Cooper and Barry Swadron, a Toronto doctor and lawyer respectively, in a report submitted to Mayor Mel Lastman of the Borough of North York (Cooper, 1973) set forth fifteen suggestions to be carried out by the borough. The North York Committee on Child Abuse was composed of both professional and non-professional people and limited its definition of abuse to physical damage. The recommendations of the committee, however, were never implemented. It was felt that structuring a system of communication could only lead to inflexibility and that there are "many ways to skin a cat."

The Child Welfare Act of 1965 sets out the powers of the Children's Aid Society to enact the law, but because known abusers move around the country, its ability to enforce its powers is severely impaired.

The concept of a registry on Child Abuse was suggested by William H. Ireland in the United States and quickly gained acceptance by Canadian social agencies (Ireland, 1966). A central registry of child abuse cases became mandatory in the State of Illinois and has been reasonably successful in that state in locating abusers who move from one location to another in an attempt to avoid apprehension. The Canadian Central Registry located in Ottawa has met with minimal success, however; Canadian social workers contend that all too often workers fail to report abuses (Beyer, 1973).

In 1971 the State of Michigan enacted legislature which made mandatory the duty of a social worker to accompany all children involved in suspected cases of abuse to medical doctors and to prepare a report thereon. Such legislation put pressure on the social worker to report the incident to the Central Registry. This procedure, as reported by De Francis fulfilled the legal requirement that the culpability of a parent requires proof beyond a reasonable doubt (De Francis, 1970).

There are two courts in Canada in which the hearing of the suspected abuser may be heard. The first and most infrequently used is the Criminal Court. The abuser is tried under the category "Assault," and in order to enforce a conviction, "assault with intent to do bodily harm" must be proved. This presents two problems. First, the assault must be witnessed, and secondly, the matter of "intent" must be dealt with. Assaults are rarely witnessed, except in blatant cases, such as the Toronto father who cut both arms off his son. The police came upon the scene, and the man was charged with criminal assault. The problem of intent is aptly put by William Downs:

> It is very difficult to define the duties of parents in this regard. It is hardly appropriate to say there is a legal duty of love and affection toward one's children. How do you command one person to love another? (Downs, 1963, p. 132).

It is mandatory within the Criminal Court system that a person be tried on the basis of a single assault. Therefore if the parent has had frequent contact with the Family Court, all pointing to abuses which have had a cumulative effect on the child, such evidence is inadmissible in Criminal Court. Information flows between Criminal and Family Court are virtually non-existent.

Needless to say, very few people are convicted of child abuse in Criminal Court.

In 1972, Mary Van Stolk attempted a study of child abuse in Canada which would focus on the larger problem in contrast with the province-wide studies (Van Stolk, 1972). Van Stolk's book reeks with sensationalism and lacks a sensible unfolding of the facts. Van Stolk concludes that what is sorely needed is a restructuring of Canadian law as it affects child abusers. The irony lies in the fact that her statistics are American, as well as most of her references. Laws governing child abuse in the United States are state laws. Canadian law governing abuse is provincial, with overriding federal law. The difference in Canadian and American laws affects not only the judiciary, but the actions and attitudes of social workers and police officers. To suggest that changes be made in Canadian law based on statistics which rest on United States law is sheer folly. A comparison of social and pathological forces between countries may indicate useful parallels, but is hardly relevant to our legal procedures.

Lastly, one must recognize the body of literature which is designed for the sole purpose of pressing for laws to rescue already abused children from their caretakers. Generally, and as discussed hereinafter, such research projects are undertaken by social workers.

Boardman, director of social service at Children's Hospital in Los Angeles, describes the project to prevent children already hospitalized from returning to their homes (Boardman, 1962). Boardman's research was based on her experience in the hospital and her observations that parents are likely to protect each other when abuse is suspected, leaving no one to act in the interest of the child. Boardman and her team of researchers forced a crucial issue into the courtroom. In California, as in

Canada, assault is a criminal offence and is extremely difficult to prove. Prior to the Boardman project, parents exonerated in Criminal Court retained custody of their child. What was established by the project was a precedent action to clarify a separation of two court actions. One action is in the Criminal Court where the offending adult is charged. A second action is in the Juvenile Court where the Juvenile Court is to act on behalf of the child. This is not to be confused with what we in Canada call Family Court, which stands in much the same position as the Juvenile Court of California. As a result of the clarification of these laws, the State of California was able to retain custody of the child even after the parents had been cleared of guilt in criminal court. Such a separation of court issues tended to free doctors and other special witnesses to give evidence in juvenile court after the criminal case had concluded; doctors did not want to get involved in lengthy and costly criminal cases.

THE PSYCHOPATHOLOGICAL MODEL

The dominant theme in research related to child abuse falls within a psychopathological model. Early childhood experiences of the abuser result in adult psychopathic states. The focus of attention is the character disorder of the abuser.

Helfer, in particular, related child abuse to the early experiences of the abuser. His research indicates that abusers were, as children, also abused, and that the potential to protect and mother has never been developed and nurtured in these persons (Helfer, 1970). Because the adult has never learned how to parent, the adult looks to the child for fulfillment, rather than the reverse. As a child, the parent was expected to fulfill his parents' emotional needs and not to expect much in return. The learned function of accepting help from others and communicating with others has not been established. Since parents cannot communicate with others, they build a wall of isolation around themselves and look to their own children to fulfill their needs. Helfer is saying that there is a cycle of abuse which repeats itself.

Kaufman and Zalba, as well, discovered that abused parents have been abused themselves as children, or neglected either physically or emotionally (Kaufman, 1962, Zalba, 1975). Steele and Pollock concur with Kaufman and Zalba and demonstrate that parents recreated patterns of child rearing similar to their own (Steele and Pollock, 1968). The children of these parents were deprived of both basic mothering and a deep sense of being cared for from the beginning of their lives. The defect in "motherliness" in the parents refers not to the ability or willingness to perform the mechanics of child care, but to the attitude and means with which this was accomplished.

Fontana viewed such parents as emotionally handicapped, unable to handle children because of traumatic circumstances in their own childhood (Fontana, 1968). Parents acted in accord with past experiences of loneliness, lack of protection and lack of love by dealing with their children in this manner.

In support of the hypothesis that former childhood experiences are an agent in child abuse, Kavisarak found in his study of abusing families the emotional loss of a significant parental figure early in the life of an abusive parent to be a striking statistic (Kavisarak, 1966). Support for establishing that the abusive parent was once an abused or neglected child is found in most major articles on child abuse (Kempe, 1962; Nurse, 1964; Zalba, 1966).

Acceptance of the hypothesis of a deprived childhood on the part of abusers led investigators to agreement that abusing parents labour under misconceptions of the nature of child rearing and generally look to the child as a source of satisfaction for their own needs. The abusing parents generally possess high expectations and premature demands are made on their children (Steele and Pollock, 1968). Galdston (Galdston, 1966) found similar results and added that the parents were incapable of understanding the particular stages of development of the child. Melnick and Harley found in the mothers severely frustrated dependency needs and an inability to empathize with their children (Melnick and Harley, 1969).

The possibility that the abusive parent is psychotic and that abuse stems directly from this has been entertained by many investigators. There appears to be little support for this hypothesis, except in a few cases. Kempe found only 5 per cent of the families had one parent who was psychotic (Kempe, 1971). Although lack of impulse control is commonly found with abusive parents, few severe psychotic tendencies are evident (Wasserman, 1967).

No one set of factors, demographic, parental history, parental attitudes toward child rearing, or severe personality disorder, could account for cases of child abuse. With the realization that very divergent paths may lead to child abuse, various researchers have attempted a typological approach.

Merrill presented the first major typology at a National Conference on Social Welfare in 1962 (Bryant *et al.*, 1967). He identified three distinct clusters of personality characteristics that were applicable to both the mother and father and a fourth that applied to fathers alone. These characteristics included aggressiveness, rigidity, compulsiveness, passivity and dependence.

Zalba presented a typology much like Merrill's, but added two categories: the psychotic parent and the impulsive, but generally adequate, parent with marital conflict (Zalba, 1967). It is the psychotic, according to Zalba, who is responsible for the greatest number of infanticides and child homicides. The impulsive parent's abuse is generally the result of marital conflict displaced onto the child. Despite extensive literature on the topic, Zalba's categories have never been validated empirically through field research.

Zalba, a consistent figure in child abuse literature, is adamant in his position that it is character-disordered parents who make up the majority of child battering parents. The following passage is typical of the stance of the proponents of the psychopathological model:

> Child-battering and serious child abuse are inflicted by parents with a variety of problems ranging from violent and episodic schizophrenia to immature and impulse-ridden character disorder, who displace and act out their anger over marital conflicts onto their children. The common element among them is that children are used as targets of abuse and injury in the process of projecting, displacing, and denying intrapsychic and other-object-oriented hostility and aggression (Zalba, 1975, p. 219).

Model 1
The Psychopathological Model

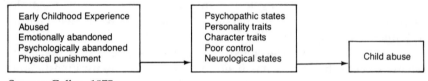

Source: Gelles, 1975

THE SOCIAL MODEL

Most researchers have concerned themselves with psychopathological studies related to child abuse. Gil, however, while granting a correlation, notes that instances related to psychopathology are not independent of certain basic cultural dimensions. Child abuse cannot be explained solely on the basis of psychopathology. Rather, it is related to two cultural factors, namely: the socioeconomic status of the abuser; and the "culturally sanctioned and patterned use of physical force in child rearing" (Gil, 1975).

A variety of nationalities flourish in Canada. These ethnic groups differ in their child-rearing philosophies as well as in actual practice. The variables which are related to social and economic strata are related as well to child abuse. For example, both education and income are negatively correlated with incidence rates. Furthermore, minority groups have no recourse to external societal violence, which in time leads to frustration and violence against one's own group. In support of this contention Gil points out the relatively high rates of homicide among minority group members.

Poverty may be a precipitating factor whereby undue stress is placed upon the deprived in terms of environmental, psychological and socio-economic deprivation. Gil stresses the lack of alternatives for expression of aggression among the minority groups. The families of minority groups are large yet their living space is inadequate.

Socialization differs with social class as well. Aggressive impulses are expressed through direct action in the lower socioeconomic classes. The middle classes tend to use psychological approaches in the disciplining of their children. While Gil acknowledges that psychological interaction may be more devastating than physical force, he contends that middle-class families are spared the pressures of poverty, thereby lessening the overall stress factor.

Gil then turns to what might be done to lessen the incidence of child abuse. His emphasis is on societal conditions rather than parental makeup. Says Gil, "For social policies to be effective they must be based on a causal theory concerning the etiology of the condition which is to be corrected or prevented" (Gil, 1975). Because of the various links between poverty, discrimination, pathology and child abuse, Gil sees the route toward reducing abuse in the elimination of poverty and social inequalities. His remedial suggestions require long-range planning as follows: change public attitude toward aggression; eliminate poverty; and improve family social services.

Wasserman, as well, is interested in the social implications of child abuse (Wasserman, 1967). According to Wasserman, the public, by and large, view themselves as righteous and far removed from battering parents. Labelling the parent as a child batterer is a defence mechanism used by society which serves to release it from any responsibility to understand the needs of the abuser. To label is to deny that we all possess the potential for violence. "But stripped of our defences against such instincts and placed in a social and psychological climate conducive to violent behaviour, any of us could do the 'unthinkable' " (Wasserman, 1967, p. 224).

Wasserman points to the defective socialization of the abused. While claiming not to be interested in a sociological approach, he claims that we are what we have learned to be. Wasserman offers a solution as to why a particular child is abused. The child abuser, in particular, has had associations with other people who have taught him the importance of immediate gratification and have convinced him to focus his life on his own needs. When such a person does not have his immediate needs gratified, he selects a "hostility sponge" upon whom to vent that rage. The object of that rage is somebody who is competing for and getting something which belongs to him or somebody who represents an unconscious symbol of something which once caused pain. To help the parent, claims Wasserman, we must break the socialization chain learned by the parent. We must come to grips as well, with the larger issue, that of a moral code which condemns violence in one form and permits it in another. Regardless of the difference in socioeconomic status of the family, Wasserman contends, the rules are not clear. Model 2 illustrates the positions of Gil and Wasserman.

Model 2
The Social Model

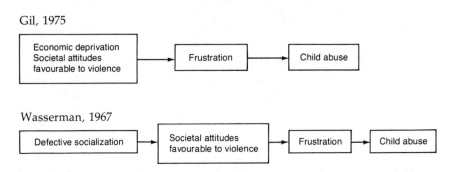

Gil, 1975

Wasserman, 1967

Şara Davidson describes a group of people who are committed to Wasserman's suggestion: breaking the learned cycle of abuse. The group is known as Parents Anonymous, a self-help citizen volunteer group. Each Parents Anonymous group meets on a weekly basis, at which time parents with abuse problems discuss the commonalities in their behaviours and look to each other for help in what they term "the vicious cycle of abuse." Davidson states that Parents Anonymous has elected Dr. Ray Helfer, well-known authority on child abuse, to their Advisory Board. They have adopted Helfer's position that abusive parents have lacked a model of healthy parenting. Helfer fully supports Parents Anonymous groups, seeing the advantage of treating the symptoms and "short-circuiting abusive habits" (Davidson, 1973, p. 190).

Young denies the association of poverty with child abuse as stressed by Gil and claims that child abuse is common in all social strata. According to Young, child abuse is the result of "the perverse fascination with punishment as an entity in itself, divorced from discipline and even from the fury of revenge" (Young, 1975, p. 189).

THE SOCIAL-PSYCHOLOGICAL MODEL

Gelles's social-psychological model below accepts neither a psychological nor a sociological explanation of child abuse (Gelles, 1975). It includes psychological, cultural and social situational factors. Double lines indicate additions made by this author to be elaborated later.

Model 3
The Social Psychological Model

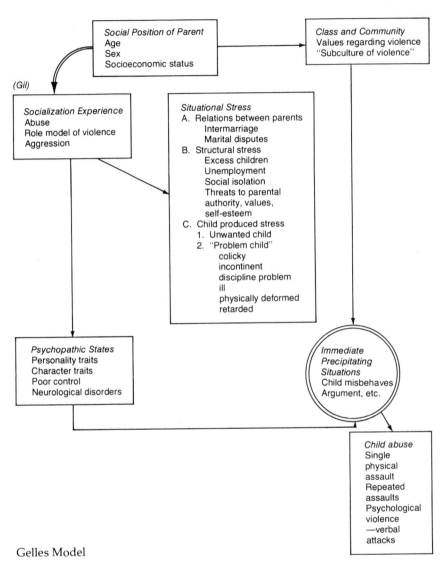

Gelles Model

A review of Gelles's model would substantially replicate the earlier part of this paper. It is where Gelles's model leads us that is of interest. The psychopathological approach, says Gelles, cannot account for most cases of child abuse. This is because it attributes child abuse to a single, causal variable. Variables are ignored which may be even more important. Psychological explanations dominate the literature on child abuse.

The common theme is as follows: "Anyone who would abuse or kill his child is sick . . ." The illness presumption assumes that abusers have distinctive personality traits, the roots of which can be traced back to the childhood of the parent. Gelles points out that advocates of the psycho-pathological model are quick to explain that social variables are not the cause of child abuse. Gelles is critical of the authors of the psychopatho-logical approach for what he calls their "blatant contradictions." An abusing parent is said to be a psychopath and, at the same time, no different from other members of society. His second criticism is that authors do not agree on what characteristics represent the pathology, and thirdly, very few studies attempt to test the hypotheses. This is so because the analysis takes place after the fact, which leads to the logical conclusion that the abuser lacks emotional control. Gelles uses the argu-ment of Thomas Szasz: people who are labelled mentally ill are thought to be suffering from mental illness, ergo people who are child abusers are suffering from uncontrolled aggression.

A final criticism of the psychopathological approach relates to the sampling technique. Subjects in child abuse studies are not representa-tive of the child abusing population. They are generally cases from medical and psychiatric practitioners. No attempt has been made to compare child abusers with non-child abusers. Thus, we do not know whether abusers differ from the rest of the population in terms of causal variables.

Gelles looks at three aspects of child abuse: the social characteristics of the abuser, the characteristics of the victim and the properties of the act of abuse. He finds that the socioeconomic class of the abuser is generally low (Gil, 1975), that the lower classes use violence more frequently than the upper classes (Gil, 1975), and that mothers appear to be more abusive-prone than fathers. The child who is abused is often not yet old enough to be capable of meaningful social interaction, which may create a source of frustration for a parent attempting interaction. Gelles tells us that most studies of abuse have failed to look at possible social causes of psychological stress and that even the structural aspect of stress alone does not explain why all families under similar stress situations don't abuse.

Gelles proposes his social-psychological model which emphasizes the complexity and the interrelationship of factors which lead to child abuse. The social-psychological perspective sees child abuse as a "form of deviant behaviour instead of being seen only as a result of individual pathology" (Gelles, p. 199). This behaviour is in part determined by the abuser's own childhood socialization. Gelles suggests the use of Miller's frustration-aggression approach. This author does not support Gelles's suggestion, since Miller's approach assumes aggression always follows frustration and this is certainly not the case in many instances.[7] Gelles suggests also that a Mertonian structural approach to such behaviour be researched. Once again, this does not explain the fact that most people under similar structural conditions do not abuse.

Gelles's solution is much like Gil's: the elimination of poverty, the removal of the stigma attached to aborting unwanted children and the development of programs which teach parenting.

Gelles makes a valuable contribution to the literature by bringing to light the shortcomings of the relevant research in the field of child abuse. His Social-Psychological Model combines the efforts of many into one model. Perhaps the only major researcher he has not done justice to is Gil. The author has added an arrow to Gelles's model to include Gil's point of view. Gelles makes a major error in suggesting that a structural model will explain child abuse. He is guilty of some of his own criticisms of others. His model has not been put to the test, nor does he suggest a control group in order to determine whether "normal families" under similar stress situations behave in the same was as do abusing families.

His most valuable contribution, set out in the double circle, entitled "Immediate Precipitating Situations," has been only vaguely mentioned in many studies, yet invariably such situations precede child abuse. It is this "circle" which is worthy of elaboration and further research.

TOWARD AN INTERACTIONAL MODEL OF CHILD ABUSE

The foregoing portion of this paper comprises various models, separated by interest and focus of the researcher. A number of important considerations have not been dealt with.

Models 1 and 2 are psychological and sociological causal models. All models suggest that the problem can be reduced to either a simple psychological or social cause, or some combination of the two. In Model 3 Gelles demonstrates the acknowledged and never dealt with variable, the factor which immediately precipitates the abuse. While Gelles has constructed the only model demonstrating an active link between static factors such as personality traits or socioeconomic status, he has chosen merely to link causal factors and not to elaborate on the importance of "Immediate Precipitating Factors."

Studies all too often focus on the motivation and behaviour of the attacking person. Such an approach disregards the dynamics of conflict. An abusive act depends upon the behaviour of the perpetrator, and it also depends on the reaction of the victim to this behaviour (Gil, 1970).

Research focuses on child abusers or abused children rather than families in which a child is abused. The stress factor merely mentioned in other studies is not experienced only by an abuser or an abused. It is experienced by the entire family immediately preceding the abuse and it is, therefore, important to look at child abuse as one manifestation of conflict in a family.

In England, John and Elizabeth Newson have begun international comparative studies in an attempt to seek differences in family dynamics leading to physical punishment.

> The point, explain the Newsons, in trying to discover under what circumstances some parents resort to physical or verbal violence, is that punitive acts themselves cannot be isolated from the complexity of attitudes, values and clashes of tension in families (Blumberg, 1975, p. 149).

The following factors are suggested as indicators of future directions in the study of child abuse:

1. Child abuse is seldom found in the absence of conflict. Those factors which precipitate child abuse may prove to be the variables which can be manipulated in order to reduce its incidence.
2. An interactional model of child abuse would be functionally relevant to family dynamics. Child abuse may well be only one manifestation of conflict in a family.
3. Control groups have not been used in previous studies of child abuse. Many researchers have found that child abusers have been abused themselves as children. This finding can only be substantiated if a comparable control group proves not to have been abused as children.
4. Research has been conducted on socially labelled or "agency child abusers," lumping them all into a single category and assuming their guilt on identical grounds. Future studies would do well to dichotomize examples. For example:
   (a) Abuse of a child in a crib may differ significantly from abuse of an active two-year-old.
   (b) Abuse in intact families may differ from that of the broken home.
   (c) Mode of detection of the abuser may significantly alter this offence.
   (d) Cultural differences may account for and explain a variety of types of abuse. For example, within the black population of America it is common to find abuse in the form of a parent-child fistfight. Child abuse in large Canadian cities frequently takes the form of abuse to the head. Within ethnic pockets of Canadian cities abuse takes on a variety of distinct characteristics.

In conclusion, it is our feeling that the concept "child abuse" needs reexamining. It needs clarification and specification. While we intend to investigate the abuse of children in greater detail in subsequent papers, presenting a viable theoretical model, it is our hope that this classification and qualification of the relevant research will suggest some bases for future exploration.

NOTES

[1] "For a Broken Child," *The Globe and Mail*, Dec. 27, 1974. See also "22-Day Ellis Inquest Is One of the Longest, Most Expensive in Ontario, Costing $250,000." *The Globe and Mail*, July 23, 1977.

[2] A recent attempt at interprofessional research can be found in *Child Abuse and Neglect*, Report to the House of Commons, First Session, 1974-75-76.

[3] To be discussed at length under b) Legal problems.

[4] In 1972 Van Stolk estimated the Canadian child abuse rate to be 7,000 cases per year based on U.S. criteria. In 1975 this figure was adjusted to 5,524 (Van Stolk, 1975, p. 1).

[5] See *Child Abuse and Neglect, ibid.*

[6] See also Dickens, Bernard M., *Legal Issues in Child Abuse*, Centre of Criminology, University of Toronto, 1976.

[7] The debate over the "Frustration-Aggression Hypothesis" began in *Frustration and Aggression*, Dollard, J., Miller *et al.*, Yale University Press, 1939, wherein violence was said to have been the result of frustration. After considerable criticism Miller modified his theory in "The Frustration-Aggression Hypothesis," in *Psychological Review*, 1941, Vol. 48, to the effect that frustration produces a number of responses, one of which is violence. There is consensus that the theory is still inadequate (Hartung, Frank, *Crime, Law and Society*, Detroit: Wayne State University Press, 1965) for the following reasons: an individual may respond violently at one time, yet not at another; and the theory is the result of an experimental finding and its application to real-life situations requires caution.

REFERENCES

Beyer Gammon, Mary Alice
    1974   "Child Abuse: Toward an Interactional Model," unpublished paper, Toronto, University of Toronto.

Blumberg, Myrna
    1975   "When Parents Hit Out," in *Violence in the Family*. Suzanne K. Steinmetz and Murray A. Straus (Ed.) New York: Dodd Mead and Co.

Boardman, Helen E.
    1962   "A Project to Rescue Children from Inflicted Injuries," in *Social Work*, January: 43-51.

Bowker, Marjorie Montgomery, LLD
    1977   "Child Abuse: Social Work Aspects," paper presented by the Second World Conference of the International Society on Family Law, McGill University, June.

Bryant, H. D., *et al.*
    1967   "Physical Abuse of Children: An Agency Study," in *Child Welfare*: 125-130.

Cooper, Jerry and Barry Swadron
1973   *Report of the Committee on Child Abuse,* submitted to Mayor Mel Lastman, Borough of North York, September.
Davidson, Sara
1973   "At Last! Help for Child-Abusers," in *Woman's Day,* March.
De Francis, Vincent
1970   *Child Abuse Legislation in the 1970's: Protecting the Battered Child.* The American Humane Association, Children's Division: vi. Denver: Oceana Publishing Co.
Dickens, Bernard M.
1976   *Legal Issues in Child Abuse,* Centre of Criminology, University of Toronto.
Dollard, J., Miller, et al
1939   *Frustration and Aggression,* Princeton: Yale University Press.
Downs, William T.
1963   "The Meaning and Handling of Child Neglect—A Legal View," in *Child Welfare,* March: 131-134.
Etzioni, Amitai
1971   "Violence" in Contemporary Social Problems, Third Edition, Robert K. Merton and Robert Nesbet (Eds.), New York: Harcourt, Brace, Jovanovich, Inc.
Fontana, V. J.
1968   "The Maltreated Child: The Maltreatment of Children," in *New York State Journal of Medicine:* 2214-2215.
Frazer, Murray F.
1973   *Child Abuse in Nova Scotia: A Research Project About Battered and Maternally Deprived Children.* Province of Nova Scotia.
Galdston, K.
1966   "Observations on Children Who Have Been Physically Abused and Their Parents," in *American Journal of Psychiatry:* 440-443.
Gelles, Richard J.
1975   "A Sociological Critique and Reformulation," in *Violence in the Family,* Suzanne K. Steinmetz and Murray A. Straus (Ed.), New York: Dodd Mead and Co.
Gil, David G.
1970   *Violence Against Children: Physical Abuse in the United States,* Cambridge: Harvard University Press.

1975   "A Conceptual Model of Child Abuse and Its Implications for Social Policy," in *Violence in the Family,* Suzanne K. Steinmetz and Murray A. Straus (Ed.), New York: Dodd Mead and Co.
Greenland, Cyril
1973   *Research Report No. 3 to the Ontario Ministry of Community and Social Services, Research and Planning Branch,* Province of Ontario, The Queens Printer.
Hartung, Frank
1965   *Crime, Law and Society.* Detroit: Wayne State University Press.
Helfer, Ray E. and Henry C. Kempe (Ed.)
1968   *The Battered Child.* Chicago: University of Chicago Press.
Hepworth, Philip
1973   "Looking at Baby Battering: Its Detection and Treatment, in *Canadian Welfare,* Vol. 49: 13-25.
Ireland, William H.
1966   "A Registry on Child Abuse," in *Children,* Vol. 13, No. 3: 113-115.
Kaufman, J.
1962   "Psychiatric Implications of Physical Abuse of Children," in *Protecting the Battered Child,* V. D. Francis (Ed.). American Humane Association, Children's Division, Denver: Oceana Publishing Co.

Kavisarak, R.
1966   "Clinical Evaluation of Child Abuse: Scarred Families, a Preliminary
            Report," in *Juvenile Court Judges Journal*, (Wayne County, Michigan) Vol.
            66-70.
Kempe, C. H.
1971   "Paediatric Implications of the Battered Baby Syndrome," in *Archives of
            Disease in Childhood:* 28-37.
Kempe, C. H., *et al.*
1962   "The Battered Child Syndrome," in *Journal of the American Medical Associa-
            tion:* 17-24.
Melnick, B. and Harley, J.
1969   "Distinctive Personality Attributes of Child-Abusing Mothers," in *Journal
            of Consulting and Clinical Psychology:* 746-749.
Miller, N. E.
1941   "The Frustration Aggression Hypothesis," in Psychological Review, Vol.
            48, pp. 337-342.
Nurse, S.
1964   "Familial Patterns of Parents Who Abuse Their Children," in *Smith College
            Studies in Social Work:* 11-25.
Steinmetz, Suzanne K. and Murray A. Straus
1975   *Violence in the Family.* New York: Dodd Mead and Co.
Silverman, Frederic N.
1968   "Radiologic Aspects of the Battered Child Syndrome," in *The Battered
            Child*, R. E. Helfer and C. H. Kempe (Ed.). Chicago: University of Chicago
            Press.
Steele, B. F. and C. B. Pollock
1968   "A Psychiatric Study of Parents Who Abuse Infants and Small Children,"
            in *The Battered Child*, R. E. Helfer and C. H. Kempe (Ed.). Chicago:
            University of Chicago Press.
Van Stolk, Mary
1975   "The Abused Child and the Law, in *Reports on Family Law*, p. 1.
_____
1972   *The Battered Child in Canada.* Toronto: McClelland and Stewart.
Wasserman, S.
1967   "The Abused Parent of the Abused Child," in *Children.* 175-179.
Young, Leontine
1975   "Parents Who Hate," in *Violence in the Family*, Suzanne K. Steinmetz and
            Murray A. Straus (Ed.). New York: Dodds, Mead and Co.
Zalba, Serapio R.
1975   "Treatment of Child Abuse," in *Violence in the Family*, Suzanne K. Stein-
            metz and Murray A. Straus (Ed.). New York: Dodd Mead and Co.
_____
1974   "Battered Children," in *Intimacy, Family and Society*, Arlene Skolnick and
            Jerome H. Skolnick. Boston: Little Brown and Co.
_____
1967   "The Abused Child: A Typology for Classification and Treatment," in
            Social Work: 70-79.
_____
1966   "The Abused Child: A Survey of the Problem, in *Social Work:* 3-16.

Chapter 6

WEDNESDAY'S PARENT AND
THE ROLE OF THE PARAPROFESSIONAL

Barbara Warme and Sharon Thomas

*Although it has been shown that the occurrence of child abuse is not confined to
a particular socioeconomic level, sex, religious affiliation or educational background, there seems to be emerging an identifiable pattern of key variables in
terms of the adult caretaker, the child, the situational stresses and the precipitating crisis. Warme and Thomas present this pattern and the manner in which it
has provided the basis for the development of a new paraprofessional role in the
therapeutic and preventive approach to child abuse. The Toronto Lay Therapist
Project was designed as a multi-disciplinary undertaking to explore the use of
the paraprofessional in the rehabilitation of the abusing parent. A small group of
lay therapists, provided with intensive training and close, supportive supervision, was given the task of working with abusing mothers or fathers on a one-to-
one basis. This chapter examines the process of attempted rehabilitation as is
unfolded in a single case, over a period of two and one-half years.*

*Research in the area of violence rarely utilizes a long-term approach such as
that of Warme and Thomas. The difficulty of engaging an entire family over a
period of years generally precludes such research. Families in which children are
abused often move from one province to another to avoid provincial agency procedures. The case-study approach as employed here is of pedagogical value and is
found frequently in anthropological studies where it has provided stimulating
insights in "relatively unformulated areas" (Selltiz, 1976). Our researchers
have chosen to confine themselves to a small group, in this instance a family, in
order to study it intensively, rather than to conduct a more superficial, large-
scale examination. The case history will dig deeper, but lose in generality. It
lacks the controls of experimental research and relies heavily on the integrative
powers of the investigators. Its critics conclude that it may reflect the predisposi-
tions of the researchers rather than the object it is to study.*

*The case study approach is an appropriate procedure when one chooses not to
be limited to the testing of hypotheses or causal relationships, or by theory
which, utilized a priori, may be irrelevant to the task. It is intended not to test
but to evoke hypotheses. Its theoretical value emerges. Patterns of behaviour
which might otherwise be treated as a series of traits to be tabulated are viewed as
units which typify a particular family pattern. In this instance it is demonstrated that the therapist-client relationship is embedded in a matrix of impera-
tives, many of them conflicting and operating at cross purposes.*

---

* An original article written for this volume.

INTRODUCTION

Our purpose here is to examine the role of the lay therapist in a single family in which child abuse has been identified and a therapeutic, rather than punitive, orientation to one of the parents has been attempted. Such an examination provides an opportunity to identify some of the complex issues involved in the development and use of the paraprofessional role as a component of rehabilitative intervention. While we are aware of the severe limitations of the case study approach, we are also concerned that the idea-generating value of clinical observations has had to be sacrificed in the recent spate of large-scale epidemiological studies (Smith, 1975). Clinical material may also serve as a corrective to the tendency, noted by Merton in his discussion of sociological euphemisms, to analyze human problems in terms of an elaborate, impersonal conceptual apparatus, "as if these persistent problems did not involve the suffering of actual human beings" (Merton, 1972).

THE LAY THERAPIST PROJECT

It is not uncommon for families with a child abuse problem to be receiving a massive infusion of social services—welfare payments, subsidized housing, family counselling, subsidized day care, the assistance of public health nurses, homemakers, child care workers, help with job retraining and a multitude of other ministrations provided by social agencies in order to relieve pressures in the home environment. And yet, more often than not, the abuse continues—or at least the home continues to be a pressure cooker in which the children are considered to be at risk. It has long been recognized that social workers with characteristically heavy caseloads do not have the luxury of sufficient time to spend with these needy, insatiable parents whose diagnosis is "insufficient mothering" (Kempe and Helfer, 1972). Nor do volunteers find it easy to persist in working with this type of ungratifying client. Individual psychotherapy is also not a realistic plan, for there are not enough therapists to go around, nor is psychotherapy the intervention of choice for many of these persons (Kreindler, 1975). Organizations like Parents' Anonymous and distress centres can rarely connect with abusive parents in the early stages, because of the latter's inability to reach out voluntarily to help that is available (Smith, 1974; Baher, 1976).

It was with this in mind that the Lay Therapist Pilot Project was conceived and initiated in a Canadian metropolitan area in 1974. Inspired by the work done at the University of Colorado Medical Center by Kempe and his associates (Kempe and Helfer, 1972)[1], this paraprofessional role was viewed as a contribution to the multi-disciplinary approach generally agreed to be so necessary in dealing with parents who physically harm their children. The lay therapists were to work in close co-operation with the child protective agency; it was to be clear that the agency should actively exercise its legal responsibility for the protection of the child, while the lay therapist would focus as exclusively as possible on one of the parents. The role of the lay therapists was to provide, over a long period of time, a positive nurturing experience for uncommunicative, isolated and chronically deprived individuals. The goal was to help such parents to develop a sense of being valued and a sense of self-esteem which would eventually permit them to find sufficient gratification in the adult world and so be better able to parent their own children. The relationship with the therapist would become a model for other trusting relationships. The parent would also learn, it was hoped, to reach out to other individuals and agencies in the community for help, when needed.

In concrete terms the job of the therapist was to listen, in a non-directive and non-critical way, to whatever the parent wanted to talk about and to be responsive to the parent's needs. Twenty-four hours a day accessibility by telephone would be supplemented by home visits as often as necessary—usually no less than twice a week and, at times of exceptional stress, every day. Sometimes the contact would involve going out for a cup of coffee or a meal, or out for an evening of bingo, although often these parents are at first fearful of leaving their home even to venture to a nearby coffee shop. When appropriate, the lay therapist would offer practical assistance in potentially stressful or disruptive situations—in job hunting, the move to a new apartment, a visit to the doctor, an interview at the school, the arrival of a new baby, the return of a child from foster care, or even the monumental struggle with a new recipe. The task was to be alert to the particular types of situations which might constitute stress for that particular parent (Warme, 1975).

In looking for candidates for training, the project directors (a psychiatrist and a sociologist) were seeking people who had sufficient supports to draw upon in their own private lives and who had experienced the pleasures and strains of being parents themselves. Flexibility in schedules, compassion, the capacity to be non-judgmental and the ability to resist rushing around and "getting things done" were also qualities sought. It seemed important to find people who would not be impatient for quick, tangible results. They would need to be able to endure, for example, the boredom of endless hours spent watching afternoon television shows with the parent, often without conversation or any gesture of hospitality. They would also have to tolerate the banality of months of chitchat unrelieved by any "significant unburdening" or indeed any manifest indication that what they were doing was at all worthwhile. They would have to learn not to be seduced by superficial co-operation, palliative offerings such as dramatic bits of self-revelation, and other signs of pseudo-improvement. Abusive parents have characteristically had a lifetime of learning to please others and tend to be adept at providing what they think is expected of them.

THE MACDONALD FAMILY

The MacDonald family consists of two parents, Ruth and David, in their early thirties, two boys, Blair and Greg, both ten, and one girl, Heather, who is five. This is a common-law relationship. Blair is David's son by a previous common-law union; Greg, Ruth's son, is the product of an earlier common-law relationship which she was never prepared to discuss with the lay therapist. Heather is Ruth and David's own daughter. Both parents have relinquished children from earlier legal marriages to their respective estranged spouses. David recently received his divorce; for financial reasons, Ruth's marriage is not yet dissolved.

Four generations live in a crowded row house in the low income urban area. Ruth's paternal grandmother of ninety-five lives with them, paying rent for her room. The grandmother firmly believes that women should stay in the home; those that go out (like the lay therapist) are "responsible for all the problems with children today."

For several years, Ruth's father had also lived with them. He was at the time unemployed, alcoholic and only occasionally paying rent. He and Gran would sit on the living room couch most of the day, watching television and objecting if the children joined them or in any way disturbed them. Since they did not like the meals Ruth prepared for the rest of the family, Ruth prepared separate meals for them. The father believed and frequently told Ruth that once the Children's Aid Society was "in" you could never get them "out," and that if they took one child they would eventually take them all. Her father was also the man who tried to assault Ruth sexually throughout her childhood.

The extended family played a large part in the MacDonalds' life. Ruth's older sister had "married up" and only called when she needed David's help, perhaps to move or to deliver something. Carol, Ruth's younger sister, lived in the same neighbourhood with her common-law husband and four children. In fact, the two families had recently exchanged houses. Carol, too, made many demands on Ruth and David. She also acted as a communication link between David and his former wife, Blair's natural mother. Ruth always resented her younger sister's "tattle tale" role in family affairs.

David's brother, an unemployed trucker who lived in the country, spent a great deal of time at the MacDonalds' home. He often visited during the day and he and his wife regularly played poker at the MacDonald's on the weekend. Both Ruth and David frequently lost all their cash on a Friday night. The MacDonalds purchased a small second-hand pool table and all the relatives continually dropped in to play pool until late at night. Ruth finally said that she wished they had never purchased it. When David's sister had her third baby her husband was in jail, so Ruth looked after the older children. In all these relationships Ruth and David never seemed to be able to say no.

As is common in working-class families, the MacDonalds maintained contact with siblings and parents to compensate for loneliness, rather than developing friendships of their own (Wilmott and Young, 1960). Contrary, however, to the picture evoked by current nostalgia surrounding the disappearance of the extended family system in our society, these relatives were a source of severe and chronic stress rather than of support. Baher (Baher, 1976) noted that only one family in their study received emotional support from parents. Despite the number of relatives constantly present, the MacDonalds were socially isolated, such isolation being one of the "constellation of characteristics common to abusive families" (Elmer, 1967). More needs to be known about the ways in which being enmeshed in a large web of relatives who mirror one's own failures and vulnerabilities can be dysfunctional for the nuclear family.

David, the husband and father, owns his own truck; operating from his own home, he does odd moving and repair jobs, and collects scrap. He is very proud of being able to pay his own bills. The importance attached to the "provider role" (Gelles, 1973) and the pride in "going it alone" (Baher, 1976) are characteristics that have often been noted in the literature on abusive fathers. David worked long and irregular hours, "Saturdays if he could," according to Ruth, and he demanded that she stay home during the day to answer the phone for him in case a job came up. Consequently, the degree of Ruth's isolation was increased, as was the amount of time she was left to cope with the children by herself.

Through Ruth, the lay therapist eventually learned that David was regularly beaten as a child, with the frying pan if that was handiest; he was expected to do all the dishes and also had the responsibility of washing his mother's hair. His parents separated and David and his mother's subsequent common-law husband did not get along; David therefore left home at the age of fourteen, shortly after the common-law husband moved in. His natural father presently lives near by and frequently asks for David's assistance with various jobs.

In his mid-twenties, David spent some time in jail. Ruth was unsure of the length of his sentence (one-two years?) and of the reason for it. After his release he took custody of Blair and arranged for Ruth to be his babysitter/housekeeper in exchange for room and board for herself and Greg. A year or two later they began to live together in a common-law relationship.

The lay therapist first met David when he unexpectedly picked Ruth and her up after bingo. On that evening the conversation between David and his wife had the flavour of teasing teenagerish banter; this was seen again on their good days. They were never, according to Ruth, able to "talk serious." If a problem was brewing, David would get drunk, start an argument, and occasionally hit Ruth, but "nothing was ever settled." During the lay therapist's involvement there were several serious marital rows; Ruth was kicked out once (she went to her sister Carol's) and David left once (he also went to Carol's). Ruth, in a conversation with the lay therapist, wondered out loud how other married couples were able to settle their problems.

The main source of disagreement between them was the children's discipline. David would lay down the law and then leave Ruth to enforce it. This might involve keeping the children in their room all day. Insecurity with respect to the common-law relationship complicated their disagreements. With David, social workers or child care workers, Ruth hesitated to discuss her problems in dealing with Blair, because he was not hers. She believed that David thought she favoured her own children and picked on Blair. She felt that "if David really loved me he would get the money somehow to pay for my divorce." David's former common-law wife, with her erratic demands for custody of Blair and for visiting rights, was also a source of marital friction. Ruth showed jealousy and possessiveness even when other children played up to David. She once admonished a four-year-old nephew, "That's *my* David."

Blair is the severely abused child in the family. However, according to Skinner and Castle's data, there is a 13 to 1 chance that where the first child is abused, a subsequent child will be injured. Smith (1972) also cautions against the over-optimistic view that only one child in a family is affected. Certainly in this family Blair's siblings, Greg and Heather, "fared little better emotionally" (Baher, 1976). Actually, as the case progressed the lay therapist worried that Ruth was beginning to preceive Heather's behaviour as similar to Blair's and hence more difficult to tolerate.

The school nurse called the Children's Aid Society in mid-winter, having noted welts on Blair's arm. She pursued that observation to discover that belt marks covered his trunk and to learn that he was regularly beaten. On investigation, the social worker learned that his parents were at the "end of their rope." Blair was given the strap almost daily by one parent or the other. They described him as the "bad boy" and Greg as the "good boy." Blair's behaviour with animals was cruel and bizarre, he lied, stole, wet his bed, generally misbehaved and had his parents "at each other's throats." His behaviour relates to the question raised by Goode (Goode, 1971) concerning the contribution of the victim to the dynamics of violence, a notion that is only now beginning to receive systematic attention. Blair was removed from the home and placed in the Children's Aid Receiving Centre for protection and assessment.

Several months later, the family's social worker presented the case to the agency's abuse committee. With abusive families, data at intake are usually "seriously incomplete or incorrect" (Baher, 1976), and this raises practical problems for the social agency. Accurate assessment is essential before treatment goals and most effective treatment methods can be determined. However, based on data available it was decided that a lay therapist might effectively work with Ruth.[2] Although David was also known to have abused Blair, it was thought access to him would be less feasible. The therapist was introduced simply as someone who would help get Ruth out of the house.

It was fully six months later that Ruth reintroduced the lay therapist to her grandmother as "the lady who keeps me from killing the kids."

Before discussing in detail the relationship with Ruth, it is important to summarize the family's involvement or contact with other institutions and individuals over the two-year period. After leaving the Receiving Centre, Blair was under the care of a residential treatment centre and then at home under the auspices of a Home Care Program. The latter intervention was based on the theory of behaviour modification; in no respect did it obviate the parents' need to punish Blair. As Goode has noted, " . . . nothing less than severe punishment (for the child) will right the injustice they (the parents) have experienced" (Goode, 1971). In addition, the role-playing involved in the behaviour modification program only served to increase their sense of inadequacy.[3] The program was discontinued after six weeks at the parents' insistence. At a much later date Ruth told the lay therapist, "We didn't fight them. We didn't understand." The MacDonalds met with two psychiatrists, a psychologist and three child care workers. They were in family court on three different occasions, represented by a lawyer only on the first occasion. In light of this rather complicated series of agency interventions, one can appreciate the value of the *continuity* of the lay therapist's involvement. The importance of a consistent relationship is stressed in the literature (Wasserman 1967; Zalba, 1966); the personality of the abusing parent poorly equips him/her to cope with worker turnover.

The lay therapist first met Ruth with the social worker. They sat in the kitchen, over coffee, having a fairly easy social conversation. When leaving, the therapist asked if she might return on the next Monday and Ruth concurred, "That would be fine." This easy entry into the home was not typical of each lay therapist's involvement. For two years Ruth was visited quite regularly, twice a week. The length of the therapist's visits varied from an hour and a half for coffee at the house to six hours on the occasions she accompanied her to bingo—Ruth's only recreation outside the home. The lay therapist usually called her several times a week, being one of the first "outsiders" to have access to the MacDonald's unlisted number. The therapist gave Ruth her phone number and it was clearly understood that Ruth was to call before, as Ruth put it, she "reached the end of her rope." In the second year of their relationship Ruth would call when she was very upset regarding the children or a marital problem. Whenever the therapist was away on holidays she kept in touch by letter and several long-distance phone calls.

When discussing the lay therapist's involvement with an abusive parent, people generally find it difficult to accept that much time and attention is being given to the abuser rather than to the abused. There is an emotional response of anger that overrides the intellectual understanding that the *long-term* result of a lay therapist's intervention might be protection for the children now in the family and perhaps for children not yet born.

Like most abusive parents, Ruth suffered severe physical and emotional abuse in her own childhood. For almost one year the therapist had understood that Ruth's father and stepmother had been "very strict"—that brief comment being the only reference she had ever made to her childhood. Ruth intended the comment as a favourable comparison with David's childhood experiences. However, in response to an innocuous question posed by the therapist concerning Ruth's playing as a child, she was thoughful, then replied flatly that she did not remember playing; she did not remember having a toy or celebrating a Christmas. She had always wanted a doll, a very particular doll, one that sits on the bed with a large skirt up over the pillow. Asked about what she did remember, she replied *"work."* She was constantly responsible for the care of her sister, eight years younger. She prepared all meals, did all the dishes, and the cleaning. If it were discovered that the cleaning was not done—and frequently this was detected at supper time—she was denied her supper but was forced to sit at the table. Ruth commented mildly that missing supper the first night was not too bad, but the next day having had no breakfast or lunch it was very hard to sit at supper again and watch the others eat.

Ruth's other sister, older by one year, did not have to do any work. She was "the good one," Ruth the "bad one," a situation which, as we have noted earlier, is recapitulated with Greg and Blair. Ruth remarked to the therapist that she guessed this was the case in every family. When finally allowed to have a boyfriend, she could go out once a week but had to take her younger sister with her—so that if she did anything wrong her parents would know "before I got in the door." For doing something wrong (and this is her term), like having a coke with friends after school or staying late at school to do a project, she was beaten with the buckle end of the belt.

Once, when a menstrual period was late, her stepmother took Ruth to the hospital emergency, convinced that she was pregnant (despite Ruth's protests that this was impossible). This experience exemplifies the pattern of teenager abuse noted by Gil (Gil, 1968) and perhaps reflected in the findings reported by Greenland (Greenland, 1973). The doctor confirmed that Ruth had had no sexual intercourse and suggested that the problem was likely one of emotional upset. Almost as an aside, Ruth told the lay therapist that she had received a lot of beatings prior to this incident. Her stepmother's response was one of fury at the doctor, at his diagnosis and at Ruth.

To escape this abuse and her father's sexual advances, Ruth began to run away from home, only to be returned by the police each time. Finally, Ruth was sent to a reform school when her parents declared her impossible to manage.

Ruth's history reflects the deprivations described by Steele and Pollock (1968). Smith's findings are at variance with their claim that baby batterers have been deprived both of basic mothering, and of the deep sense of being cared for all their lives. Significant proportions of his sample did, however, admit to having been physically maltreated in childhood, by parents whom they often experienced as being unreasonable and harsh. This, too, is consistent with Ruth's experience (Smith, 1972).

At five years of age Ruth picked up a cigarette from an ashtray and mimicked the adults' smoking. Her father, in order to teach her not to smoke, burned the tip of each finger. As if out of idle curiosity, Ruth wondered aloud to the therapist why the school had not done anything about her father's actions. She claimed that her kindergarten teacher, upon learning how and why her fingers had been burned, merely admonished that little girls should not smoke. Twenty-five years later, can we be sure that incidents like this would be quickly reported by the teacher in the interests of the children? In fact, according to Ruth, Blair's principal was very angry with the school nurse for reporting his abuse to the Children's Aid Society.

From Ruth and David's generation to Blair's, the "cycle of abuse" referred to in the literature is clearly illustrated here (Steel and Pollock, 1968; Goode, 1971). In both families, one child was perceived by the parents as being good, the other child as being bad. Physical abuse by the buckle end of the belt was administered indiscriminately to the so-called bad child. There are many other parallels, and the frustration was that Ruth recognized them with the help of the lay therapist without resolving to change. She identified with Blair and believed that his future would, like hers, be a reform school when people would not tolerate him any longer. Ruth's sense of being powerless, another of the characteristics common to abusive parents noted in the literature (Elmer, 1967; Baher, 1976) is clearly demonstrated here. This, and the characteristics noted above, all contribute to "a kind and degree of constant stress not known by nonabusive families" (Elmer, 1972).

The first responsibility of the lay therapist was to give this woman the "mothering" she had missed in her own childhood. It was important for her to listen supportively whether Ruth was discussing her own miserable childhood (this adjective was the therapist's, not hers) or the tremendous anger and dislike she felt for Blair. Ruth seemed weighted down with her unwieldy, even crippling, baggage of distorted perceptions— distorted perceptions of her own parents, of her childhood, her liaison with David, her children and their capabilities and indeed of the world outside her door. Several times Ruth described an incident that occurred just before the protective agency became involved. She was banging Blair's head against the wall and stopped, suddenly aware of what she was doing. "The next time," she reported, "I may keep bashing until his head is off—*and then he'll be sorry.*"

Some of the simple, direct gestures that the therapist made were to wash Ruth's hair, to bring her juice and flowers when she was ill, to accompany her to the doctor (an ordeal for her) and to buy the antibiotic she could not afford. After hearing of Ruth's lifelong wish for a doll, the therapist gave her one. It was a fancy velvet and lace-trimmed one that, carefully protected by saran wrap, had a place of honour in the living room. The goal was to give Ruth at thirty-two some of the childhood pleasures which she had missed, so that hopefully she would reach a stage where she could comfortably permit her children to enjoy childhood themselves.

The lay therapist's focus is on the parent and this is often very difficult to remember in a family where the children are so needy. When the lay therapist first began visiting Ruth, Heather would stand beside her chair ready to climb onto her lap. Greg, the prototypical "good boy," who has learned that the best way for him to survive is through compliance, was attentive to the point of being obsequious. Ruth, although not aware of the role reversal that was so evident in their relationship, did underline the special bond she felt with Greg in her observation. "We've been through a lot together." The therapist studiously avoided paying attention to the children so that eventually, although always happy to see her, Heather rarely tried to hold her hand and Greg no longer admired her coat or sweater. Fortunately, however, the lay therapist's presence did bring some small, immediate advantages to the children. On one outing, for example, Heather at five enjoyed her first streetcar and escalator rides, and her first walk through revolving doors. She joined her mother and the therapist occasionally for lunch or a snack at the restaurant, although this was a mixed blessing. Ruth frequently seemed to resent Heather's presence and this resulted in a very negative interaction between mother and child.

The importance of remembering for whom the lay therapist was there was clearly demonstrated one winter day. Getting the children ready for school, Ruth was haranguing Blair whom she felt was too slow in putting his boots on. He was near tears, struggling at his boots and protesting that they did not fit. Ruth's rage increased until the therapist, feeling acutely uncomfortable for the child, suggested that it was often difficult to get boots on over shoes with large heels. Ruth whirled on her with anger to say that it was *not* difficult, Blair was not trying, he never tried. Instantly, but too late, the therapist realized that she should have said, "It is frustrating trying to get three children dressed and off to school isn't it?" Probably that statement, acknowledging Ruth's feelings, would have defused the situation.

Perhaps the most difficult experience for the lay therapist was to find herself/himself in the home when the child was being maltreated in a variety of ways, and not to interfere. The Denver project had shown that if the therapist makes a move to protect the child in this situation, then the latter may only be safe for as long as the therapist remains in the home. In other words, the child might be placed in a heightened state of risk with the therapist's inevitable departure. Davoren cautions, "I have tried interfering in quiet ways . . . as well as authoritatively. It never worked . . . I think every worker will have to try for himself, because it is hard to believe that protecting a child when you cannot continue the protection beyond the moment may be the cruelest thing for him" (Davoren, 1972, p. 162). Such a limitation on the role of the paraprofessional emphasizes the urgency of constant vigilance on the part of the protective agency's worker who is responsible for the case, and the necessity for swift and constant communication between therapist and worker. It was a fundamental tenet of the project that efforts to rehabilitate battering parents should never be at the expense of the safety of the child (Smith, 1975). While the validity of such a tenet might seem obvious, if not simplistic, it is one that is often overlooked in the current trend toward keeping biological families together at all costs (Goldstein, Freud and Solnit, 1973).

To focus on the parent's needs was difficult for another reason. Ruth's expectations of the children, like those of most abusive parents, were unrealistic in the extreme. The lay therapist, having young children of her own, was especially aware of how Ruth set herself up to be disappointed. As noted by Baher (1976), although there is considerable variation in the parent-child relationships studied, "the mother's inconsistency and unreasonableness is striking." During a visit, Ruth would tell Heather to sit and watch television, expecting her to do exactly that, not to go upstairs, not to touch something on the coffee table and not to move from the couch. When Heather failed to remain motionless she was sent to her room and the therapist was told that Heather never did what she was told. Ruth's frustration and anger were very real, but it is difficult to accept these reactions when they result from such ludicrous demands. The cycle of defeat was inevitable under these conditions.

Lacking those life experiences necessary for the development of a sense of self-esteem, Ruth, when the lay therapist first met her, never used the pronoun "I" and indicated no sense of having control over her own life. Seven months later they spent many visits discussing the problems which resulted from her father's presence in the home. With the therapist's support, Ruth was eventually able to tell him that, now that he was working, he must find his own place. This was the first sign of her growing self-esteem. A few months later, she was able to distinguish what *she* wanted from what her husband wanted; she became willing to express *her* opinions—if only to the lay therapist. Then, during a marital row, Ruth told David he could get out and take Blair with him. For her, this was an incredible show of strength. A pattern of behaviour typical of all project cases was an abrupt pulling back or retrenchment on the part of the parent after showing increased trust in the therapist. After telling David he could leave and later discussing this fight with the therapist on the telephone, Ruth missed their next appointment, going on a job with David instead. At the next meeting between the lay therapist and Ruth, she had reverted to her old pattern of speaking: "David says . . ."

There is the danger that in concentrating on fostering a friendship one forgets the severity of the case. After Halloween, Ruth asked the therapist if she had heard on the radio about the child who had been poisoned. The therapist replied affirmatively, adding (probably sounding horrified) that the child's father had done it, hadn't he. Ruth said, "Yes, but you don't know what the child was like, he might have been a rotten kid."

Before the therapist became involved with this family, Blair had been removed for his protection and treatment. Once back in the home, he was only strapped several times a month, sent to bed after supper when kept late at school with a detention (usually two to three times a week) and made to stand in the corner an hour or more for misbehaving. He was still verbally abused and rejected by Ruth, even though an occasional, genial exchange was observed. However minimally the childrens' situation had improved, the MacDonalds had moved from physical abuse as defined by present law to a grey area of childrearing practices about which there is no consensus in society. What are the tolerable limits of discipline? Can agreement be reached regarding what is psychological abuse, and how to prevent it?

Ruth was then verging on readiness to accept some form of guidance—perhaps marital counselling, child care instruction or further treatment for Blair. It was not the lay therapist's role to undertake these specific professional tasks. Hopefully, her interventions would enable Ruth to reach out for, and benefit from, the kinds of assistance the community is able to provide.

CONCLUSIONS

Though little is yet known about prevention of child abuse, otpimism has been expressed (Schneider, Helfer and Pollock, 1972) that high-risk families can be identified as early as the antenatal stage. In truth, even after abuse *has* occurred in a family and the child has been allowed to remain in the home or to return home after a period of removal, case management on the part of protective agencies is not effectively geared to the prevention of further abuse. It has been our repeated observation that harrassed social workers have not been provided with the kinds of attention, supportive supervision, and agency insistence on the importance of preventive measures that will convince them to devote time to high-risk families where "nothing much seems to be happening." On the contrary, *the present system of supervision and case review tends to reward the crisis*. It is the worker who is dealing with an emergency who receives a flurry of attention in the form of supervisory support, the opportunity to present the case to his peers and also to a panoply of experts at the agency abuse committee session. While this kind of attention may be necessary to meet the crisis, we must argue that it is only when the gratifications of encouragement and supervision are given for the much less dramatic efforts of preventive work that an agency can move on to attempt operating successfully at this level. This argument was the rationale for the close supervision and structured peer group consultation that were essential elements of the Lay Therapist Project. Subsequent attempts to institutionalize the paraprofessional's role (the goal of the project) were in fact hampered by social worker resentment of such "pampering" which was so foreign to their own experience.[4]

The MacDonald case, with its high turnover of workers, numerous agency transfers, unco-ordinated provision of services and treatment attempts, underlies the importance of a multi-disciplinary team effort with leadership and a clear allocation of responsibility. While whatever social worker was associated with the case at a particular time had *de jure* responsibility for the children, the lay therapist was obliged to assume *de facto* responsibility in the absence of agency initiative. This watchdog function not only detracted from her work with the parent, but also jeopardized the progress that had been made. While it might seem obvious that the paraprofessional's role with the parent should always be supplementary rather than primary, in the management of child abuse cases (Baher, 1976) it is clear that his or her deep involvement is a temptation to an overburdened agency to relax its vigilance or even to abdicate. A team effort will also help to avoid the territoriality disputes and the unproductive scapegoating which are common when a number of institutions are involved (eg., school, hospital, agency, church).

It must be reiterated that the safety of the children must always be the paramount concern in dealing with families where abuse has occurred. The use of paraprofessional assistance to the abusive parent does not imply that the child should not be removed from the home. Kempe urges (Kempe, 1973): "Society has worked out a way to manage failure in marriage; it is called divorce. We should be prepared to accept failures in totally unregulated, random parenthood by permitting, without social stigma, either voluntary or involuntary termination of parental rights . . ." In fact, it might well be a major task of the lay therapist to support the parent in coping with the removal of the child. Rehabilitation of the parent is, then, no less necessary, since there may be other children left in the home, or a child born later.

We are in firm agreement with those who insist that the only possible way of significantly reducing child abuse in our society is to attack the problems at the macro-social level. This requires addressing environmental factors such as poverty, unemployment, discrimination, and the cultural sanctioning of the use of force in the service of many types of authority (Gil, 1972; Steinmetz and Straus, 1975; Gelles, 1973). We would add that the idealization of marriage and of motherhood also creates many dilemmas in modern society.

Without a commitment to resolution of these fundamental problems, the provision of social services is at best a band-aid approach. There are those who question the effectiveness of therapists' intervention with response to reported cases of child battering (Polansky, 1968). However, the amelioration of societal conditions is at best a long, irregular, arduous and controversial process. Some writers have emphasized the importance of developing child-rearing programs to teach people alternative means of raising their children (Gil, 1970; Gelles, 1973). We question, however, the prophylactic value of information giving and advice giving *per se*, and doubt their efficacy if administered in a vacuum to young people who have yet to face strains surrounding marriage and child-rearing.

Smith (Smith, 1975) has carefully documented the absence of consensus about the management of cases in which a child was injured by his custodians. The approach we have described here represents merely one modest attempt to engage only one dimension of the problem, ie., parental needs. Enlisting the participation of able lay persons in such an endeavour would seem to allow for a more efficient use of expensively trained professional personnel who are faced with escalating demands on their time. Obviously, the validity of such an approach can only be determined under research conditions which were far beyond the scope of the project.

NOTES

[1] The project was funded by the Laidlaw Foundation and the Dept. of Manpower & Immigration under the Local Initiatives Program.

[2] This was the beginning of a two-and-a-half year involvement.

[3] Howells has observed that the very services created to help battered children add to the risks these children face (1974).

[4] Resentment was also encountered by two further factors: 1. The lay therapist had the luxury of being able to devote a great deal of time to the parent because the case load was limited to a maximum of three families. This is, of course, not possible for social workers; 2. Since protective agencies have the responsibility for legal action, the worker often had to play the punitive role while the lay therapist was expected to continue to help the parent through the ordeal of court appearances.

REFERENCES

Baher, Edwina *et al.*
1976   *At Risk: An Account of the Work of the Battered Child Research Department,
NSPCC.* London: Routledge and Kegan Paul.

Bennie, E. H. and A. B. Sclare
1969   "The Battered Child Syndrome." *Paediatrics* 45, 1003-1007.

Davoren, Elizabeth
1972   "The Role of the Social Worker"—*Helping the Battered Child and his Family,*
C. H. Kempe and R. E. Helfer (eds.). Philadelphia: J. B. Lippincott.

Elmer, Elizabeth
1967   *Children in Jeopardy.* Pittsburgh: University of Pittsburgh Press.

Galdston, Richard
1969   "Dysfunctions of Parenting: The Battered Child, the Neglected Child, the
Exploited Child" in John D. Horvell's *Modern Perspectives in International
Child Psychiatry.* New York: Brunner/Mazel.

Gelles, Richard J.
1973   "Child Abuse as Psychopathology: A Sociological Critique and Reformulation." *American Journal of Orthopsychiatry*, 43 (July): 611-621.

Gil, D. G.
1970   *Violence Against Children.* Cambridge: Harvard University Press.

————
1968   "Incidence of Child Abuse and Demographic Characteristics of Persons
Involved" in *The Battered Child*, Ray E. Helfer and C. Henry Kempe (eds.).
Chicago: University of Chicago Press.

Goldstein, Joseph, Anna Freud and Albert J. Solnit
1973   *Beyond the Best Interests of the Child.* New York: The Free Press.

Goode, William J.
1971   "Force and Violence in the Family." *Journal of Marriage and the Family*, 33
(November): 624-636.

Greenland, C.
1973   *Child Abuse in Ontario.* Ontario Ministry of Community and Social
Services, Research and Planning Branch.

Howells, J. G.
1974   *Remember Maria.* London: Butterworth.

Kempe, C. Henry and Ray E. Helfer (eds.)
1972   *Helping the Battered Child and His Family: A Preliminary Report.* Philadelphia: J. B. Lippincott.

Kempe, C. H.
1973   Position Paper for Hearings of the Subcommittee on Children and Youth
of the Committee on Labor and Public Welfare. United States Senate
(March). Unpublished.

Kriendler, Simon
1975   "Some Considerations Regarding the Psychiatric Assessment and Treatment of the Abusing Parents." Presented to the Ontario Psychiatric Association (January). Unpublished.

Merton, Robert K.
1972   "Sociological Euphemisms." *American Journal of Sociology* 78 (July).

O'Brien, John E.
1971   "Violence in Divorce—Prone Families." *Journal of Marriage and the Family* 33 (November): 692-698.

Polansky, N.
1968   The Current Status on Child Abuse and Child Neglect in this Country. Report to the Joint Committee on Mental Health for Children.

Schneider, Carol, R. E. Helfer and C. Pollock
1972   "The Productive Questionnaire" in *Helping the Battered Child and His Family: A Preliminary Report*, C. H. Kempe and R. E. Helfer, (eds.). Philadelphia: J. B. Lippincott.

Seltiz, Claire, L. S. Wrightsman and Stuart W. Cook
1976   *Research Methods in Social Relations*. New York: Holt, Rinehart and Winston.

Skinner, A. E. and R. L. Castle
1969   *Seventy-Eight Battered Children: A Retrospective Study*. London: National Society for the Prevention of Cruelty to Children.

Smith, S. M.
1975   *The Battered Child Syndrome*. London: Butterworth.

Smith, S. M., R. Hanson and S. Noble
1974   "Social Aspects of the Battered Child Syndrome." *British Journal of Psychiatry* 125:569-582."

Steele, B. F. and C. B. Pollock
1968   "A Psychiatric Study of Parents Who Abuse Infants and Small Children", in *The Battered Child*, Ray E. Helfer and C. Henry Kempe (eds.). Chicago: University of Chicago Press.

Steinmetz, Suzanne K. and Murray A. Straus
1974   *Violence in the Family*. New York: Dodd, Mead and Company.

Warme, Barbara
1975   "Breaking the Cycle of Child Abuse: The Lay Therapist's Role", presented to the Ontario Psychiatric Association (January). Unpublished.

Wasserman, S.
1967   "The Abused Parent of the Abused Child." *Children* 14 (September-October): 175-179.

Willmott, P. and M. Young
1960   *Family and Chaos in a London Suburb*. London: Routledge and Kegan Paul.

Zalba, S. R.
1966   "The Abused Child, Part I: A Survey of the Problem." *Social Work* II (October): 8-16.

Chapter 7

VIOLENCE IN THE FAMILY

Dr. James Wilkes

Dr. Wilkes has been a child and adolescent psychiatrist in private practice in Toronto for many years. He has served as well as Director of the Division of Child and Adolescent Psychiatry at Scarborough Centenary Hospital. His brief chapter which follows reflects his vast experience with the realities of child abuse. We have discussed in Chapter 5 the extent of this phenomenon in Canada and the difficulties encountered by various social and legal agencies in contending and assisting with the cases. Chapter 6 outlines the difficulties encountered by the lay therapist and paraprofessional in providing support and rehabilitative services. Wilkes here makes clear that no professional or lay body can solve the problem alone. The solution lies in the creation of a society which provides a climate which is conducive to the nurturance and love of children. It lies as well in the combined efforts of family, social and legal agencies and of dedicated lay personnel.

In coming to terms with the reality of violence in family life, its causes, its effects and its prevention, it seems that one is caught up in a mass of interacting forces and influences.

There are influences from society at large, such as the prevailing political and economic climate, the prevading value systems, the degree of community solidarity. These and other factors impinge on the family from outside and influence the possibility for violence within its membership.

There are influences from within the family, such as the amount of affection and caring existing in the family members and the quality of communication between them. The clarity and ease of decision making, the rules and norms of family functioning, these and other factors influence the possibility for violent action between its members.

The mental health of each individual is another important influence: the capacity to deal with stress, to face ambiguities and uncertainties, the capacity to delay gratification for a greater good, to create one's life and meaning out of conflicting forces, and the capacity to accept the impossibility of absolute certainty, security and perfection in oneself, in

* Dr. Wilkes was the guest speaker at a public forum held in Toronto's St. Lawrence Centre in 1977 entitled *Violence in the Family*. The forum was sponsored by Mental Health—Toronto. This paper is a reconstruction of that speech.

one's life, or in the world at large. One's capacity in these and other individual mental struggles influence that individual's propensity for violence, and the likelihood of his stirring up violence in the other members of the family.

With these interrelating social, family and psychological forces as a background, one is enabled to see more clearly the nature of individual acts of violence.

When a man returns from work and enters his home it is unlikely that within two hours time he will have beaten his child severely enough that the child will sustain broken bones. If the man returns home jobless the chance is slightly greater. If the night before his wife and he had a quarrel and are not talking, the chances increase. The chance increases again if the child is crying, angry, belligerent or raging with frustration. The chances increase further if there are other children running about and quarreling, further still if there is no place he can go to get away from the noise, further still if his meal is burned or unavailable. The chance is increased still more if he himself as a child lived in circumstances where he was neglected, brutalized and shamed, and where violence was modelled for him in acts on him and on his siblings, in circumstances which meant that instead of growing up with a general sense of himself as good and capable and secure, he has a sense of himself as bad, weak and afraid.

In such circumstances he has likely learned that power is used arbitrarily and that to delay gratification of one's wishes means that they will seldom, if ever, be gratified. If a man is brought up in such circumstances, he is that much more likely to be violent.

The story and the stresses can be rewritten. Instead of the father we can talk of the mother or both parents together as instruments of violent behaviour. Instead of anger showing in physical abuse, we can talk of it showing in indifference and ignoring. We could add other areas of stress and violence to the picture, such as excessive and hurtful fighting between the siblings as they fight for the little parental affection available, or they discharge their anger for the lack of parental affection on the safer target of their brother or sister. These angry children move into the world outside stirring up anger and rejection in school, in the community, and return home angrier and more needy than ever. We could talk of excessive alcohol or drug consumption. We could talk of the lack of community support systems to deal with high-risk families already identified, or inadequate and ideologically remote mental health facilities. We could talk of many things and change the story many ways, but the meaning is the same. Every man and every woman may be violent, and the major influencing variables have much to do with forces beyond volition, beyond the free decision of the people involved.

There is no mistaking the point that we, like our parents, are capable of inflicting violence on our children.

The parent-child relationship is reciprocal in the sense that negative or positive feelings and responses in one stir up similar feelings and responses in the other. When an infant does not accept feeding well or when it resists cuddling, the mother's self-confidence in her mothering is undermined and she is thereby likely to show some rejection herself. The same is true of the rejecting response an older child engenders in his parents when he is defiant or a behaviour problem. The parental rejection in turn leads to further defiance and behaviour problems. The circular effect also works the other way: a child's accepting response allows a parent to be giving, and a parent's acceptance allows a child to be responsive. In the matter of acceptance one of the greatest difficulties parents have is to allow their children to be unhappy. When a child feels fear or loneliness or other negative feelings, parents often act as if these feelings have become the parents' responsibility. In such circumstances a parent may shame the child for his feelings or react in annoyance. "How can you be so unhappy, I've given you so much," "You're nothing but a sissy." The child learns to reject his negative feelings and may learn to avoid them through violent reaction. Another difficult task, made more difficult for parents who are feeling inadequate about themselves, is to allow a child to move to independence. If independence is not gained by gradual process, too often there are disruptions and confrontations and in adolescence the adolescent leaves home, not after loving consideration but after violent exchanges of orders, threats and perhaps blows.

Broken bones we can identify and care about, but we have more difficulty identifying and caring for broken hearts and broken spirits. Yet it is tragic that children are neglected and exposed to destructive influences so that they grow up academically impoverished, with narrow interests and emotional insensitiveness. Such an outcome is usually the result of a long process of repeated rejection. Each incident of rejection lacks the vividness and horror of actual physical trauma but, when combined, they accumulate to an outcome which does violence to our image of what a child should become. Perhaps the use of violence in this context is stretching its meaning beyond our purposes, but it could be argued that there is a large overlap in the factors leading to ongoing rejection and those leading to flagrant violence. At least it is clear that when one is dealing with forces which lead to the rejection of children, one is also dealing with the forces which lead to their physical abuse.

If we are to direct our attention to the prevention of violence it is important that we accept the violence within ourselves or else we are likely to pursue the current scapegoat pushed from within by our own disguised violence. Too often we react as if violence is imposed on us and on our society from outside, instead of accepting the reality that it arises from within us all. The point is to recognize the broad base of our violence, to agree that each element is worthy of attention, but to move exclusively in one area is the result of dangerous over-simplification. The forces of violence in the family are best met with measures which improve the social and mental well-being of the community at large.

PART THREE

VIOLENCE AND
THE ADMINISTRATION
OF JUSTICE

Addendum

LEGISLATION IMPENDING AT TIME OF PUBLICATION

On May 1, 1978 the federal Minister of Justice introduced a bill (C-52) in the House of Commons to amend the Criminal Code with respect to the offence of rape.

The Bill that was introduced would change the present law dealing with rape in the following particulars.

1. The crime of rape would be replaced by offences of indecent assault and aggravated indecent assault.
2. Both men and women would be protected under the new bill. At present, under the Criminal Code, only women can be raped.
3. Sexual penetration would be redefined to include sexual penetration "of any bodily orifice" (Section 149.2).
4. Married couples living separate and apart at the time of the alleged offence could bring an action for assault or aggravated indecent assault under the proposed Bill.
5. In the trial of an offence of indecent assault or aggravated indecent assault, an order direction that "the identity of the complainant and his/her evidence taken in the proceedings shall not be published in any newspaper or broadcast," can be granted if: a) the complainant so requests, or b) if in his or her discretion, and in the absence of a request by the complainant, the presiding judge or magistrate so directs.
6. It is mandatory for the presiding judge or magistrate to advise the complainant of his or her right to the above order "at the first reasonable opportunity;" and failure to do so will be grounds for an appeal.

There are three particular weaknesses with the proposed Bill. First, there is no specific definition of the words indecent assault, aggravated indecent assault, or what will constitute severe psychological or physical damage. Second, the whole question of consent is still undefined; and it would appear from the wording of the proposed bill that consent will still be a vital element of the offence. Three, previous sexual conduct with a person or persons other than the accused is still admissible, subject to the judicial discretion of the judge decided at an *in camera* hearing at the request of the accused. It appears to be the Minister's view that the traditional argument, that a woman who has consented to sexual intercourse on one occasion with one person is more likely to have consented to sexual intercourse with the accused on the occasion in question, is still valid.

Maureen McTeer

Chapter 8

RAPE AND
THE CANADIAN LEGAL PROCESS

Maureen McTeer

Step by step McTeer unfolds in legalistic fashion the options available to the victim of rape. As might be expected, most rapes are not reported, but when they are, it is generally to a police officer and it is at his discretion that a charge is laid. The length of time which elapses between the rape and the complaint of the victim may seriously affect the outcome. McTeer and Kasinsky (in Chapter 8 and 9 following) stress the importance of preserving battle scars to present proof of actual physical resistance. Yet police departments advise women that resistance could mean death.

Once again, the issue of laws which lag far behind needed social change comes to the fore. Many years ago, W. F. Ogburn referred to this period of delay as "culture lag." The term implies that legal and judicial change are generally the result of social change, following at a disconcerting pace. For example, the newly invented automobile required drastic improvements in road systems and the development of techniques of traffic control. Instead, unsuitable laws developed for horse-drawn carriages were passed.

In time, the reverse situation was noted, that is, laws may be used to bring about social change. Soviet Russia, for example, made use of the law to expedite and regulate social change. An important question remains unanswered: Even if pressure groups are successful in forcing legal change, what, if anything, will trigger a change of attitude toward women by the judiciary, which is the body responsible for the interpretation of the law? As McTeer concludes, a change in law without an accompanying change in attitude falls short of the mark.

At times, a change in the law will have little effect on the people it serves. In the Arab States laws were passed imposing a minimum age for marriage. The law was intended to bring about social change. However, marriage was closely linked with the religious beliefs of the people who began to contract marriage privately in order to circumvent the laws. The example illustrates the fact that laws appear to have a greater impact on activities which are instrumental than it does on activities which are emotionally charged. The same logic may be applied to the problem of rape. Like abortion, it touches the core of one's basic values. Public opinion, judicial and legal change become interacting forces and the victims of their indecisiveness proliferate.

---

* An original article written for this volume.

INTRODUCTION

The Canadian Criminal Code reads that "a male person commits rape when he has sexual intercourse with a female person who is not his wife, without her consent, or with her consent if the consent is extorted by threats or fear of bodily harm, is obtained by personating her husband or is obtained by false and fraudulent representations as to the nature and quality of the act."[1]

According to the case law, sexual intercourse, within the meaning of the Code, "is complete upon the penetration of the labia, either majora or labia minora, no matter how little, even though the hymen was never touched nor is there any penetration of the vagina."[2]

The trial for the offence of rape is fraught with complex evidentiary rules and exceptions, due mainly to the nature of the offence. Rape has been described for centuries as an offence easy of complaint but difficult of proof, a description which has shaped our laws to this day.[3]

A man's fear that he might, at some time, face a false rape charge made by a woman out to seek revenge on him has had a direct bearing on the treatment of the charge of rape, and its victim both at pre-trial and trial stage.

This article is not written to bemoan the injustices of the past centuries. Its purpose is to set out, as accurately as is possible, the rules of evidence applicable in a rape case. Further, it contains comments on the 1975 Criminal Code amendments, and sets out some of the more progressive legislation in Michigan State, passed in 1975.

Over the past five years there has been an increase in the number of reported rapes both in Canada and the United States.[4] The growth of Rape Crisis Centres in a number of Canadian urban centres has given women someone other than the police or family to help them. But even with what at face value appears to be an increase in the number of reported rapes, it is estimated that rape continues to be the least reported of all crimes.[5] According to one author, "In Canada in 1971, less than half (45.2%) of 1,230 reported rape cases was cleared of the charge, as opposed to almost three-quarters of reported murders which were so dispensed with."[6]

There are a number of reasons why the crime of rape goes unreported, or, if reported, why no charge is laid. Such rapes are said to be "unfounded" by the police. This term means simply that, for whatever reason, the police have decided not to lay a charge.

Most complaints subsequently "unfounded" by police involve at least one of the following factors: a) evidence that the victim was intoxicated, b) delay in reporting by the victim, c) lack of physical condition supporting the allegation, d) refusal to submit to a medical examination (an examination not required of the accused), e) the previous relationship of the victim and the offender, and f) the use of a weapon without accompanying battery.[7]

But the major reason is that, in the end, the police must inevitably make a value judgment on whether or not the woman herself and/or her case will stand up under the pressures of a rape trial. A member of the Ottawa Police Force once told me that the most credible victim and the one most likely to succeed in court that he could imagine would be the wife of a senior public servant who was happily married with three children and was wearing a two-piece suit at the time of the assault. He was serious in his comments—and he is right.

The courtroom is an intimidating and alien place for most Canadians. For the complainant in a rape case, it is one of the most humiliating experiences she will ever encounter.

Mr. Justice Haines wrote:

> Most judges, lawyers and those experienced in the trial of rape cases would tell a female member of their household if she were raped, that it would be much better not to complain about it because to the victim the trauma of a rape trial can be often more serious than the original assault.[8]

Realistically, there are four options available to a woman who has been raped.

The first is to do nothing at all and to try to forget the incident ever happened. Most women choose this option.

The second is to make a complaint to the police, who will decide whether or not to lay a charge. The problems with this method are set out in this paper.

The third is to begin a civil assault action for damages. Although a criminal conviction is not a condition precedent for bringing such an action, where such a conviction has been registered, the chances of a woman winning her case are quite good. This is because the criminal burden of proof beyond a reasonable doubt is higher than the civil burden of proof on the balance of probability. However, to choose a civil route as an initial step in lieu of a criminal trial is not advisable. For one thing the court will wonder why a woman, convinced of the strength of her case, would choose a method which will perhaps afford damages, but will not remove her alleged rapist from society. Further, any such action assumes that the alleged rapist has enough money to pay any judgment the court may award.

The fourth option is to bring an application before the Provincial Criminal Injuries Compensation Board. This method is often chosen where the victim does not know who the offender was, or whether the offender, although known, is insolvent. In Ontario, since the inception of the Board in April of 1968, 75 of a total of 4,789 applications dealt with victims of rape. Generally, the awards made by the Board are minimal with an average award of around $2,000.[9] And, once again, the rapist is not taken into custody.

This paper will deal in detail with only one of these four options, that being an action under Section 143 of the Criminal Code.

THE COMPLAINT

The initial step that brings a complainant into contact with the judicial process is the complaint. This is often her first encounter with the police. Generally, the police have to be very certain of their chances at trial before they will lay a charge in a rape case. In an attempt to determine whether there is sufficient evidence to warrant a charge, the police conduct a thorough investigation of the woman involved, questioning her on every intimate detail of the incident. The purpose of this method is two-fold. First, it determines whether the evidence is sufficient to lay a charge of rape or of some lesser offence; and second, it helps the police decide whether the woman would stand up under questioning by defence counsel in court. Taking all their observations into consideration, the police then decide whether or not to lay a charge.

The fact of having made a complaint or not, and its particulars, are usually crucial to the woman's case. To be admissible, a complaint must have been made at the first reasonable opportunity, without leading or intimidating questions, and must relate only to the alleged offence.[10]

The trial judge must decide whether the complaint was made at the first reasonable opportunity by taking into consideration all the surrounding circumstances. The onus is on the Crown to show that there was no reasonable opportunity to complain,[11] but the case law is conflicting as to what can be considered an acceptable delay in making the complaint. In *R. v. Hill*, the court recognized the preference of a woman to complain of her rape to a non-stranger such as her husband, friend or family member, even though she had almost a day during which she could have made a complaint to some other person.[12]

When there has been no complaint, or where the complaint is held to be inadmissible as not having been made at the first reasonable opportunity, the judge must instruct the jury that the absence of such a complaint gives rise to an exculpatory inference inconsistent with her evidence at trial that intercourse was without her consent. According to recent case law, the jury must be charged as to such exculpatory inference and the absence of such instruction is fatal to a conviction and will necessitate a new trial.[13]

The complainant's evidence as to what she did does not have to be confirmed in all details by the person to whom she made the complaint. Such evidence would be admissible even if that person was not called as the witness to confirm the facts and some particulars of the complainant's testimony. There is little doubt, though, to call the person to whom the complaint was made, or to have that person confirm the facts and particulars set out by the complainant would affect the weight the jury would give to the complainant's evidence.

It is the responsibility of the trial judge to direct the jury that the evidence of the complaint is not thereby evidence that the woman was raped;[14] and that the single fact of having made the complaint does not corroborate the woman's testimony, because it lacks independence.[15] To be considered independent in such a case, evidence would have to be able to stand on its own, rely in no way on the complainant's testimony.

Once the trial judge has admitted the complaint as complying with the three conditions above, he or she must instruct the jury that it can only use the complaint to determine whether the woman's conduct was consistent with first, her testimony under oath that she had not consented, and second, with the conduct that would be expected of a truthful woman under the circumstances.[16]

The myth persists that a raped woman will become hysterical and tell the first person she meets.[17] Workers at Rape Crisis Centres have observed, however, that many women respond to rape by going into a state of numb shock. The latter response could be quite damning to a complainant in the eyes of a jury.

The police must indicate the "state" of the victim when they first see her and that witnesses are called to testify as to her condition immediately after the rape. Courts expect hysteria, tears, etc. to be reported, and accused rapists have been released because such emotions are not reported as being manifested.[18]

As mentioned previously, to be admissible a woman's complaint must have been made without leading, or intimidating questions, and the trial judge must decide whether the questions leading to the complaint were suggestive or leading, making the complaint inadmissible.[19] However, lack of spontaneity in making a complaint will not necessarily be fatal, provided the question soliciting the complaint was not suggestive or leading.[20] Finally, a second or subsequent complaint that is separate and distinct from the initial one will be inadmissible on the grounds that it may have been planned, and therefore is not spontaneous or completely true.[21] Therefore, the use of the complaint, where admissible, is as evidence bearing on the complainant's credibility. It relates only to the consistency of her conduct. Because the complainant's evidence is not independent, it cannot be deemed to corroborate her story, and cannot be used to negate any consent.[22] However, as long as the jury has been instructed properly by the trial judge as to the onus and burden of truth, it may convict on the uncorroborated evidence of the complainant.[23]

Finally, where no complaint was made, or where a complaint, although made was held to be inadmissible for whatever reason, the trial judge may instruct the jury that the complainant's silence following the alleged rape can be taken to contradict her story that the intercourse had taken place without her consent.[24] The theory is that a woman, having been raped, will tell anyone as soon as possible.

Judging from comments made by workers at the Ottawa Rape Crisis Centre, there are a number of women who do not report a rape to anyone for some time following its occurrence. The reasons vary from not knowing what to do, to fearing the rapist's revenge, to losing a husband who would blame her for the rape. Regardless of the reason, under the present system, these women would have little, if any, recourse to the Courts.

CORROBORATION

In Canada, the victim in a rape case, who is also the main witness for the Crown, is governed by a rule which requires the trial judge to instruct the jury that, although they may do so if convinced of the accused's guilt beyond a reasonable doubt, it is not safe to find the accused guilty on the uncorroborated testimony of the victim. Accomplices in crime, children and the victims in other sex cases are the only other witnesses subject to this rule.

Black's Law Dictionary defines the verb corroborate as "to strengthen; add weight or credibility to a thing by additional or confirming facts or evidence." This rule of evidence did not exist at common law.[25]

Independent evidence that could be termed corroborative of the victim's testimony includes other witnesses to the incident, or witnesses who saw the victim immediately following the incident, physical signs of injury consistent with resistance such as bruises, lacerations, ripped clothing, or the presence of semen on the clothing or body of the victim.[26]

Three reasons are usually given for this exceptional evidentiary rule in rape cases: the frequency of false rape charges; the predisposition of a jury to favour the victim in a sexual case; and the difficulty for an accused to disprove the charge of rape. But at least one author disagrees with all three reasons. He writes:

> . . . Repeal (of the corroboration rule) will not leave the innocent defendant without protection against the false charges of a lying or deluded complainant. In large part, the goals and purposes of the corroboration requirements are served by two ordinary safeguards in our criminal law—the jury trial and the judge's power to set aside or direct a verdict based on insufficient evidence.[27]

This same author continues:

> The corroboration rule may be based plausibly on the laudable purpose of protecting the innocent against false accusations; but this is a purpose of criminal procedure to be filled in all cases. If the traditional safeguards are not functioning properly to fulfill that purpose,

the solution lies in reform of criminal procedure as a whole, not in a special rule for cases involving the crime of rape.[28]

Until 1975, the trial judge was required to give a mandatory charge to the jury that it was unsafe to convict the accused on the uncorroborated evidence of the victim, unless the jury was certain beyond a reasonable doubt that the accused was guilty as charged. The judge was then required to set out all the evidence in the case that could be considered by the jury as being corroborative of the woman's testimony.

The practical effect of the mandatory charge was two-fold. First, except in exceptional circumstances, the police would counsel a woman not to proceed in the absence of corroborative evidence; and second, the jury was left with the impression that no matter how convincing the woman's case appeared, they were to view the truth of her testimony with extreme caution before convicting the accused, where the only supporting evidence was the woman's testimony.[29]

The Criminal Law Amendment Act, 1975,[30] an omnibus Bill introduced to deal with a number of criminal matters, repealed section 142 of the Criminal Code which required a mandatory charge by the trial judge in cases where there was only evidence which had not been corroborated in a material particular by evidence implicating the accused.[31]

The recent Court of Appeal decision in *R. v. Camp*[32] has held that by repealing section 142, the Canadian Parliament returned the law in this regard to its pre-1955 position, where the judge's charge to the jury in *all* sexual offences was regarded as a rule of practice, and not a rule of law as it was under section 142.

Dubin, J.A., speaking for a unanimous Court of Appeal wrote:[33]

> I am of the opinion that it is no longer a *rule of law* that it is dangerous to convict on the uncorroborated evidence of the complainant with respect to those offences which had been enumerated in the former section 142, and an instruction to the jury in the language therein prescribed is no longer appropriate. On the other hand, the effect of the repeal does not limit the discretion of a trial judge, nor relieve him of the duty in appropriate cases, while commenting on the weight to be given to the evidence of a complainant, to caution the jury in simple language as to the risk of relying solely on the evidence of a single witness, and to explain to them the reasons for the necessity of such cautions. In so doing, the trial judge ought not to resort to the term "corroboration," but is free to point out to the jury any evidence which, in his opinion, supports the trustworthiness of the testimony of a complainant, even if such evidence does not meet with the test set forth in *R. v. Baskerville*.[34]

The decision to caution the jury and the choice of words to do so, remain in the trial judge's discretion. According to the judgement of the Court of Appeal, he or she also has a further duty, when they think it necessary, to caution the jury about the risks of relying on the evidence of a single witness.[35]

No criteria for determining "appropriate cases" are set out, and the only limits on the content of the caution is that it must be in simple language and must not contain the word corroboration or any of its derivatives.

The appeal in the *Camp* case centered around the trial judge's charge to the jury. In finding that the repeal of former section 142 did not prevent the trial judge's particular instructions to the jury, Dubin, J.A. wrote:

> Although the trial judge did caution the jury as to the danger of acting on the evidence of the complainant alone, he did not state the proposition as a rule of law, but only as a matter which the jury should consider in determining the weight to be given to the complainant's testimony. The term corroboration was not used.[36]

Thus it would appear that although no longer mandatory by law, the practice of cautioning required by the previous section 142 will continue as before, subject only to judicial discretion, but without any substantive guidelines for its exercise and without an explicit technical explanation of the law of corroboration. It is the author's view that the *Camp* decision effectively frustrates Parliament's attempt at reform on this most serious matter.

CONSENT

Consent or no consent, when in issue, is the most important element in the offence of rape. The onus is on the Crown to prove beyond a reasonable doubt that, where it is in issue, the complainant did not consent to intercourse with the accused; or if she did, that such consent was obtained either by threats or fear of bodily harm by the accused personating her husband, or by false or fraudulent representations as to the nature and quality of the act.[37]

Although the last two conditions provide the reader with some rather incredible fact situations, they are not of major concern here. As such, this comment will deal only with situations where there was no consent or where the consent was vitiated by threats or fear of bodily harm.

"Consent" is not defined in the Criminal Code, but is given the meaning of "voluntary agreement or compliance" by the *Concise Oxford Dictionary.*[38] An American case defined it as follows:

> It means voluntary agreement by a person in the possession and exercise of sufficient mentality to make an intelligent choice to do something proposed by another.[39]

The Canadian Criminal Code sets out a number of cases that provide statutory protection for certain classes of women. Among these are mentally incompetent women and women under the age of fourteen years.[40] When such women are raped, the accused will be denied the defence of consent.

Studies show that the majority of those rapes reported have taken place in the accused's car or his home.[41] The result is that it is usually the complainant's word against the accused's as to whether or not the rape took place, whether the accused was the rapist, and whether or not the complainant consented to intercourse with the accused.[42]

Assuming that the first two conditions are established to the satisfaction of judge and jury, the sole issue to be resolved would be that of consent. It is at this stage that the rules of evidence have traditionally worked against a complainant.

The general rule is that the character of an accused is not an issue in a rape trial unless he chooses to put it in issue by presenting evidence as to his good character, and therefore by becoming a witness in his own defence. Then and only then, can the Crown bring evidence to contradict his story either by questioning the accused or some other witnesses as to his character. However, the usual practice is for the accused to say nothing, and in such cases the Crown cannot bring forward any evidence as to the accused's character. This ban includes previous charges or convictions for the same crime.

Unlike the accused, the complainant in a rape trial is often the Crown's sole witness. An accused is allowed to ask any and all questions that are relevant to the just determination of his case. The trial judge, however, retains the final say on what is relevant in each case. Until 1975, any and all questions about the complainant's sexual relationships could be asked of her in an attempt to impeach her credibility. There were two main reasons for allowing this type of questioning. First, the theory was that a woman who had consented to previous sexual relationships with one or more men was the "type" of woman who would consent to intercourse with the accused on the occasion in question. And second, such questions were deemed relevant as tending to show the credibility or veracity of the victim as a witness; a woman of bad moral character would probably lie in the witness box.[43]

Section 143(b)(i) deals with the issue of a consent that was "extorted by threats, or fear of bodily harm." Fear is an important element of the crime of rape. This section merely says that fear for her life and well-being forced a complainant to consent to the act of intercourse with the accused.

But what will be held to constitute reasonable fear? In *R. v. Jones*, Macdonald, C.J. wrote:

> It is not enough for a woman to say "I was afraid of serious bodily harm and therefore consented"; she must prove in evidence that she had dire reason to be afraid, and that she took every reasonable precaution to avoid the outrage.[44]

Thus, where a complainant's testimony is uncorroborated, there should be signs of physical injury. Colour pictures taken soon after the assault showing injury are particularly important. It would not be sufficient, where there was no weapon to merely claim that she was afraid. Further, the test of fear is an objective one. Would a reasonable woman have had reason to be afraid in the particular circumstance? The answer to that question, though, is subjective, dependent upon the judge and/or jury.

It is to be noted in passing, that while courts expect physical injuries consistent with resistance, police departments across North America actively advise women that to resist could mean death. This requirement of active, physical resistance in a rape case is contrasted with an assault case, where a person need only show that force was threatened and that he or she believed their attacker had the ability to carry out his or her threat. No force need even be applied.

As improbable as it may seem, the material time of consent is at the stage of penetration.

> And the all important negation of consent or proof of an extorted consent is, *of course*, related to the time the act is committed, for if there was no violence, as here, there could have been a genuine consent *at the last moment*.[45] (Author's emphasis)

In 1975, the federal government introduced an amendment to the Criminal Code to eliminate what a number of national and regional women's organizations had termed legalized character assassination. It was felt that the legislation would put the complainant and the accused on a more equal evidentiary footing. The law as it now reads is that where an accused is charged under one of the enumerated sections, of which rape is one, then:

> . . . no question shall be asked by or on behalf of the accused as to the sexual conduct of the complainant with a person other than the accused unless
> (a) reasonable notice in writing has been given to the prosecutor by or on behalf of the accused of his intention to ask such questions together with particulars of the evidence sought to be adduced by such question and a copy of such notice has been filed with the Clerk of the Court; and
> (b) the judge, magistrate or justice, after holding a hearing *in camera* in the absence of the jury, if any, is satisfied that the weight of the evidence is such that to exclude it would prevent the making of a just determination of an issue of fact in the proceedings, including the credibility of the complainant."[46]

The 1975 Canadian Criminal Code amendments, while removing in part some of the most blatant inequalities with respect to the rape victim, still leave a number of important matters unresolved. While the amendment appears on its face to eliminate the right to question a complainant about past sexual experiences, judicial discretion still determines whether or not a woman's past sexual conduct with a third party is to be considered relevant to the issue of consent or credibility. No guidelines for determining the question of the relevance of such evidence are set out in the Code or other regulations to assist the trial judge; and the fact that the hearing to determine the admissibility of such evidence is *in camera* effectively frustrates any review of judicial decisions on this matter.

According to the recent Ontario court of appeal decision in *R. v. Camp*[47] there continues to be a duty on a trial judge to warn the jury[48] that in a rape case they should be cautioned, in simple language, against relying solely on the evidence of a single witness.[49]

The sentence of life imprisonment,[50] while, rarely if ever imposed, still appears on the books and continues to prove to be a deterrent to the conviction of accused rapists.

Men continue to go unprotected by the rape laws.[51]

And finally, very few police forces have men or women on their staffs who have been specially trained to deal with rape victims. For a number of reasons rape continues to be one of the least reported of all criminal offences. As such, a substantial number of Canadians are without any protection in this respect under the law.

The State of Michigan

The State of Michigan enacted Criminal Sexual Conduct Statutes in 1975.[52] The purpose of this legislation was to change the "Carnal Knowledge" law of rape and replace it with legislation dealing with "Criminal Sexual Conduct." Under the new law, the single offence of rape requiring sexual penetration, however slight, has been replaced by four degrees of sexual assault. The severity of each depends on the presence or absence of a deadly weapon, physical injury to the victim, and whether the victim suffered sexual penetration or merely sexual contact. The sentence for the convicted offender ranges from six months to life, depending on the degree of sexual assault.

The new law introduced a number of changes in an attempt to make the law dealing with rape more humane and fair to the victim. It includes the following:

1. Although the victim may raise the question of consent as an affirmative defence in certain situations, the onus is no longer on the victim to prove that he or she did *not* consent to the assault. In effect, after presenting testimony as to the identity of his or her attacker as being the accused, and asserting that the assault took place without his or her consent due to real or apprehended force, the onus is on the defendant to show real consent.

2. Any person, male or female, may be the victim of a rape.

3. The use of actual force, as well as the threat of force and other types

of coercion (i.e., kidnapping) may be sufficient to support a finding of sexual assault.

Previously in Michigan the law required that the rape had to be accomplished by force and that the victim had to . . .

> do everything she could under the circumstances to prevent the defendant from accomplishing his purpose. Otherwise it is not rape.
> . . . Resistance must have continued from the inception to the close.[53]

Now the victim need not put his or her life in danger by resisting in futile and dangerous situations. The victim need only show that he or she believed that the attacker had the ability to execute his or her threats of assault.

4. While Michigan courts never required corroboration of the victim's testimony, the new law statutorily recognizes that such corroborative evidence is not required; the jury may find the accused guilty if they are convinced beyond a reasonable doubt that the victim is telling the truth.

5. Any and all evidence of the victim's previous sexual activities with persons other than the accused is not admissible. The policy decision behind this section is three-fold. First, the highly prejudicial nature of such evidence far outweighs its probative value. Second, a person's chastity is irrelevant to the question of whether or not that person had been sexually assaulted or is worthy of belief in this or any circumstance. Third, the traditional safeguards against false charges such as police investigation and questioning of the victim, the right of the defence counsel to cross-examine the victim concerning consistency of her actions and statements during and after the assault, the traditional burden of proof on all plaintiffs to prove their charge in a criminal case beyond a reasonable doubt and, finally, the ability and duty of the jury (where the defence chooses such a trial) to evaluate and decide upon the issue of the victim's credibility are sufficient to ensure the accused is given a fair trial.

To this date, in Michigan no defendant has successfully argued that a denial of cross-examination of a woman's past sexual history with a third party has affected his constitutional right to a fair trial on the basis of a denial of his right to cross-examination.

CONCLUSION

The rape laws in Canada are outdated and no longer serve their original purpose of protecting women from what is "the ultimate violation of self short of homicide."[54] The fact that rape continues to be the least reported of all crimes with the lowest conviction rate for all criminal offences indicates how in need of reform are the laws related to rape.

But the law alone is not responsible for this state of affairs. A judicial system that has allowed defence counsel to destroy a woman's credibility and personal dignity in court by painting her as a whore who would likely consent to intercourse with anyone has also played a major role in making a farce of our rape laws.

The *Camp* case is but one indication that piecemeal attempts at reform will never result in a fair rape law. Only comprehensive legislation recognizing, as a fundamental principle, a woman's right to freedom of movement and participation in society, coupled with a change of attitude towards women by the judicial and legal professions, will afford women any real protection from physical violation of their bodies.

NOTES

[1] Criminal Code, R.S.C., 1970, c. C-34, s. 143.

[2] *R. v. Johns* (1956), 25 C.R. 153, 20 W.W.R. 92, 116 C.C.C. 200 (B.C.) per Clearihue, Co. Ct. J.

[3] ". . . an accusation easily to be made and hard to be proved, and harder to be defended by the party accused, tho never so innocent." 1 M. Hale, Pleas of the Crown 636 (1680).

[4] No studies are available to show that this is due to changes in the rape laws in some American States and in Canada, but I would assume this is one of the prime factors.

[5] Neil Brooks, in his article "Rape and the Laws of Evidence," (1975) 23 *Chitty's L.J.* pp. 1-11, wrote: "Although in many jurisdictions the number of rapes reported has increased more rapidly in the last few years than for any other crime against the person, rape is still the most under-reported of all crimes against the person; estimates of the number of rapes reported compared to the number actually committed run as low as 5%, and never higher than about 30%. The number of rapes that are reported compared to the number in which suspects are arrested and brought to trial is lower than the rate for any other crime against the person; in the U.S. in 1972 only 57% of the reported forcible rapes were cleared by arrest, and in Canada in 1973 only 50% were cleared by a charge. If by chance a rape case gets to trial the chances of the accused being convicted are lower than for any other crime; in the U.S., in 1972, only 30% of the persons prosecuted for forcible rape were convicted of that offence, and in Canada in 1971 only 51% of the prosecutions resulted in conviction."

Nationally, the rate for crimes of violence, which include all sexual offences, increased by 6% in 1975 over 1974, the most recent year for which these statistics are available. According to Statistics Canada's service bulletin on law enforcement, judicial and correctional statistics (July, 1976), the percentage change in the number of rapes in Canada between 1974 and 1976 was 2.2%. In 1975, the statistics show 1,852 rapes compared to 5,106 indecent assaults and 20,703 assaults causing bodily harm. The actual number of rapes in 1976 is reported as 1,834.

[6] Marcia Rioux, "When myths parade as reality: A study of rape," (discussion paper prepared for the Advisory Council on the Status of Women) April, 1975, p. 13.

[7] Camille E. LeGrand, "Rape and the Rape Laws: Sexism in Society and Law," California Law Review, 61:919 at pp. 928-929.

[8] Mr. Justice Haines (1975) 23 *Chitty's L.J.* p. 57.

[9] Information obtained from an employee at the Board in Toronto, Ontario, September 30, 1977. Marcia Rioux's article, *supra*, also contains some figures for similar Boards in other provinces, at page 74.

10 *R. v. Kistenday* (1975), 29 C.C.C. (2d) 382 (Ont. C.A.) has held that not only will a failure to complain at the first reasonable opportunity affect the credibility of the complainant, but that an explanation of the lateness is irrelevant and inadmissible. But see *R. v. Mace* (1975), 25 C.C.C. (2d) 121 (Ont. C.A.).
Further on these three requirements are the following cases:
R. v. MacNeil (1976), 16 N.S.R. (2d) 366 (C.A.)
R. v. Davidson (1975), 24 C.C.C. (2d) 161 (Ont. C.A.)
R. v. Hill (1928), 49 C.C.C. 161, 61 O.L.R. 645, which held: "The material point, however, is not whether her complaint was made on the first opportunity, but whether it was made on the first reasonable opportunity. . . . It was the province of the trial judge to decide whether the statement was made under circumstances which rendered it properly admissible." at page 162-63.
R. v. Ashley (1944), 82 C.C.C. 259.
R. v. Osborne, /1905/ 1 K.B. 551 where it was held that "In each case the decision on the character of the question put, as well as other circumstances, such as the relationship of the questioner to the complainant, must be left to the discretion of the presiding judge. If the circumstances indicate that but for the questioning there would have been probably no voluntary complaint, the answer is inadmissible. If the question merely anticipates a statement which the complainant was about to make, it is not rendered inadmissible by the fact that the questioner happens to speak first." p. 556.
R. v. Hunt (1964), 1 C.C.C. 219 (Ont. H.C.)
R. v. Gordon (1924), 25 O.W.N. 572.
R. v. Hall (1927), 31 O.W.N. 451, 49 C.C.C. 146 (CA)
R. v. Dunning (1908), 7 W.L.R. 857, 14 C.C.C. 461 (Sask. C.C.)
R. v. Jones (1945), 84 C.C.C. 299 (P.E.I.S.C.)
11 *R. v. Jones (supra)* per Campbell, J. at p. 301: "The onus is on the Crown to show that there was not a reasonable opportunity to complain." If it does or not, "subsequent complaints will therefore not be admitted."
12 *Supra*, footnote 10.
13 *R. v. Davidson (supra* footnote 10); *R. v. Boyce* (1975), 23 C.C.C. (2d) 16, 7 O.R. (2d) 561, 28 C.R.N.S. 336; *Thomas v. The Queen* (1952) 2 S.C.R. 344, 4 D.L.R. 306 (S.C.C.); *The Queen v. Lillyman,* /1896/ 2 Q.B. 167; *R. v. Adam* (1972) 8 C.C.C. (2d) 201 (Ont. C.A.).
14 *R. v. Osborne, supra* footnote 10, where it was held that:
"It (the complaint) applies only where there is a complaint not elicited by questions of a leading and inducing or intimidating character, and only when it is made at the first reasonable opportunity after the offence which reasonably offers itself. Within such bounds we think the evidence should be put before the jury, the judge being careful to inform the jury that the statement is not evidence of the facts complained of, and must not be regarded by them, if believed, as other than corroborative of the complainant's credibility, and, when consent is in issue, of the absence of consent." page 561.
15 *Thomas v. The Queen, supra* at footnote 13, per Cartwright, J. at p. 356: "It is no longer open to doubt that before evidence can be properly described as corroborative in cases where corroboration is required either by statute or under the rule of practice at common law it must be shewn to possess the essential quality of independence. It must be made plain to the jury that the witness whose testimony requires corroboration can not corroborate herself."
Also, see *R. v. Evans* 64 O.L.R. 181; *R. v. Coulthread* (1933), 24 C.A.R. 44; and *Rex v. Whitehead,* /1929/ 1 K.B. 99 (at p. 102) where the judge said: "In order that evidence may amount to corroboration, it must be extraneous of the witness who is to be corroborated."
16 See footnote 14, *supra.*
17 ". . . in early times it was incumbent on the woman who brought an appeal of rape to prove that while the offence was recent she raised "hue and cry" in the neighbouring towns, and shewed her injuries and clothing to men, and that the appellee might raise as a defence the denial that she had raised the hue and cry. . . . The hue and cry was the phrase used generally for the pursuit of a felon; but we have not found any other case than rape in which it was for the prosecution to shew that they had raised it, or in which it was a defence to shew that it had not been raised." *R. v. Osborne, supra* p. 561.
18 *Op. cit.,* Marcia Rioux, p. 19.

[19] See footnote 10, *supra.*

[20] *Ibid.*

[21] *R. v. Lebrun* (1951), 100 C.C.C. 16, 12 C.R. 31.

[22] See footnote 15, *supra;* also, *R. v. Plantus,* 1957 O.W.N. 338, 118 C.C.C. 260 (Ont. C.A.)

[23] *R. v. Kribs,* /1960/ S.C.R. 400, 127 C.C.C. 133, C.R. 57 (S.C.C.)

[24] See footnote 13, *supra.*

[25] It is the legislatures and the courts that have chosen to make this special evidentiary rule.

[26] However, the jury must decide whether any of these can be said to corroborate the victim's testimony in any given fact situation.

[27] "The rape corroboration requirement: repeal, not reform." (1972) 81 *Yale L.J.,* p. 1365.

[28] *Ibid.*

[29] The previous Criminal Code s. 142 (now repealed) read: "Notwithstanding anything in this Act or any other Act of the Parliament of Canada, where an accused is charged with an offence under section 144, 145, subsection 146(1) or (2) or subsection 149(1), the judge shall, if the only evidence that implicates the accused is the evidence, given under oath, of the female person in respect of whom the offence is alleged to have been committed and that evidence is not corroborated in a material particular by evidence that implicates the accused, instruct the jury that it is not safe to find the accused guilty in the absence of such corroboration, but that they are entitled to find the accused guilty if they are satisfied beyond a reasonable doubt that her evidence is true."

[30] 1974-75-76 S.C. c. 93. Bill C-71 was passed by the House of Commons on January 27, 1976. Section 8 deals with the offence of rape.

[31] Section 144 deals with the punishment for rape; s. 145 with attempted rape; s. 146(1) with sexual intercourse with a girl under 14 years, and section 146(2) with sexual intercourse with a girl over fourteen and under sixteen; and section 149(1) deals with indecent assault on a female.

[32] Decided in the Ontario Court of Appeal in April, 1977.

[33] Page 18 of the Court of Appeal judgement.

[34] *R. v. Baskerville,* /1916/ 2 K.B. 658.

[35] Page 18 of the Court of Appeal judgement in *R. v. Camp.*

[36] *Ibid.* p. 21.

[37] *R. v. Bursey* (1957), 118 C.C.C. 219 (Ont. C.A.).

[38] *The Concise Oxford Dictionary of Current English,* 5th ed. Oxford University Press, 1964.

[39] 44 Cal App. 345, 186 P. 388, 389.

[40] It is interesting to examine the sexual offences set out in the Criminal Code to see the penalty attached to each. Note that there are still sections that contain the words "of previously chaste character."

s. 145 —attempt to commit rape; ten years maximum sentence.

s. 146(1)—sexual intercourse with a female under 14 years; life imprisonment maximum. Before its repeal, could also be sentenced to be whipped.

s. 146(2)—sexual intercourse with a female over 14 and under 16. If the victim is of previously chaste character, then there is a five year maximum. If not of previously chaste character, the victim must bring an ordinary action for rape. Because of that wording, such a victim would begin with everyone knowing she had had previous sexual experience. In addition, s. 146(3) reads: "where an accused is charged with an offence under subsection (2), the court may find the accused not guilty if it is of the opinion that the evidence does not show that, as between the accused and the female person, the accused is more to blame than the female person."

s. 148 —sexual intercourse with feeble-minded, insane, idiot or imbecile of female gender: maximum of five years.

s. 149 —indecent assault on a female: maximum of five years. Until recently, this section also provided that a convicted person could be whipped.

s. 150 —incest: maximum of fourteen years.

s. 151 —seduction of a female "of previously chaste character" aged 16 to 18 years by a male aged 18 years or over: maximum of two years.

s. 152 —seduction under promise of marriage: maximum of two years.

s. 153(1)—sexual intercourse with a step-daughter, foster daughter or female ward: maximum of two years.

s. 153(2)—sexual intercourse with a female employee "of previously chaste character" and under the age of 21: maximum of two years, with the same qualification regarding blame as in s. 146(3).

s. 154 —seduction of female passengers on vessels by the owner or master of the vessel: maximum of two years.

s. 155 —buggery or bestiality: maximum of fourteen years.

s. 156 —assault with intent to commit buggery, or indecent assault on a male: maximum of ten years. Until recently, this section also provided that a convicted person could be whipped.

s. 157 —acts of gross indecency with another person: maximum of five years.

[41] *Supra,* footnote 27. That author points out that although these statistics are high for Canada, the situations of rape continue to make it a private crime with few, if any witnesses.

[42] The following quote was taken from a practice note following the headnote in the case of *R. v. Bursey, supra,* footnote 37:
"Consent or non-consent must of course be determined by the jury on the facts in evidence and it will be found in practice that the facts of 'non-consent' are generally those stated by the complainant herself and that her evidence stands alone and uncorroborated. In the result, the jury may have to decide between the acceptance of the story of the prosecutrix and the story of the accused as to consent."

[43] See *Rex v. Cargill,* /1913/ 2 K.B. 271; *Regina v. Taliberte,* /1877/ 1 S.C.R. 1175; *Rex v. Bell* (1938), 53 C.C.C. 80 (Alta. S.C. App. Div.); and see generally, Leggett, *The Character of the Complainant in Sexual Charges,* 21 *Chitty's L.J.* 132 (1973).

[44] *Supra,* footnote 11.

[45] *R. v. Bursey,* per LeBel at p. 175.

[46] *Supra,* footnote 30. The premise of the Amendment, as written, appears to be that a woman's past sexual conduct is *prima facie* irrelevant to whether or not she consented in the situation in question. It remains to be seen whether our criminal court judges will respect the spirit of the amendment when it is raised for their consideration. As before, the complainant can still be questioned as to any previous sexual relationship with the accused, and if she denies any, evidence can be brought to contradict her.

[47] *Supra,* footnote 32.

[48] This is over and above the usual warning given concerning uncorroborated evidence in any indictable offence.

[49] The Attorney General's office in Toronto, Ontario has suggested that even in light of the

Chapter 9

THE RISE AND INSTITUTIONALIZATION OF THE ANTI-RAPE MOVEMENT IN CANADA

Renée Goldsmith Kasinsky

Language is a product which emerges over time by consensus in society. Words emerge and become modified with usage and what the term violence embraces changes. An act or a failure to act may be interpreted as violence, depending on who is doing the defining. Historically, rape has not been considered a violent act. Kasinsky defines the cultural definitions of sexuality through time. The private property of a man consisted of, among other things, a woman. In North America, the violation of one person by another is commonly understood as a means of "getting ahead." Man is expected to fulfill the virility mystique, which exalts power, dominance, assertiveness and strength. In this context, rape can be understood as an act of over-conformity by a man trying to fill society's expectations of him. Women across the world have responded differently to the challenge inherent in the double standard. Canadian women view the emergence of rape crisis centres as the only viable immediate alternative to a legal process which will take years to change. A rape crisis centre insures the anonymity of the woman, advises her of her legal rights, and attends to her medical, physical and emotional needs. Kasinsky views rape as a social problem and not as an individual one.

PART I.   RISE OF THE RAPE PROBLEM

INTRODUCTION

This article will explore the rise of the anti-rape movement in Canada as a by-product of the feminist movement. It will discuss the rise of rape as a social problem within the historical context in which it arose and was defined. Rape in relation to the Canadian law and criminal justice system will be analyzed. The anti-rape movement in Canada and the ideology and structure it has taken . . . in rape crisis centres . . . will be examined in an overall theoretical framework that emphasizes social movements and interest group formation.

One cannot understand the rape problem in the late 1960s and early 1970s without also considering the various feminist interest groups

---

* An original article written for this volume.

which formed part of the women's movement. The interest in the anti-rape movement in Canada is understandable in view of the overall context of women becoming more involved in groups in an attempt to control the direction of their lives. Women began to investigate the solution to their own problems, problems with which men showed little concern. Womens' health collectives dealing in issues of birth control, sex education and abortion, sprung up in Canadian cities. In all of these concerns women insisted on the right to have control over their own bodies. In the early seventies, rape crisis centres became part of the women's health movement. This movement focuses upon what women can do *for themselves* rather than relying solely upon professionals for their physical and mental health.

Inez Garcia, a Spanish-American woman of thirty, was raped by two men who threatened to kill her. In self-defence, she responded by shooting one of her assailants. She was arrested and charged with homicide, and a California jury sentenced her to five years to life imprisonment, while her rapist has not even been charged! Inez Garcia has become a symbol for North American women of the double standard of justice inherent in our rape laws and practices. Anti-rape women's groups defended her and said that Inez Garcia had acted as she did because "she had no alternative for redress in this sexist society." These women spoke of the failure of police and the courts to prosecute rapists of women. They gave evidence of the humiliation and degradation women face at the hands of police, prosecutors and courts during a rape investigation. On October 4, 1976, two years after the initial trial, Inez Garcia underwent her second trial for her self-defence against rape. After two years of lobbying by the anti-rape movement in the United States, she was acquitted of murder.

The above case articulates some of the key internal dynamics of the interaction among the rapist, his victim and the response of society. It violates the normative situation only inasmuch as the victim, rather than acting in a so-called typically feminine manner, defended herself.

In general, it is men who force sexual relations, and it is women who are blamed for their occurrence. If a woman agrees to have a drink with a stranger or to hitchhike in a stranger's car (the two standard examples of provocative or consensual behaviour), she will find that men interpret this as giving sexual carte blanche. She will have difficulty proving afterwards that she did not consent to intercourse. The concept of provocation hinges primarily on male definitions of expressed or implied consent to sexual relations. It is shaped by traditional, restrictive stereotypes of women.

LEGAL PERSPECTIVE

Our present rape law reflects such a stereotype. The Criminal Code of Canada, Section 143, states:

A male person commits rape (forcible rape) when he has sexual intercourse with a female person who is not his wife, without her consent, or, with her consent if the consent is extorted by threats or fear of bodily harm (Criminal Code, R.S.C., 1970:C-34).

Also included as rape is the act of a man impersonating a woman's husband or the fraudulent representation of the act of sexual intercourse. Let us examine the elements involved in this definition of forcible rape.

There are at least three important facts regarding the position of women under this definition. Firstly, the principal offender must be a male and the victim a female. There is no intrinsic reason why the victim-offender roles are thus ordered, since rape is also a reality to men, especially homosexual rape which reaches epidemic proportions within prison walls. For example, in the United States it was estimated by one investigation that about 1,880 forcible rapes had occurred within a Philadelphia prison during a 20-month period (David, 1968:8-16). Certainly men subjected to this kind of sexual assault should be guaranteed equal protection by the law.

Secondly, under this definition, a wife cannot be raped by her husband. This rule has survived from Common Law to today. The sixteenth-century Common Law rationale for this, according to one of the earliest commentators, Sir Mathew Hale, was that: "By their mutual matrimonial consent and contract the wife hath given up herself in this kind unto her husband, which she cannot retract" (Hale, 1800:15). Modern North American criminal codes have retained this rule, similarly arguing that sexual relations among married persons involve consent on the part of the women.

This rule is related to the third premise, under the definition that if a woman consents to sexual intercourse under threats which do not involve those related to bodily harm, it is not considered rape.[1] A rule of evidence that applies to victims in rape cases (and few other cases) requires the judge to instruct the jury that "it is not safe to find the accused guilty in the absence of corroboration, but that they are entitled to find the accused guilty if they are satisfied beyond a reasonable doubt that her evidence is true." The issue of corroboration was introduced into the Criminal Code in 1955; it meant that it is dangerous for the jury to convict in the absence of corroboration. This provision was removed from the Code in April 1976, but the issue is still before the British Columbia Court of Appeal. In a separate but similar case in July 1977, the Ontario Court of Appeal upheld the removal of corroboration. In 1978 the issue will be heard in The Supreme Court of Canada (*Vancouver Sun*, July, 1977).

This type of cautionary statement is not expressed in other types of criminal cases. Why is it necessary? Why does our society have a special concern expressed through rape laws for sexual assaults on females to begin with? To answer, it is important to make clear who is protected by the crime of rape. Rape laws and practices protect male interests. The law itself is the creation of male lawyers and judges, and the administration of this law for the most part is also in the hands of men.

The law supports the middle-class notion that defines the "good woman" as one who is "chaste" and "pious" and who, in good conscience, voluntarily subjects herself to her husband's will. It also makes clear that the sexuality of a married woman becomes the legal property of her husband. The woman who is "possessed" at the time of the rape by a husband or a lover is often referred to thereafter as despoiled, her value as a desirable sexual object being diminished according to the man. This perception of the woman as the possession of man has been borne out empirically in a study by Linda Holmstrom on the reactions of husbands to the rape of their wives. The two most common reactions were that they themselves had been hurt and that they should seek revenge on the assailants (Holmstrom, 1974). Legal writers analyzing rape laws have concluded that they protect male interests!

> Rape laws bolster and in turn are bolstered by a masculine pride in the exclusive possession of a sexual object. They focus on a male's aggression, based on fear of losing his sexual partner, against rapists rather than against innocent competitors. Rape laws protect the male from any decrease in the "value" of his sexual possession, which results from forcible violation (LeGrand, 1973).

The underlying assumption that women often make false rape charges and that this might result in the conviction of innocent men has not been substantiated by recent research. Let us turn to the statistics and the treatment of rape victims by the agencies of social control: the police and the legal structure.

In comparison with other crimes against the person, rape is the most unreported crime—only 5 percent to 30 percent are reported (LeGrand, 1973). Furthermore, the figures diminish from the initial reporting of the rape through the laying of a charge and conviction rate. In Canada in 1973 there were 1,522 reported rape incidences (*Statistics Canada*, 1973), and only 50 percent resulted in a charge by police. Using 1971 statistics, although 119 persons across Canada were charged with rape, only 65 of them, or 54 percent of the total number, resulted in convictions. This compares unfavourably with the rate of 86 percent convictions for other indictable criminal offences (*Statistics Canada*, 1971). The most striking fact is how little we actually know about rape, since those rapes which do come to the attention of the police are one-tenth or less of the total number of rapes committed. Thus, of the total of 233 reported rapes in Metropolitan Toronto in 1973, there are 2,330 or more actual rape cases, the bulk of which are not reported and of which we know nothing (Kostash, 1975:62-71). I would suggest that the fact that rape is one of the most unreported of all crimes is directly related to the treatment the rape victim receives by the police and judicial agencies.

Most studies of rape based upon official police statistics suggest that these are skewed samples, since the majority of victims are from the lower-income group. Data supplied by the new rape crisis centres suggest that victims come from all social classes.

Only the minority of women have enough courage and stamina to undergo the drilling of a police interrogation, a preliminary hearing and a trial, especially if the victim may lose her friends and family support in the process. The rape victim is often processed brutally by the agencies of social control which are frequently insensitive to her subjective plight and sometimes openly hostile to her. To explain this legal process in terms of a reliving of the initial rape trauma is an understatement; it is a caricature and objectification of the game of male domination and humiliation of the woman.

The social construction of her experience as a "rape case" by the police is an example of what Dorothy Smith describes as a structuring procedure which becomes the "official version" of the rape incident (Smith, 1973). It is very revealing in terms of providing us with information about how such male-dominated social organizations as the police, hospital pathologists, and the court view rape. But it tells us nothing about how the women subjectively experienced rape and how they viewed it. Officials' views and those of the law itself are largely based on the traditional attitudes that have already been discussed regarding sexual mores and the subordination of women to men.

In the police station, hospital and courtroom the woman is treated as a sexual object rather than a sentient human being, much as in the initial rape incident. The court transcripts read more like a pornographic book written and read to debase the woman even more. In addition, defence lawyers thrive on giving evidence of a woman's past sexual history, though that of the defendant is inadmissible—an example of the double sexual standard. Studies of the courtroom process have demonstrated that, in fact, the rape victim is treated both socially and psychologically as if *she* had committed the crime and is on trial: the old game of "blaming the victim."

Thus, the rape laws and practices of the criminal justice system in dealing with rape victims enable men to exercise power over women and place them in a vulnerable position. These practices assault and challenge her sense of personal autonomy and integrity and strip her bare.

In addition to controlling and psychologically assaulting the rape victim, the law and legal practices also exert social control over the entire female population through the wide fear of rape. The law and court process help legitimize the assailants' actions through the lack of prosecution. Women soon learn that they cannot rely upon the authority of the State, controlled by male interests, to protect themselves from rape.

HISTORICAL PERSPECTIVE

It is important to view rape and rape justice within a historical context rather than as an isolated phenomenon, since it is defined differently in various societies and at different historical periods. Rape flourishes in an atmosphere of sexism and exploitation for individual or collective gain. Rape, as part of the booty of conquest, has been tolerated as part of a soldier's plunder from antiquity to recent times in many societies. In medieval times, rape was considered as much a blow to the economy of the victim's family as it was an offence against the person. Punishment was often in the form of military reprisals, ransom or monetary compensation, and marriage of the victim. In England before 1066, the victim of a rape or her kin would seek redress. According to Anglo-Saxon law, trial was by ordeal and the sanctions were largely some kinds of civil restitution. After the Norman conquest, the mode of trial was wager of battle and no redress of the injured person was given. The death penalty was imposed, and the offender forfeited his goods to the Crown. The victim gained nothing and her relatives had to expose themselves to a combat with the accused. Henry II introduced prosecution by indictment, which is the procedure the law takes today (Partridge, 1960). Seventeenth-century Anglo-Saxon laws about women were influenced by the general changes in the forms of class justice. For example, Common Law implicitly assumed that a woman's "honour" and "chastity" should be more highly valued than her life; therefore, it was the duty of a chaste woman to resist the shame of rape to the death if necessary (George, 1973).

The cultural attitude of the Arapesh of New Guinea towards sexuality stands in sharp contrast to North American cultural attitudes. The Arapesh are a small-scale cooperatively organized society and the concept of private ownership is unknown to them. The survival of the group where resources are scarce is dependent upon communalized economic and social arrangements. For the Arapesh sexual intercourse is a natural culmination of the relationship between a husband and his wife who have been living together in the family. Sex is part of a total relationship and no emphasis is placed on the act of sex *per se*. The Arapesh view aggression and extreme sexuality as antithetical to nurturance and growth (Russell, 1974). Thus, rape is practically unknown and would indeed be viewed as a deviant act.

IDEOLOGY OF THE SOCIAL SCIENTISTS

Before the consolidation of feminist views on rape, ignorance has often remained the benchmark of both scientific and common sense theories. There has been little empirical research on the experiences of the rape victims and the social context of forcible rape incidents. This is in sharp contrast to the voluminous literature focusing upon the psychopathology of rapists and other sexual offenders. Most social scientists writing on the topic of rape prior to the sixties have been males who for the most part have belittled the problem or indulge in what I have characterized as the ideology of "blaming the victim" (W. Ryan, 1971). They have been accused by feminists scholars and writers of perpetuating unfounded assumptions and myths about rape.

Sutherland, a noted criminologist, has written that:

> . . . charges of forcible rape are often made without justification by some females for purposes of blackmail and by others . . . who have been engaged voluntarily in intercourse but have been discovered, in order to protect their reputations . . . [M]any cases reported as forcible rape have certainly involved nothing more than passive resistance (Sutherland, 1950:544).

Another common myth is that it is impossible to rape a woman of normal strength. According to another criminologist: " . . . forc[ing] a woman into intercourse [is] an impossible task in most cases if the female is conscious and extreme pain is not inflicted (Glaser, 1972:61). A closely related myth is that women enjoy being raped and almost always do something to provoke it. According to psychologist David Abrahamsen:

> But women take the position that women are always playing a seductive role and ask to be aggressed upon. Many a young girl without realizing it has wanted to have sex with a particular man, and has seduced him in order to be attacked, thereby becoming a victim of her seduction, in accordance with her unconscious self-destructive desires (Abrahamsen, 1973).

The views above have in recent years been given the stamp of legitimacy through the study of victimology. It emphasizes the responsibility and role of the victim in precipitating a criminal act. It involves the notion that a woman assumes a certain amount of risk when she enters a "vulnerable" circumstance. For example, having a drink with a stranger has been interpreted as behaviour precipitative of rape, leading the police to categorize the complaint as "unfounded" or the jury to discount the victim's testimony. Feminists have strongly criticized the concept of "victim precipitation" as it applies to rape victims. They claim that victimologists like Amir (1971) who study rape are implicated in a process which perpetuates sexual stereotypes and "blames the victim."

CONSEQUENCES OF MALE IDEOLOGY

It is not surprising that, in a society dominated by men, women for the most part have accepted many of these sexual myths as well. They have been taught that men are their protectors, rather than their predators. What are the consequences of and who benefits from the myth that, for example, there is no such thing as rape? According to feminist research, one of the consequences is that many women don't view themselves as rape victims, especially if they were not subject to much violence or if their rapist was someone with whom they were acquainted. Their denial and suppression of these experiences can be psychologically damaging. Those women who do tell others of their experiences leave themselves vulnerable to being "twice victimized," first by the rapist and then by other persons who don't believe them because "they had consented" (Russell, 1974). Thus, this myth serves quite a different function for women than for men. While the myth protects a man's image in the eyes of women, it destroys a woman's veracity by convincing other women that the raped woman is responsible for her victimization. This skeptical point of view "puts down" the victim and questions her veracity at the outset. The effect is that if the woman was raped by a date, a doctor or an ex-lover, (if the rapist was not a complete stranger), the police and many other people are unlikely to believe the victim's story. This is confirmed in Russell's study: out of 85 rape victims, only those who were raped by strangers reported it to the police, with only three exceptions. Clearly, this myth allows the man to have the upper hand and maintains the woman in a dependent subordinate position.

FEMINIST IDEOLOGY

Rather than view rape as an act by a perverse male or "bad woman," feminists feel that it is more meaningful to regard rape as essentially an exaggeration of the dominant conception of sex roles and of duality in the context of North American society. According to this perspective, it is the outcome of a conflict situation which reflects the sexual politics that are part of the collective exploitation and oppression of women. It is regulated by the same culturally defined values and norms which establish how men and women relate to each other.

This argument is viewed sympathetically by the Vancouver anti-rape collective. They argue: "In our society men are taught to be sexual aggressors and women are taught to be the passive objects of that aggression. The laws around rape and sexual offences are designed to deal with only the violent extremes of this oppression of one sex over the other. Seduction, manipulation, psychological threats, all games except physical power games, are condoned by our society." It would seem, then, that rape may be best understood as an overconforming act of men to what has been characterized as the "masculine mystique" (super-masculine qualities of power, dominance, assertiveness, toughness), highly valued attributes in our competitive society. The Vancouver collective sees the resolution of this struggle accomplished by an attitudinal change on the part of both men and women: "It demands firmness and decisiveness on the part of women, and demands that men see women as persons capable of knowing what they do and do not want to do."

In the remaining portion of this article, I will trace the rise of rape crisis centres in Canada as a new social movement in the middle and late seventies. We will examine the rise of rape as a social problem and as part of the feminist movement, the coalescence of the rape movement structured around rape crisis organizations, and, finally, how the anti-rape movement in Canada has become institutionalized in the late seventies and is taking an acceptable place within the health and social defence network of Canadian institutions.

Social problems arise as social movements, through the political activism of certain interest groups. These social movements have a "natural history" consisting of stages through which they usually evolve. Looking at the problem of rape in this context, we can examine the anti-rape movement: its origin, its coalescence as a movement, and eventually its institutionalization.

PART II—RISE OF THE CANADIAN ANTI-RAPE MOVEMENT

FEMINIST ORGANIZING

Feminist analysis, ideology and organization are inseparable from the rise of the anti-rape movement in the seventies throughout North America. Two long-term goals seem to be paramount for the anti-rape movement: (1) substantial revision of the present rape laws, and (2) a concomitant change in traditional attitudes and assumptions concerning rape which both reflect and are reinforced by existing laws. These goals are to be accomplished by rendering assistance to rape victims in the short term and eliminating rape in the long term.

During the late sixties, women's groups across North America met in consciousness-raising sessions and developed a communications network that enabled them to organize around such issues as abortion, labour laws, and eventually rape laws (Freeman, 1973). In the early 1970s in the United States, the first rape workshops and conferences were held throughout the country, and "speak-outs" were held featuring public testimony by rape victims (Connell and Wilson, 1974). The Rape Crisis Center began the first rape crisis telephone line for receiving emergency calls from victims in Washington, D.C. in July 1972 (Wasserman, 1973). It has served as a prototype for services both in the United

States and Canada. The U.S. National Organization for Women (NOW) in 1975 had approximately two hundred rape task forces organized throughout the United States, including one at the national level. In most major cities and college communities in the United States some form of crisis telephone line for rape victims is available. Thus, by the midseventies, the anti-rape movement in the States progressed from a fledgling movement to a crystallized social movement, with high priority on the national agenda. In Canada the development of this movement followed a parallel development, although somewhat less dramatic.

In the early seventies the movement against rape in Canada began to coalesce around the concept of a rape crisis centre.

CANADIAN RAPE CRISIS CENTRES

The year 1972 marked the formal development of the anti-rape movement as it got underway in Canadian cities. The goals, ideological underpinnings and organizational format in Canada took a very similar form to those centres south of the border, with their U.S. "sisters." But rather than the Canadian centres being a response to the American rape crisis centres, "they arose primarily out of the local needs expressed by different social organizations, especially those which consider themselves part of the women's movement in Toronto," according to Andrea Noell, a Toronto counsellor. Canadian counsellors in other cities agreed that the centres were a direct response to meet the needs presently not being met by other distress centres or agencies. Rape counselling was felt to be a delicate issue, "too hot" to handle in conjunction with other types of counselling, and needed its own specialized, trained staff. The U.S. experience was an asset, though. The Seattle Rape Relief provided a useful model for the Vancouver women to observe.

In the earlier stages of the movement, letter correspondence, an exchange of pamphlets and a few personal visits between centres had been the main source of communication. Janet Torge, a Vancouver counsellor, begins a six-page letter in response to a fledgling Edmonton group inquiry into their modus vivendi:

> We are always glad to share our information and what we have learned with others who are just starting—it would be nice if there existed some established Canadian resource exchange service for women's groups—but I suppose that's more a dream for the future.

Almost all the existing Canadian centres have developed in the framework of women working together with their "sisters," trying to do something positive about how rape is handled or simply ignored by other societal agencies. In Toronto, women from Women's Place began planning a crisis centre one year before the Toronto Rape Crisis Centre opened its doors on Valentine's Day.

In Vancouver, it also took half a year of thinking and organizing before the Rape Relief began a full-time service. A major consideration was whether to become closely associated with the Vancouver crisis centre or the Women's Health Collective. It was resolved finally in favour of working closely with the latter, since it was felt their major emphasis was on follow-up, education, and long-term support, rather than simply a short-term crisis. The Vancouver handbook explains:

> It took a lot of time and a lot of explaining to help people understand how we saw ourselves dealing not with just a crisis but with the whole area of sexual politics between men and women (where rape is an extremely violent instance of sexual power-tripping).

The Montreal anti-rape squad made a similar decision to make their initial home within the Women's Information Referral rather than join the Distress Centre. The flavour and dynamic quality of these centres reflects the small core of activists who initiated the centres and continue to provide enthusiasm for the new counsellors.

The Canadian rape crisis centres are attempting to silence rape myths by aiding the rape victim and providing information on the rape experience seen through the victim's eyes. They are serving victims of both emergency and past rape. The rape crisis centres have two major objectives which reflect the basic aims of all rape crisis centres.

1. To provide supportive service for victims of rape and sexual assault (providing accompaniment and referral service).
2. To conduct research and educate women, as well as the community, on issues relating to rape in order to alter attitudes.

When rape happens to be by a friend or relative, most people feel at a loss and often do things which don't effectively help the woman. One rape victim recalls to a counsellor:

> There was nobody to talk to about it. There wasn't anybody around who understood. It was a totally foreign world to them. So you had to shut it up. That was bad. It should have been allowed to come out then. . . . You need somebody to talk to . . . so you can hear what you're saying.

Another woman's response to her doctor, one of the first persons she consulted, was, "He came in with the entire attitude that only prostitutes get raped. He asked me questions that he had absolutely no business asking, like, 'Did I enjoy it?' "

It has been shown that a rape victim who can talk about the experience of rape shortly after it has happened will experience less severe emotional effects. According to Verne Price, counsellor at a rape crisis centre, "The first question rape victims usually ask is, 'Tell me, did I do the right thing?' They desperately need reassurance in the form that someone else acknowledges that the rape occurred." Giving emotional support to the victim of a rape is the number one priority.

Whether or not the woman decides to report a rape, the services of the rape crisis centre are open to her—the decision is a personal one and she needs emotional and moral support regardless. According to the Toronto leaflet, "If she does not wish to go to the police, our volunteers will see that she gets medical treatment and assist her in whatever ways they can." Often those who decide not to report may have the rape centre file a third party report anonymously with the police department. Those who decide to report the rape are offered support from the crisis centre to deal with the police and hospital, as well as through the court proceedings, which may string out over many months. Volunteers are also available to aid the woman and speak on her behalf.

All of the crisis centres have put out information leaflets advising women of the police investigation, medical procedures, and the court process and legal procedures that are relevant if a woman wants to report a rape. A bright yellow leaflet from the Vancouver centre gives the following advice:

If You Want to Report a Rape
Preserve the evidence.
Call the police immediately.
Call a friend and/or Rape Relief for support.
Get medical attention.
Write down the details of the rape.

Preserve the Evidence
Until you have had a medical examination, *Do Not* wash, change your clothes, nor bath or douche. *Do* save torn clothing, articles which may have fingerprints, anything broken in the struggle, or any weapon used by the rapist. Try to remember the licence plate number, the description of the rapist, his car, etc.

Call the Police Immediately
Call the police as soon as possible. This will help them find the suspect. Initial investigators will come immediately to take down a statement. They will take you to the emergency ward of a hospital for a medical examination to obtain evidence. Take a change of clothing with you. You do have the option to call your own doctor.

Within the next day or two, detectives will contact you for a more detailed interview. They will question you thoroughly about your description of the suspect and the rape situation. Some of the questions may seem irrelevant, or even humiliating; don't hesitate to ask for an explanation.

At the Trial
It is the trial that finally decides the case. It may take place several months after the preliminary hearing. The case is generally heard before a jury, but the defence can elect to have it heard by a judge. The trial is open to the public and usually lasts several days. The same individuals are present at the trial as at the preliminary hearing, plus other relevant witnesses for the defence (character witnesses, private investigators, etc.).

If You Decide Not to Prosecute
Make sure you get proper medical treatment for injuries and possible VD or pregnancy. Even if you are not going through with the prosecution, it is still possible to make an informal report to the police. Any information they have helps in identifying repeating rapists and/or identifying suspects. If you do not want to involve yourself, you may ask Rape Relief to file a *Third Party Report*, in which the circumstances will be reported to the police, but your name will never be used. *Remember, that even if you report the rape to the police, you can drop the case at any time.*

What We Do at Rape Relief
We give support and counselling to women who have been raped—be it recently or long ago.

We are available in crisis situations on a 24-hour, 7-day week basis.

We will accompany a woman through the police investigation, medical procedure and/or the court process if she so desires.

We will provide information about the police investigation, medical needs and legal procedures.

We have an educational programme. Speakers and reading materials are available through our centre at 4197 John Street.

We will provide medical and psychiatric referrals.

We will file Third Party Reports.

There is a similar thread running through Canadian rape crisis centres. They are all providing a critical service to a rape victim who has few other places where she can go and feel at home. They are providing a lay counselling service in which the key ingredient is emotional support by another woman who is prepared to act in a crisis, do extensive follow-up and lend a helping hand wherever it is needed, whether it be protection during the pre-trial period, housing referral or emotional catharsis. A common problem from which rape victims suffer is the lack of financial support they receive from their local communities because of the controversial nature of rape. Funding is vital to this much needed service and will determine the nature of the commitment of the various communities in dealing with their rape problems. The centres are run by young, enthusiastic women, backed up by a dedicated volunteer group of women from all walks of life. Many of the staff, as well as the volunteers, have experienced a rape or sexual assault or have friends who have. The full-time staff are comprised more than likely of women of a feminist orientation, whereas their clients more often than not have had no contact with any women's organization. Many tend to "blame themselves" after they were raped, and only gradually with the aid of a sympathetic counsellor begin to understand their reaction and understand that any woman in that situation, very probably, would have reacted in a similar manner.

INSTITUTIONALIZATION OF THE RAPE MOVEMENT

The coalescence of the Canadian anti-rape movement during the mid-seventies, indicates that the movement has reached its apex or institutionalized stage. It is at this stage in its life cycle that the movement has gained acceptance and has become a prominent issue for formal organizations and societal institutions to contend with. In short, the problem has a place on the national agenda and it is sustained by a well-organized and nationwide program.

In the spring of 1975, the first national convention was held by the major Canadian rape crisis centres, utilizing a grant by the Secretary of State. Three years later there were 25 operating rape crisis centres and a "National Assister," a coordinator paid by a National Health and Welfare grant. She was appointed by a five-person national review committee consisting of representatives from Halifax, Victoria, Waterloo Edmonton, and Montreal. Her duties were to: (a) establish a National Clearing House on rape, (b) coordinate and standardize statistics from the individual rape crisis centres (c) publish a bi-monthly newsletter (d) coordinate a legislative lobbying campaign and (e) provide aid to fledging rape crisis centres. Thus in a few years the rape crisis centres developed a coordinated network system which provided closer communication and more efficient operation. The centres developed a standardized method of collecting monthly statistics. In British Columbia, a coalition was formed of rape crisis centres from Vancouver, Vancouver Island, Kamloops and Nanaimo to share resources and better coordinate activities around anti-rape issues. Similar to other groups throughout Canada, it is commonly funded by "establishment" sources.

Recognition on the national level was the net result of the success of the rape crisis centres. Their skills were solicited by the National Film Board. They were invited to provide seminars for the local police and hospital personnel. In Vancouver, the rape crisis centre obtained a research grant from the Directorate on the Non-Medical Abuse of Drugs.

However, in exchange for public acceptance and more stable funding, some might argue that rape crisis centres have been coopted by established power groups in society. The centres have been encouraged to focus upon short-term service-rendering activities to rape victims and put aside more radical long-term preventive goals, such as feminist education of young males and females of the meaning of rape and broader sex role options.

The priorities that were enunciated at the third annual National Conference in the Spring of 1977, are:

1. formation of a national association, commencement of federal incorporation procedures;
2. ways and means of obtaining permanent funding, possibly by restructuring centres so as to fulfill mandates outlined by National Health and Welfare/provincial social affairs health cost-sharing programs;
3. formation of national coalition to construct a plan of pressuring for amendment of the criminal code as it pertains to rape and sexual assault;
4. sharing of information and internally published handbooks, etc.;
5. election of new regional representatives for the Hiring and Review Committee, to which the National Assistor is responsible.

These goals give credence to the moderate goals and the institutionalization of the rape crisis centre movement.

SUMMARY AND CONCLUSIONS

We have traced the rise of the anti-rape movement in Canada through the stages of its incipiency, coalescence and finally its institutionalization as an acceptable institution within the community.

This anti-rape movement has begun providing effective support for women victims of forcible rape as evidenced by their own statistics, and has encouraged rape victims to report rape to the official social control agencies.

Laws, police, hospitals and court mediation procedures still have to be altered to deal with the primary concerns and trauma of the victim.[2] The fear of rape, as well as the way rape is defined and prosecuted in the courts, serves to maintain social control over the entire feminine population and to maintain the domination of men. Our social and economic structure generates rape and certainly does nothing to discourage it. To eliminate rape as a social problem we have to deal with its root causes. We have to be committed as a society to encourage the economic and physical independence of women, rather than perpetuate their dependency. The counterpart of this would be to provide men with a greater role in the socialization and nurturing process of their children. This would begin to alter their views of sexuality to more closely coincide with those that most women presently hold, and sensitize men to woman's total being, rather than viewing her as a sex object. This will involve a total resocialization process which has to begin with the ways young girls and boys are taught to regard themselves and their place in the world.

The forthcoming community and governmental support of the anti-rape movement reflects a changing attitude toward the rape problem. A dialogue has begun on a once taboo topic, and rape myths are slowly being eroded. Basic changes in the law and more equitable and humane treatment for victims of rape, though, have yet to be instituted on a universal basis. It still remains unclear as to whether the efforts of the rape crisis centres will be able to successfully address the basic issues that will eventually lead to reducing and eliminating the incidence of rape.

NOTES

[1] Recently proposed American legislation involving the laws of evidence of rape laws in California and elsewhere have been amended and provide for a rape offence as a result of "any threat that would render a female of reasonable firmness incapable of resisting." National Commission on Reform of Federal Criminal Laws, Proposed New Federal Criminal Code, Sec. 1642 (1971). The Evidence Project of the Law Reform Commission in Canada has also proposed such changes. See for example, Neil Brooks, "Rape and the Laws of Evidence," *Chitty's Law Journal* (vol. 23, No. 1 1975: 5-8). Retrogressive rape legislation has also been forthcoming. In the English House of Lords, May 1975 a decision was handed down that mere belief of the man, however unreasonable, that the woman consented was sufficient evidence that he could not be convicted of rape.

[2] For example, in Canada, the rules of evidence in rape cases should be amended so that evidence of the character of the victim should be inadmissible. This was recommended three years ago by the Evidence Project of the Law Reform Commission of Canada, Paper No. 4, Proposed Legislation Sec. 3. In 1974, Otto Lang, Minister of Justice, put forward amendments to the Criminal Code which, although not as far-reaching as those proposed by the Law Reform Commission, would take into account the rape victim to a limited extent.

REFERENCES

Abrahamsen, David
1973   *The Murdering Mind*, New York: Harper and Row.
Amir, M.
1971   *Patterns of Forcible Rape*. Chicago: University of Chicago Press.
Connell N. and C. Wilson
1974   *Rape: The First Sourcebook for Women*. New York: New American Library.
1970   *Criminal Code*, R.S.C. C-34.
Davis, Alan J.
1968   "Sexual Assaults in the Philadelphia Prison System and Sheriff's Vans," *Transaction* (Dec. 8-16).
Freeman, Jo
1973   "The Origins of the Women's Liberation Movement," A.J.S. 78 (January p. 792-811).
George, Margaret
1973   "From 'Goodwife' to 'Mistress.' The Transformation of Woman in Bourgeoisie Culture," *Science and Society* XXXVIII: 152-177.

Glaser, Daniel
  1972   *Adult Crime and Social Policy*. Englewood Cliffs, New Jersey: Prentice Hall,
                p. 61.
Hale, Sir Matthew
  1800   *The History of the Pleas of the Crown*. London: E. Rider, Little-Britain.
Holmstrom, Linda
  1974   "Rape: An Indicator of Woman's Family Role," paper presented at I.S.A.,
                August 1974, Toronto.
Kostash, Myrna
  1975   "Rape." *Maclean's*. pp. 62-71.
LeGrand, Camille
  1973   "Rape and Rape Laws: Sexism in Society and Law 61." *California L. Review*
                919-921 for estimates of rapes reported in various studies.
Russell, Diana
  1974   *The Politics of Rape: The Victim's Perspective*. New York: Stein and Day.
Ryan, William
  1971   *Blaming the Victim*. New York: Vintage Books.
Smith, Dorothy E.
  1977   "Women, The Family and Corporate Capitalism," in Marylee Stephenson
                (ed.), *Women in Canada*. Toronto: General Publishing.
                Statistics Canada, Statistics of Criminal and Other Offences 38. 1971,
                1973.
Sutherland, Edwin
  1950   "The Sexual Psychopath Laws," *Journal of Criminal Law and Criminology* 40
                (January-February), p. 544.
                Vancouver Sun, July 1977.
Wasserman, Michelle
  1973   "Rape: Breaking the Silence," *The Progressive* 37 (November: 19-23).

Chapter 10

THIRD PARTY JUSTICE:
THE PENAL RESPONSE TO VIOLENCE

John Hagan

Rape victims, Kasinsky tells us, may employ the services of a rape crisis centre to file third party reports on their behalf. Hagan in this chapter examines the role of the third party (the victim) in determining societal reaction to violence. He is concerned also with the effect of victim involvement on the criminal justice system. At each stage in the criminal justice system, the victim may be the determining factor in the continuation and outcome of the case.

"Reform" and "deterrence" are suggested as the goal of our system of justice, while the victims of violence rate highly "restraint" and "justice." Systematic research on the influence of the victim has not yet been done in Canada. Whether one assumes it should be done may depend on whether one has been raped or assaulted and on whether one is male or female.

Uncontrolled violence is commonly perceived as the ultimate threat to the social order we call society. In most societies, the legitimate use of violence is restricted in monopolistic fashion to the police and armed forces. The use of violence outside these institutions provokes relative consensus in the societal definition of deviance. The problem, then, consists of developing a societal strategy for the prevention of violence. In this paper, we will examine an *apparent* societal strategy for the control of violence, and the actual *application* of this strategy in North American systems of criminal justice. Our discussion will be based on the assumption that even the best societal blueprints usually do not describe accurately the social system in operation. In particular, we will be interested in (a) the role of victims in determining the societal reactions to violence, and (b) the consequences of victim involvement for traditional goals of the criminal justice system. Whether our legal system could operate with more consistency and rationality with regard to these goals is the issue that will concern us.

We can begin our discussion on a rather abstract level by considering

---

* This paper was presented at the Workshop on Violence in Canadian Society held in Toronto, Canada, September 8-9, 1975. Permission to print this paper has been granted by the author and the Centre of Criminology, University of Toronto. This paper also appears in the *Report of the Proceedings of the Workshop on Violence in Canadian Society*, Department of Criminology, University of Toronto.

violence and the threat it poses to the social order as this problem was conceptualized by the seventeenth century philosopher Thomas Hobbes.

THE HOBBESIAN PROBLEM OF ORDER

Thomas Hobbes (1651) is commonly credited with having stated the problem of social order in its most cogent form calling particular attention to man's presumed propensity for violent conflict. The problem begins, according to Hobbes, with the quest for power. Mankind is such that there is " . . . a perpetual and restless desire of power after power, that ceaseth only in death" (64). These deadly quarrels have three principal causes: competition, diffidence, and glory. "The first, maketh men invade for gain; the second, for safety; and the third, for reputation" (81).

While noting that in the absence of a *common* power such activities cannot be evaluated as right or wrong, just or unjust, Hobbes is clear in distinguishing between "the right of nature" and "the law of nature." The right of nature consists of " . . . the liberty each man hath, to use his own power, as he will himself, for the preservation of his own nature . . ." (84). A law of nature, on the other hand, " . . . is a percept or general rule, found out by reason, by which a man is forbidden to do that, which is destructive of his own life, or taketh away the means of preserving the same . . ." (84). In sum, " . . . *right*, consisteth in the liberty to do, or to forbear, whereas *law*, determineth and bindeth . . ." (84).

Where the right of nature prevails, unconstrained by the laws of nature and the power of a sovereign state, " . . . there can be no security of any man" and the people are " . . . in that condition which is called war; and such a war, as is of every man, against every man" (82). The way out of such a condition lies, then, in the adherence to laws of nature. One additional element, however, is required to assure adherence to the laws of nature and to put an end to the war among men. This, considered the most important factor by Hobbes, is the transfer of power from individuals to the state: " . . . the multitude so united . . . is called a commonwealth . . . that great Leviathan . . ." (112).

With the establishment of the commonwealth, we reach the end-point of Hobbes's discussion. The Hobbesian question can now be articulated. It is this: "How is social order established?" The answer lies, according to Hobbes, in the imposition of a common, sovereign power. However, one aspect of the problem remains unresolved: "Why do individuals surrender their powers to the state?" For Hobbes, the answer is found in utility: "The final cause, end, or design of men . . . is the foresight of their own preservation, and of a more contented life thereby . . ." (109). The solution, then, comes in the form of man's capacity for reason: man is able to grasp his situation and take rational steps to remedy the violent pursuit of self-interest. These actions typically take their form in the creation and application of laws, the purpose of which is to make human behaviour conform to a common social purpose.

THE SOCIAL-ENGINEERING FUNCTION OF LAW

Social and legal philosophers from Auguste Comte to Roscoe Pound have shared Hobbes's hope that society possesses the capacity to change and control itself through the rational and conscious use of laws. Pound designated this capacity the "social engineering" function of law. However, although some jurists are profoundly optimistic, the limits of law seem apparent. In a less than perfect society, a number of constraints limit the effectiveness of the law as an instrument of social change and control. Chambliss and Seidman (1971) suggest that " . . . it is an important task of the sociology of law to examine these constraints, thus to pose to the policy-makers the actual range of choice with which they are confronted. Such an empirical examination of the situation is the indispensable first step toward planned social engineering" (9).

Figure 1
A Model of Role Expectations

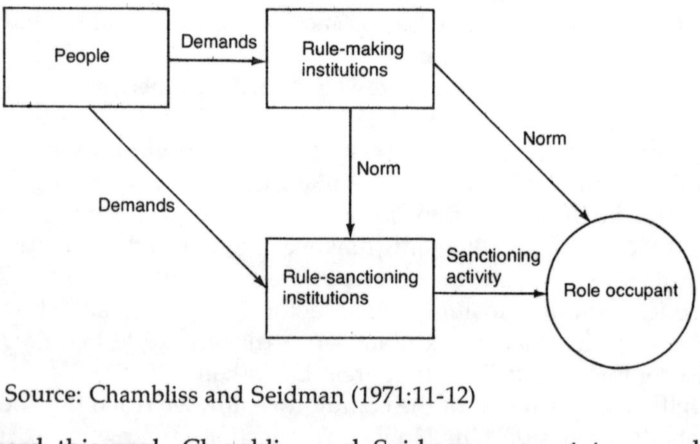

Source: Chambliss and Seidman (1971:11-12)

Toward this goal, Chambliss and Seidman suggest two models of legal activity in democratic societies (Figures 1 and 2). The first model describes the legal system as a formal set of role expectations (i.e., the law as formulated by statute). The second model is intended to more accurately reflect actual role performance (i.e., the law in action). Both models are based first on the fact that nearly every legal norm is addressed simultaneously to a role-occupant (e.g., the citizen) and a sanctioning body (e.g., the courts). Thus sections of the Criminal Code of Canada governing assault first define for the citizenry and the legal system acts to be included under this section:

> Section 244: A person commits an assault when, without the consent of another person or with consent, where it is obtained by fraud,
> (a) he applies force intentionally to the person of the other, directly or indirectly,
>   or
> (b) he attempts or threatens, by an act or gesture, to apply force to the person of the other, if he has or causes the other to believe upon reasonable grounds that he has present ability to effect his purpose.

Instructions are then provided for the judicial response to such acts:

> Section 245: (1) Every one who commits a common assault is guilty of an offence punishable on summary conviction
> (2) Everyone who unlawfully causes bodily harm to any person or commits an assault that causes bodily harm to any person is guilty of an indictable offence and is liable to imprisonment for five years.

Figure 2
A Model of Role Performance

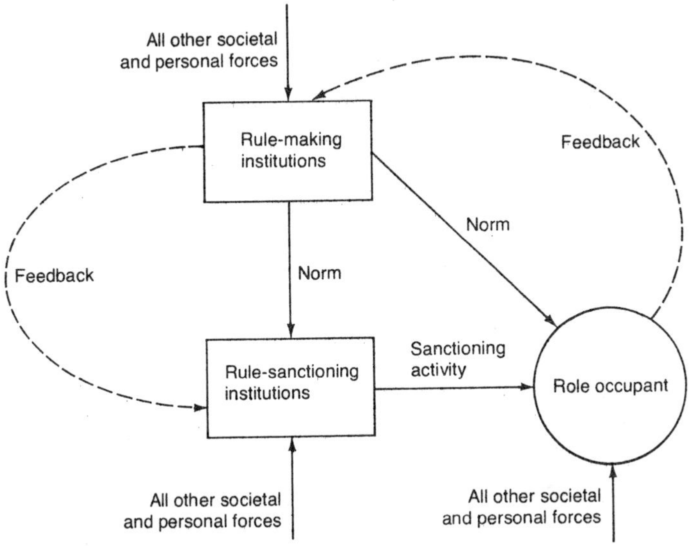

Source: Chambliss and Seidman (1971:11-12)

In operation, however, "the law" is more complex than our statutes suggest. For example, in cases of assault, charges are rarely laid, and convictions rarely obtained, without the cooperation of the victim. A variety of external forces, then, may influence "the law in action."

Chambliss and Seidman represent these possibilities with the exogenous arrows introduced in Figure 2.

Chambliss and Seidman refer conceptually to the differences between these models as a disparity between role expectation and role performance. In the remainder of this paper, we will be concerned with the manner in which victims of violence influence the role performances of sanctioning agents, and thereby produce disparities between ideal and actual models of the criminal justice system. Our interest is in how these disparities may affect the social engineering function of those laws seeking to control violent behaviour.

THIRD PARTY JUSTICE

We have noted that, ideally, laws controlling violent behaviour are addressed only to would-be assailants and sanctioning agents. We noted further, however, that the law can be influenced by a third party: the victim—particularly the victim of violence. The role of the victim in guiding the penal response to violence (a) begins with the initial decision whether or not to report the event to the police, (b) persists via the willingness of the victim to see the case through prosecution, (c) extends into the judicial sentencing process, and (d) ends with the decision whether or not to seek compensation. At each stage, this third party, the victim, can be a crucial factor in the continuation of the case. A review of existing research will help to inform our assessment of the influence of the victim in each of these phases of the criminal justice system.

1. *Victim and Police Reports.* The significance of the victim in initiating the penal response to violence is indicated in two different types of research. First, observations of police work reveal that very little victimization is discovered without an initial reporting of the event to the police. Albert Reiss (1968) makes this point in analyzing the data from a three-city American study of policemen and their encounters with the public. Thirty-six trained observers rode in patrol cars and walked with policemen on their beats on all shifts, each day of the week for seven consecutive weeks, in each of the three cities. In all, over three thousand police-citizen "encounters" were observed. Reiss then designated each of these incidents as either a "pro-active" (i.e., on-view) or "reactive" (i.e., in response to citizen report) mobilization. Eighty-seven per cent of the encounters were thus indicated as *reactive* mobilizations. The clear implication is that the police are not likely to respond to violent events unless they are summoned to the scene.

A second indication of the importance of victims in determining the penal response to violence is found in the various victimization surveys conducted in North America. The first national survey of this type reported in the United States by Ennis (1967) revealed striking differences between the occurrence of crimes of violence, and the frequency with which these crimes are officially known. For example, nearly four times as many forcible rapes are reported by victims as appear in the official data, more than twice as many aggravated assaults, and nearly one-third again as many robberies. Only homicides, among the violent crimes, are reflected with a semblance of accuracy in the official data. A Canadian survey conducted in Toronto by Courtis (1970) reveals even more startling findings. Here, more than ten times as many common and aggravated assaults are reported by interviewed victims as are reported to the police. The message of these surveys is that much violence goes undetected and unrecorded and, therefore, unrecognized by a penal system designed to control it.

2. *Arrest and Prosecution.* Victims of violence whose experiences are reported are not necessarily willing or anxious to pursue their cases to prosecution. An indication of this reluctance is found in a further consideration of the data on police-citizen encounters, as analyzed by Black and Reiss (1970). These authors report important variation among complainants (many but not all of whom were victims of violence) in their desire to see a suspect arrested. Black and Reiss found that black complainants responding to black suspects were the most insistent on an arrest taking place. It is further noted that demands for arrest from a complainant are very difficult for the police to deny. This situation contributes to a higher arrest rate among blacks. Whether this race differential is similarly a class disparity is unknown, but certainly plausible. It is in this regard that such findings become relevant to the Canadian scene.

The influence of the complainant in determining arrest decisions is made more disconcerting by research on "victim precipitated" crimes. Curtis (1974) found, in analysis of police reports from seventeen cities, that victim provocation is common in criminal homicide and aggravated assault, less frequent but still empirically noteworthy in robbery, and perhaps least relevant in forcible rape. Where the victim of violence acts as complainant, the justification of the insistence on arrest becomes problematic. Curtis summarizes the moral dilemma as follows: "In such situations, distinctions between victims and offenders are often blurred and mostly a function of who got whom first, with what weapon, how the event was reported, and what immediate decisions were made by police" (1970:597).

The fact that a charge is laid does not, of course, ensure that a conviction will follow. This is so in spite of " . . . a factual presumption that it is more plausible than not that a person suspected by the police is guilty of a crime, a presumption whose probability grows constantly higher as the accused passes through the system from stage to stage without being rejected at one point or another" (Chambliss and Seidman, 1971:272). This factual presumption suggests that something other than the guilt or innocence of the suspect and the willingness of the state determines conviction. Canadian research by John Hogarth (1974) again suggests the influence of our familiar third party: the victim.

Hogarth's study is concerned, in part, with the relationships between offenders and victims of person and property crimes in East York. Hogarth reports that in 55.2 per cent of the person and property offences, some but not all of which involved violence, the offender and victim had a pre-existing relationship. Beyond this, an inverse relationship was observed between the intensity of the prior relationship and the use of charging options. Thus, the frequency of criminal charges declined as one moved from "strangers" to "commercial" to "other friends and relatives" to "neighbours" to "family." In the presence of close social or personal ties, then, the complainant seems less intent upon having criminal sanctions applied than in summoning the police to contain a situation temporarily out of control. Further evidence for this view emerges in the finding that when the prosecutorial initiative resided with private complainants (as in cases of common assault), they tended to proceed to prosecution less often than when the decision to prosecute was primarily within police control (as in property offences and offences against the person other than common assaults). Each of these findings suggests that the victim of violence plays a formally unexpected role in determining whether a penal response to violence will occur at the prosecution stage.

3. *Sentencing.* A variety of American studies (Green, 1964; Johnson, 1941; Garfinkel, 1949; Partington, 1965; Wolfgang and Riedel, 1973; Judson et. al., 1969) consider the role of the victim in the formation of sentencing decisions. These studies are most frequently concerned with inter-racial crimes and the use of the death penalty as a sentencing option. In particular, this body of research investigates the charge that blacks suspected of victimizing whites may disproportionately receive more severe sentences. Unfortunately, most of the research does not incorporate adequate controls for relevant legal variables (e.g., offence seriousness, prior record, and numbers of charges) (see Hagan, 1974). The most convincing of this research is a study of the use of capital punishment for inter-racial rape in the southern United States.

Wolfgang and Riedel (1973) gathered and analyzed data covering a twenty-year period, including over three thousand rape convictions, in 230 counties of eleven southern states. The results reveal that black men raping white women were considerably more likely to receive the death penalty than any other racial combination of offenders and victims. Unfortunately, Wolfgang and Riedel did not include in their published analysis an actual control for the prior records of the offenders. Nevertheless, the strength of the zero-order relationship between racial contact and disposition is sufficient to raise the definite suspicion of differential sentencing.

It seems probable that at the root of such differential sentencing patterns there exist fundamental social judgments about the relative immorality of certain types of offenders seeking out specific types of victims. In the southern United States, during the early part of this century, race seems to have constituted the salient social concern. In other periods, and in different settings, other victim attributes will be salient. The more general conclusion is that the victim is again a dominant determinant of the type of penal response to violent crime.

4. *Compensation.* The prospect of compensation for victims of violence is a new and growing aspect of North American systems of criminal justice. Unfortunately, research on the use of criminal compensation has not developed as quickly as the programmes involved. Nevertheless, several hypotheses can be suggested relating to the role of the victim in compensation decisions.

Given what we know from the preceding section about the role of the victim in determining sentencing decisions, it seems reasonable to expect an extension of this influence into the assignment of compensation. For example, it seems plausible to hypothesize that compensation awards will vary inversely with the social and moral distance of the victims from those sitting in judgment. Said differently, it can be hypothesized that compensation boards will be most favourably disposed towards victims similar to themselves in social characteristics, and caught in situations that board members can most readily imagine happening to them. This hypothesis would predict, for example, a larger award to a businessman permanently injured while forcibly abducted for ransom, than for a female slum resident permanently injured during a forcible rape. In part, such patterns might be expected to mirror common conceptions of victim precipitated crime. An underlying issue, then, is whether these preconceptions are accurate (Note: the research by Curtis discussed earlier suggests that in the case of forcible rape these conceptions may be predominantly false).

A second source of hypotheses regarding compensation awards is the issue of who seeks them. It can be hypothesized that upper socio-economic status victims, equipped with legal assistance, may be most likely to seek out compensation. Again, then, victim characteristics may play an influential role in determining this final penal response to violence.

THE IMPLICATIONS OF THIRD PARTY JUSTICE

We have reviewed research supportive of our original assumption that the victim of violence is an influential third party in the legal decision-making process. The irony of this situation is that when victims assume an active role in determining penal outcomes, their concern with the traditional goals of the criminal justice system seems likely to be partial.

Thus, "The criminal law is commonly considered to be useful in achieving five ends. . . These objectives receive various titles, but they can be recognized as attempts to reform the offender, to restrain him, to deter others, to revive communion symbolically, and to achieve justice" (Nettler, 1974:32). The current judicial wisdom suggests that among these goals, reform and deterrence are most important (Hogarth, 1971:70-71). It seems unlikely that victims of violence share this view.

It is hypothesized that victims of violence are more likely to rate "restraint" and "justice" as the most important goals of penal activity. It is further proposed that victims of violence are most concerned with avoiding future victimization, and with imposing retribution for the harm they have experienced. If this proposition is accurate, then we can assume further that "third party justice" will be at variance with judicially conceived purposes of the penal response to violence. The plausibility of this disparity underlines the need to determine just how great the victim's influence in the decision-making process is, and what the consequences may be for the goals of our criminal justice system.

For example, if most victims of common assaults are concerned primarily with the temporary restraint of the offender, and thus characteristically refuse to follow their cases to conviction, then it is important for our legal system to be informed of the impact of this pattern on recidivism. Unfortunately, studies of recidivism in the past have focused on only those offenders actually convicted; the guilty, but *un*convicted, remain unstudied.

A second example of deficiencies in our knowledge involves the more serious crimes of violence. We have reviewed research suggesting the influence of victim characteristics on sentencing and, by implication, on compensation decisions. Yet, we have no systematic knowledge of the extent of this influence in the Canadian Courts, or, how this influence may correlate with rates of recidivism, or, the effects of such decision-making patterns on victim and public conceptions of justice.

Finally, research to date has focused on the role of the victim largely as that of a relatively passive participant in the penal process. Little attention has been given to how more active attributes of the victim may determine his influence in the penal process. Future research may benefit from a focus on three broadly conceived characteristics of the victim: (a) ability (as indicated, for example, by previous experience in, and knowledge about, the criminal justice system); (b) motivation (as indicated, for example, by the nature of any prior relationship between the victim and offender, as well as by the degree of injury sustained); and (c) resources (as indicated, for example, by access to legal assistance and time to pursue the case). All of these factors may help to explain variation in victim impact on the penal response to violence.

Summarizing, we are aware that "third party justice" is a significant component of the penal response to violence, but we are largely uninformed of the dimensions or consequences of this situation. An important avenue for future research is thus indicated.

REFERENCES

Black, Donald J. and Albert J. Reiss
    1970   "Police Control of Juveniles." American Sociological Review, 35 (February): 63-77.
Chambliss, William J. and Robert B. Seidman
    1971   *Law, Order, and Power*. Reading, Massachusetts: Addison-Wesley Publishing Company.
Courtis, M. C.
    1970   Attitudes to Crime and the Police in Toronto: A Report on some survey findings. Toronto: Centre of Criminology, University of Toronto.
Curtis, Lynn A.
    1974   "Victim Precipitation and Violent Crime." Social Problems 21 (April): 594-605.
Ennis, P. H.
    1967   Criminal Victimization in the United States: A Report of a National Survey. Washington, D.C.: U.S. Government Printing Office.
Garfinkel, Harold
    1949   "Research Note on Inter- and Intra-Racial Homicides." Social Forces 27: 369-381.
Green, Edward
    1964   "Inter- and Intra-Racial Crime Relative to Sentencing." Journal of Criminal Law, Criminology and Police Science Vol. 55, No. 3: 348-358.
Hagan, John
    1974   "Extra-Legal Attributes and Criminal Sentencing: An Assessment of a Sociological Viewpoint." Law & Society Review 8(3).
Hobbes, Thomas
    1651   *Leviathan*. Oxford: Basil Blackwell.
Hogarth, John
    1974   East York Community Law Reform Project. Studies on Diversion: Law Reform Commission.

    1971   *Sentencing as a Human Process*. Toronto: University of Toronto Press.
Johnson, Guy
    1941   "The Negro and Crime." Annals 271: 93-104.
Judson, Charles J., James J. Pandell, Jack B. Owens, James L. McIntosh, Dale L. Matschullat
    1969   "A Study of the California Penalty Jury in first Degree Murder Cases." Stanford Law Review. 21: 1297-1497.
Nettler, Gwynn
    1974   *Explaining Crime*. Toronto: McGraw-Hill Ryerson.
Partington, Donald
    1965   "The Incidence of the Death Penalty for Rape in Virginia." Washington & Lee Law Review 22: 43-63.
Reiss, Albert
    1968   The Police and the Public. New Haven, Conn.: Yale University Press.
Wolfgang, Marvin E. and Marc Riedel
    1973   "Race, Judicial Discretion, and the Death Penalty." The Annals of the American Academy of Political and Social Science 407 (May): 119-133.

Chapter 11

HOMICIDE IN CANADA:
A STATISTICAL SYNOPSIS

Statistics Canada, Justice Statistics Division
Paul Reed, Assistant Director, Research
Teresa Bleszynski, Senior Analyst
Robert Gaucher, Analyst

The manner in which murder statistics are recorded profoundly affects the way in which Canadians view murder as a top priority among other crimes. The following report is taken from the records of the Judicial Statistics Division, Statistics Canada. It is police-reported information which provides the basis for the accumulation of such statistics. However, not all mortality statistics emanate from the same source. For example, Vital Statistics presents figures which are based on reports from death certificates provided by the Provincial registrars, and deaths which are reported as accidental, such as poisoning, can be found in Coroners' Reports. That which is included in the definition "homicide" varies with the source of statistical information.

From time to time in the affairs of every society, one issue acquires special and continuing prominence. That issue becomes the focus of widespread individual concern and the topic of much public debate. It touches the very nerves, the most basic beliefs and values and, sometimes, the laws of that society.

Murder is just such an issue in Canadian society today. To citizens and their government, the incidence of murder is a matter of preeminent concern for a variety of reasons: for how it is thought to threaten personal and public safety, for what it is believed to indicate about the "health" of Canadian society, and for the controversy it has aroused in the process of legislating appropriate ways of dealing with this most violent of criminal acts. Much of the concern and debate is based on discussion of the amount or rate of murder and the apparent acceleration in this and other kinds of violent crime; that there are more murders every year, it is argued, should be cause for alarm and should compel us to take whatever measures are necessary to halt this increase. Too few questions have been asked, though, about the nature of murder, about

* This article is an abridged version of *Homicide in Canada: A Statistical Synopsis*, Statistics Canada, 1976. Reproduced by permission of the Minister of Trade and Commerce, Peter G. Kirkham, Chief Statistician of Canada and the Minister of Supply and Services, Canada.

what kinds of people murder what kinds of victims under what circum-stances. Perhaps this stems from the common belief that because every act of murder is so reprehensible, individual variations in the nature of the act don't really matter much. It may also stem from the widespread but questionable image of all murderers as dangerous persons, more often than not with a criminal record and generally alike in the threat they pose to the social order, and the image of victims as innocent parties to their death. As well, too few questions have been asked about how our society responds when it finds that a murder has been commit-ted, about how persons charged with murder are actually dealt with by our justice system, how many are tried, how many are acquitted or convicted and the kinds of sentences given to those who are convicted.

But whenever such questions have been asked, the answers frequently have been incomplete, difficult to get, or simply not possible through lack of necessary information. The need for more and better answers has prompted this report.

HOW MUCH HOMICIDE?

Concern in Canada about homicide in general and about murder in particular rests heavily on statistics about the increasing amounts and rates of homicide and murder. There is no single answer to the question, how much homicide and how much murder take place in Canada each year? because there are different ways of measuring their occurrence.

The most standard and basic unit for measuring the amount of murder and homicide is the number of *victims* killed within a designated period of time. Since every culpable killing of a person constitutes a criminal offence, the term *offence* is conventionally used rather than *victim*. Sometimes, though, several persons are killed by the same indi-vidual at one place and time. For this reason the term *incident* is used in referring to every single event in which homicide is committed, regard-less of whether it involves one person or more than one. Because of the occurrence of multiple-victim homicide incidents from time to time, the yearly number and rate of such incidents are always lower than the yearly number and rate of homicide *offences*. Two other terms related to murder and manslaughter incidents (but not as measures of the amount of each) are *suspect* and *offender*. *Suspects* are the persons identified (and in most cases, charged) as having committed a murder or manslaughter. (In any incident where more than one victim has been killed by a single suspect, a separate charge is usually laid against the suspect for each offence.) And murder suspects who are sent to trial and ultimately convicted are referred to as convicted *offenders*.

The so-called "murder" statistics released every year by Statistics Canada indicate the number of persons in Canada who were reported by police as having been killed by another person through an act of murder. In most of these cases a suspect is identified, charged with the murder, and eventually tried by a judge and a jury. But a considerable number of these suspects are either found to be not guilty of any offence, or are found to be guilty of manslaughter or of some lesser offence. In these latter cases, the court does not find that a murder took place as originally reported by the police. Thus, the figures reported by police represent the number of criminal homicides, not necessarily the number of murders, which occurred during the year. Because murder is an offence which is defined quite precisely by law and because only courts are empowered to determine whether a person's death was a murder or a manslaughter (or neither), the amount and rate of murder should *also* be estimated on the basis of the number of convictions for murder. Figure 1 shows that a murder rate based on the number of murder convictions is far below the rate of killings (or deaths) initially reported as murders. Although it is somewhat higher than the murder conviction rate, the rate of conviction for all homicide offences is also much less than the rate of deaths initially reported as murders. Neither police information nor court information alone can provide a true measure of the murder rate; the true rate (which probably cannot be known exactly) lies somewhere between the rate of police-reported murder offences (which is higher than the true rate) and the rate of murder convictions (which is lower than the true rate).

There are yet two further ways in which the amount and rate of initially-reported murder (or homicide) may be measured; by counting the number of offences (where one offence is counted for every victim), and by counting the number of incidents (where an incident may occasionally involve more than one victim). Tables 1 and 2 show the differences in amounts and rates produced by these two measures.

Table 1 presents yearly and total numbers of murder and manslaughter *offences* (as defined and reported by police) in Canada since 1961. Reported homicide offences have increased steadily over the past fourteen years. The sharp increases in 1970 and 1972 were the result of two large mass slayings (a senior citizens' home and the Bluebird Café in the province of Quebec) by arson, and both of these unusual increases were responsible for the apparent decrease in the following years, 1971 and 1973. Not only has the rate of reported murder increased steadily; the annual increase in this rate appears to be accelerating as well. Against an average annual increase of 0.05 in the rate during the 1961-67 period, the average increase in the rate climbed to 0.14 yearly during the 1968-74 period.

The numbers and rates of murder *incidents* provide a better measure of changes in the amount of homicide and murder because these measures are not so affected by the fluctuations caused by multiple-victim murders as are offence-based measures. Table 2 shows the upward trend in homicide incidents to be more consistent from year to year. It also shows the average annual change in the rate of incidents to be increasing even faster than the rate of offences.

There has been no consistent nor cumulative change in the number of reported manslaughter offences. Furthermore, whereas in 1961 reported manslaughter offences made up 20.5% of all reported homicide offences, in 1967 they accounted for 16.6% and in 1974 for 8.3% of all reported homicide offences. It would appear that when the distinction between murder punishable by death and murder punishable by life imprisonment was first instituted in September 1961, there was a move away from reporting homicides as manslaughter offences. A possible explanation for this is that: (a) the provision of a murder charge which did not have the death penalty as the mandatory sentence (i.e., non-capital murder) may have led to the redefinition of homicide offences (formerly defined as manslaughter, becoming defined as non-capital murder by police), and that (b) judicial administrative considerations, such as the nature and extent of plea bargaining, affected the initial definition of homicides as non-capital murder rather than as manslaughter.

Table 1
Number of Homicide Offences
Rates per 100,000 Population and Annual Change in Rates, Canada, 1961-74

Year	Number of homicide offences		Rate per 100,000 population		Annual change in rates	
	Total murder[2]	Man-slaugh-ter[3]	Total murder	Man-slaugh-ter	Total murder	Man-slaugh-ter
1961	185	48	1.01	0.26	..	..
1962	217	48	1.17	0.26	+0.16	—
1963	215	34	1.14	0.18	−0.03	−0.08
1964	218	35	1.13	0.18	−0.01	—
1965	243	34	1.24	0.17	+0.11	−0.01
1966	222	28	1.11	0.14	−0.13	−0.03
1967	282	56	1.38	0.27	+0.27	+0.13
1968	315	60	1.52	0.29	+0.14	+0.02
1969	347	44	1.65	0.21	+0.13	−0.08
1970	433	34	2.03	0.16	+0.38	−0.05
1971	426	47	1.98	0.22	−0.05	+0.06
1972	479	40	2.19	0.18	+0.21	−0.04
1973	479	66	2.17	0.30	−0.02	+0.12
1974	545	49	2.43	0.22	+0.26	−0.08
1961-74	4,606	623			+0.09[4]	0.00[4]
1961-67	1,582	283			+0.05[4]	0.00[4]
1968-74	3,024	340			+0.14[4]	0.00[4]

[1] One offence is counted for every victim by reporting police departments.
[2] "Total murder" includes all capital, non-capital, and non-specified murder offences.
[3] All manslaughter figures are taken from the Uniform Crime Reporting Program and are not revised annually, as the murder figures are.
[4] These figures refer to the average annual change in rates.

Table 2
Number of Incidents of Murder[1]
Rates per 100,000 Population and Annual Change in Rates, Canada, 1961-74

Year	Number of incidents of murder	Rate per 100,000 population	Annual change in rate
1961	173	0.95	..
1962	196	1.05	+0.10
1963	192	1.01	−0.04
1964	199	1.03	+0.02
1965	216	1.10	+0.07
1966	206	1.03	−0.07
1967	239	1.17	+0.14
1968	292	1.41	+0.24
1969	320	1.52	+0.11
1970	354	1.66	+0.14
1971	395	1.83	+0.17
1972	412	1.89	+0.06
1973	447	2.02	+0.13
1974	499	2.22	+0.20
1961-74	4,140		+0.09[2]
1961-67	1,421		+0.03[2]
1968-74	2,719		+0.15[2]

[1] Murder incidents counted here are based on the number of original charges of "Capital murder," "Non-capital murder" and "Murder, not specified." The numbers of incidents of manslaughter and infanticide were not reported prior to January 1, 1974.
[2] These figures refer to the average annual change in rates.

This latter point takes place within the context of the penalty changes noted in (a) above. These are, however, only possible reasons, and the continued absence of any increase in reported manslaughter offences remains an anomalous aspect of homicide statistics.

Not included in these tables are figures showing that the rate of increase in homicide offences has risen during the 1968-74 period (compared to the 1961-67 period) for all provinces but Nova Scotia and Alberta. Regionally, British Columbia shows the most substantial increase in rate between these two periods (up from 2.42 to 4.47) followed by Quebec (from 1.28, up to 2.72) and the Prairies (2.29 to 3.22) with Ontario exhibiting the smallest increase between periods (from 1.60 to 1.93).

Increased rates of manslaughter offences for these two periods are exhibited only by New Brunswick and the Yukon, with very small numerical increases in both instances (ten and three respectively). All other provinces exhibit either stable or decreasing rates of manslaughter offences between the periods 1961-67 and 1968-74.

Figure I displays yearly rates for various categories of homicide (i.e., offences or victims of murder, incidents of murder, and offences or victims of manslaughter) and the rate of total convictions for murder and homicide generally. The persistent increase in rates of reported offences and incidents of murder, as well as the stability of the rate of reported manslaughter offences, are clearly evident. The murder conviction rate has steadily increased but not to the same degree as the rate of reported incidents of all types of homicide. The average annual rate of homicide convictions was 79% greater in the period 1968-73 compared with the 1961-67 period, whereas the average annual rate of murder convictions increased 35% between these two periods. This compares with a 65% increase between periods in the rate of reported murder incidents.

Figure 1
Rates per 100,000 Population for Murder Offences and Incidents, Manslaughter Offences[1], and Total Convictions, Canada 1961-1974

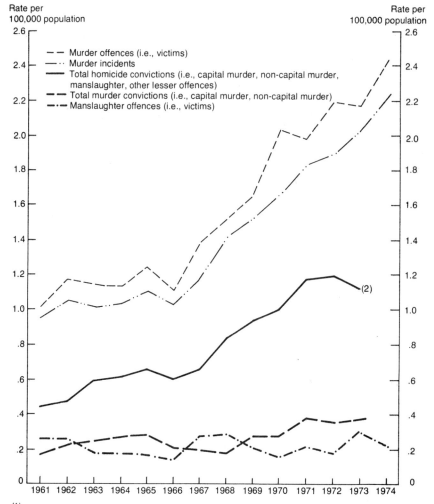

(1) Figures for manslaughter offences are taken from uniform crime reporting publications 1961-1974.
(2) 1974 figures are not included since many cases are still in the courts.

This disparity between the rate of increase in reported incidents and the rate of increase in murder convictions is noteworthy. It suggests that the definition of incidents in terms of the perceived nature and seriousness of the incident differs considerably between the police and crown attorneys (who initially define an offence as murder) and the courts (which ultimately define the offence as manslaughter). Administrative considerations are also an intervening factor. While the rate of persons convicted of homicide has increased, this increase is not nearly as sharp as that of reported murder offences and incidents.

THE KINDS OF MURDER INCIDENT

There is an extraordinary range of variation in the kinds of persons, motives, circumstances, and means of killing involved in incidents of murder and homicide. This variation is not random though; careful analysis of the statistics reveals a number of broadly distinctive kinds of murder incident, with each kind having a set of more or less typical characteristics.

This section deals with the nature of *incidents reported as murder by police* in Canada from the beginning of 1961 to the end of 1974. For this reason alone, all incidents have been referred to as murder incidents, despite the fact that a substantial number of these were later defined by the courts to have been manslaughter, not murder incidents. (Thus, strictly speaking, these incidents should really be referred to as homicide rather than as murder incidents.) The reader should clearly understand, then, that the term "murder incident" is used in this chapter to mean "incidents of killing which were initially defined by the police as murder."

All murder incidents have been placed in one of five main categories, depending on whether the murder incident was solved, whether the killing took place during commission of another crime, and whether there was a social relationship of any kind between the suspected killer and the victim. The five main categories and their several sub-categories are therefore the following:
1. Domestic relationship
   Immediate family
   Other kinship
   Common-law
2. Social or business relationship
   Lovers' quarrel or love triangle
   Close acquaintance
   Casual acquaintance
   Business relationship
3. During commission of other criminal act
4. No known relationship
5. Unsolved (i.e., no known suspect)

Table 3
Total Murder Incidents[1] and Distribution by Suspect-victim Relationship Types,
by Year and Specified Periods, Canada

		Suspect-victim relationship types				
Year	Total murder incidents	Immediate family	Other kinship	Common-law family	Lovers' quarrel and love triangle	Close acquaintance
1961	173	64	11	12	11	21
1962	196	62	12	12	10	12
1963	192	61	7	13	22	26
1964	199	57	8	15	13	25
1965	216	60	9	19	10	30
1966	206	70	9	15	11	14
1967	239	76	6	17	15	11
1968	292	88	14	19	16	18
1969	320	93	12	20	20	22
1970	354	85	13	23	17	20
1971	395	95	16	30	38	35
1972	412	97	21	33	21	39
1973	447	106	17	46	17	28
1974	499	113	28	45	13	41

		Total	Per cent	Total	Per cent	Total	Per cent	Total	Per cent	Total	Per cent
1961-74	4,140	1,127	27.2	183	4.4	319	7.7	234	5.7	342	8.3
1961-67	1,421	450	31.7	62	4.4	103	7.2	92	6.5	139	9.8
1968-74	2,719	677	24.9	121	4.5	216	7.9	142	5.2	203	7.5

	Casual acquaintance	Business relationship	No known relationship	During commission of another Criminal Act	Unsolved
1961	13	4	11	14	12
1962	20	6	17	22	23
1963	3	1	13	27	19
1964	27	5	13	23	13
1965	25	10	18	23	12
1966	29	9	17	22	10
1967	40	17	8	24	25
1968	41	5	18	34	39
1969	40	9	25	27	52
1970	58	13	25	45	55
1971	37	19	29	41	55
1972	61	9	28	42	61
1973	72	15	31	53	62
1974	76	6	43	47	87

	Total	Per cent	Total	Per cent	Total	Per cent	Total	Per cent	Total	Per cent
1961-74	542	13.1	128	3.1	296	7.1	444	10.7	525	12.7
1961-67	157	11.0	52	3.7	97	6.8	155	10.9	114	8.0
1968-74	385	14.2	76	2.8	199	7.3	289	10.6	411	15.1

[1] Murder incidents counted here are based on the number of original charges of "Capital murder," "Non-capital murder" and "Murder, not specified."

Table 3 presents the distribution, by type, of all murder incidents that have taken place in Canada from 1961 to 1974. The first seven types consist of murder incidents in which previously established social relationships existed between the suspect(s) and victim(s). These seven types comprise 69.5% of all murder incidents over the 14-year period. Murders that take place within the immediate family consistently make up the largest single type—27.2%, while all types of domestic murder (i.e., the combined total of immediate family, other kinship and common-law family sub-types) together comprise 39.3% of all murder incidents. The next most frequent types, close acquaintances (8.3%) and casual acquaintances (13.1%) together account for 21.4% of all murder incidents.

The category "No Known Relationship" accounted for 7.1% of all murder incidents occurring between 1961 and 1974. (This category actually consists of two very different kinds of incidents which have been grouped together for simplification: incidents in which there was enough information about the suspect and victim to say with certainty that there was no social relationship between them, as distinct from the remaining incidents in which there was insufficient information to permit classification; hence the term "no known relationship.")

Another important type, "During Commission of Another Criminal Act", includes *all* murder incidents other than domestic in which another criminal act (e.g., robbery, sexual assault, arson, kidnapping) was the context or the precipitating factor in the murder incident regardless of whether there was any social relationship between suspect and victim. Over the 14-year period, 10.7% of all murder incidents were of this kind. (Of all "during commission" murder incidents in which there was sufficient information to ascertain whether suspect and victim knew or were related to one another, it was found that in 34.5% such an acquaintance or relationship did exist.)

In fact, of all informationally complete murder incidents, 87.1% involved a known prior relationship between suspect(s) and victim(s). This 87.1% is comprised of homicide incidents in which there existed a prior domestic, and social or business suspect-victim relationship (82.7%), and those homicide incidents which occurred during commission of another criminal act in which there was a prior suspect-victim relationship (4.4%). In the remaining 12.9% there was no prior relationship between the suspect and victim, a portion of which (1.2%) were incidents defined as victim-precipitated (see Table 4 for details on this group). There has been no significant change in these percentages over the 14-year period.

"Unsolved" murder incidents is the last category in this set. It includes those murder incidents for which no suspect has been charged by the police but excludes those incidents in which it was physically impossible to charge a suspect with murder (because the suspect left the country or committed suicide, for example). An average of 12.7% of all murders in Canada over the period 1961 to 1974 were unsolved.

TRENDS

Figures in the preceding section clearly illustrate that the number of police-reported murder incidents occurring annually has increased steadily since 1961. This raises the questions, what types of murder are on the increase, and do any particular types account for a disproportionate amount of this increase?

One especially noteworthy aspect of the figures in this study is the general consistency in the distribution of murder incidents by suspect-victim relationship type. A comparison of the distribution (by type) of murder incidents over two seven-year periods of analysis (1961-67, 1968-74) shows signfiicant changes in the proportion of all murder incidents for only two types, "immediate family" and "unsolved." The proportion of murder incidents occurring within the social network of immediately-related family members has significantly decreased, while the proportion of murder incidents that are of other established relationship types has remained relatively stable. The proportion of murder incidents that are unsolved has increased substantially (7.1%) in the last period, almost double the proportion of unsolved incidents in the preceding seven-year period. The proportion of murders occurring during commission of another criminal act has remained stable over the two periods.

These figures indicate that the majority of murders in Canada occur within the context of domestic and social relationships. The relative proportions of these different types of murder have remained comparatively stable over the past fourteen years.

The type for which there is the greatest regional variation and the greatest change between time periods of analysis is the "unsolved" murder incident. Over the fourteen-year period, the Maritimes and the Prairies fall well below the national average of unsolved murder incidents, whereas Quebec's proportion is twice the national average of unsolved incidents and approximately double that of the next highest region, British Columbia. A comparison of the two seven-year periods indicates that the large national increase in the proportion of the unsolved murder incidents is due primarily to large increases in Quebec (where the proportion of unsolved murder incidents has doubled) and British Columbia (where the proportion of unsolved murder incidents has tripled).

To summarize: the largest proportion of all murder incidents in Canada and in each region are those which take place within the context of a prior relationship between suspect and victim. This has not changed significantly since 1961. The only kinds of murder incidents which exhibit a change in relative proportion are domestic murder incidents which have decreased in all regions, and unsolved murder incidents which have risen sharply in Quebec and British Columbia.

These figures present the distribution of different types of murder incidents in Canada for the two periods 1961-67, 1968-74.

Figure 2

Percentage Distribution of Murder Incidents[1] by Suspect Victim Relationship Category, Canada, 1961-1967, 1968-1974

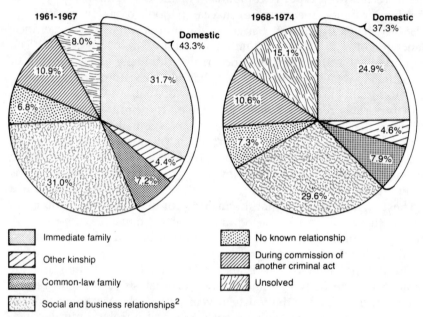

[1] "Murder Incidents" includes all original charges of "Capital Murder." "Non Capital Murder" and "Murder, type not specified."

[2] "Social and Business Relationships" includes "Lovers' Quarrels and Love Triangles," "Close Acquaintances," "Casual Acquaintances" and "Business Relationship."

Characteristics of Persons Involved in Murder and Manslaughter

What kinds of people are involved in murder and manslaughter incidents? What sorts of people are victims, what sorts are suspects? Are they young or old? Male or female? Unmarried or married? With little education or a lot?

Understanding the nature of homicide in Canada requires answers to many such questions and the figures (presented here) provide some of these answers.

Table 4
**Distribution of Homicide Victims by Age and Sex, Canada, 1961-67, 1968-74
and 1961-74**

Period	Age and sex							
	Under 1 year		1-6 years		7-10 years		11-15 years	
	M	F	M	F	M	F	M	F
1961-67:								
Number	16	13	49	46	22	24	21	24
Per cent of total	1.0	0.8	3.1	2.9	1.4	1.5	1.3	1.5
1968-74:								
Number	34	23	69	59	28	34	34	47
Per cent of total	1.1	0.7	2.2	1.9	0.9	1.1	1.1	1.5
1961-74:								
Number	50	36	118	105	50	58	55	71
Per cent of total	1.1	0.8	2.5	2.3	1.1	1.2	1.2	1.5

	16-19 years		20-29 years		30-39 years		40-49 years	
	M	F	M	F	M	F	M	F
1961-67:								
Number	40	50	178	149	193	119	142	119
Per cent of total	2.5	3.2	11.3	9.5	12.2	7.5	9.0	7.5
1968-74:								
Number	138	125	457	294	363	201	333	153
Per cent of total	4.5	4.1	14.9	9.6	11.9	6.6	10.9	5.0
1961-74:								
Number	178	175	635	443	556	320	475	272
Per cent of total	3.8	3.8	13.7	9.6	12.0	6.9	10.2	5.8

	50-59 years		60-69 years		70 years and over		All ages		
	M	F	M	F	M	F	M	F	Total
1961-67:									
Number	117	68	64	29	66	30	910[1]	671	1,582[2]
Per cent of total	7.4	4.3	4.1	1.8	4.2	1.9	57.5	42.4	100.0
1968-74:									
Number	213	109	116	54	117	65	1,907[3]	1,168[4]	3,076[2]
Per cent of total	6.9	3.6	3.8	1.8	3.8	2.1	62.0	38.0	100.0
1961-74:									
Number	330	177	180	83	183	95	2,817[5]	1,839[4]	4,658[6]
Per cent of total	7.1	3.8	3.9	1.8	3.9	2.0	60.5	39.5	100.0

[1] Includes two victims of unknown age.
[2] Includes one victim of unknown age and sex.
[3] Includes five victims of unknown age.
[4] Includes four victims of unknown age.
[5] Includes seven victims of unknown age.
[6] Includes two victims of unknown age and sex.

Figure 3

Percent Distribution of Murder Incidents by Suspect-Victim Relationship, by Region, 1968-1974

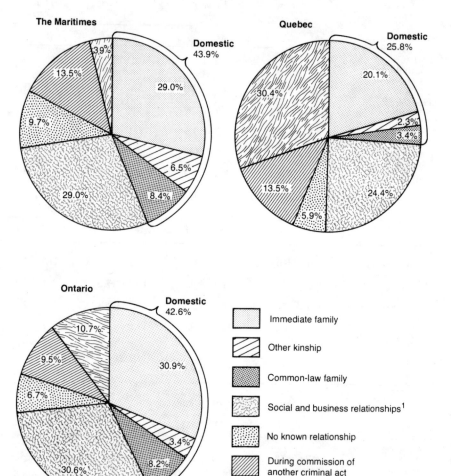

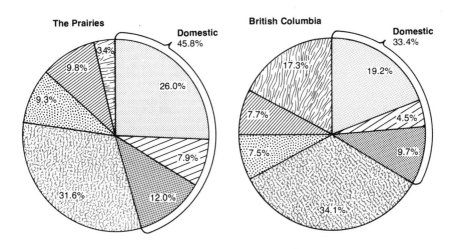

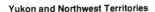

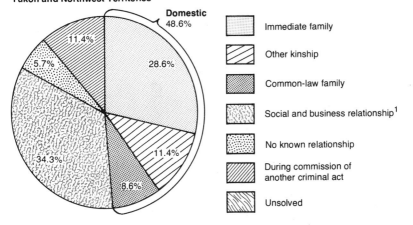

[1] "Social and Business Relationships", includes, "Lovers' Quarrels and Love Triangles," "Close Acquaintances," "Casual Acquaintances," and "Business Relationships."

Note: This shows the proportion of each type of murder incident within each geographic region.

Figure 4

Percentage Distribution of Homicide Victims by Age and Sex,
Canada, 1961-1974

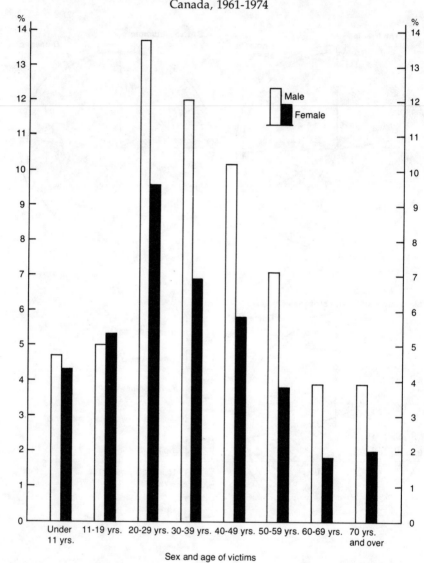

Sex and age of victims

Characteristics of Victims

Table 4 and Figure 4 deal with the characteristics of homicide victims.

Between 1961 and 1974, there were 4,658 victims of homicide in Canada. Six of every ten victims were male, four were female. The proportion of male victims has risen from 57.5% in the 1961-67 period to 62% in the 1968-74 period, with a corresponding decline in the proportion of female victims from 42.4% to 38%.

Over the 14 years, 42.2% of all victims were between 20 and 39 years of age; children under 16 and adults aged 60 years or older comprised nearly one-quarter (23.3%) of all homicide victims.

There has been a distinct decline in recent years in the proportion of all victims who were children under 16, and a distinct increase in the proportion of 16-29 year-old victims.

Male victims outnumber female victims in most age categories, with two exceptions; 7-10 year and 11-15 year-old victims are equally or more likely to be female than male (due in part to the prevalence of sexual assault murders of young females).

Table 5 indicates that persons of particular age and sex characteristics are distinctively likely to be killed in particular kinds of relational circumstances.

Of all female victims, 60% are killed in the context of a domestic relationship. This is more than double the proportion (26.8%) of male victims. These family-situated killings of women are proportionately highest for 40-49 year-old females.

Males are more typically victims of homicide involving a non-domestic relationship, no known relationship, the commission of some other criminal act, or unsolved homicide incidents. Compared to the 40.9% of domestic relationship homicide victims who are male, males comprise 76.4% of the victims of "social or business relationship" homicides, 65.7% of "during commission" homicide victims and 85.7% of "no known relationship" homicide victims; as well, 66.1% of the victims of unsolved homicide incidents are male.

Well over three-quarters of all children victims under the age of 11 years are killed by immediate relatives in family homicides, with no difference in proportion between male and female child victims.

Characteristics of Suspects

Males outnumber females eight to one as homicide suspects; this gap has narrowed slightly in recent years, though.

The largest single group of homicide suspects was that of 20-29 year-old males, who made up one-third of all suspects between 1961 and 1974. As well, this largest single group of suspects has increased considerably in recent years, growing from 29.8% of all suspects in 1961-67 to

Table 5
Age and Sex of Homicide
Victims by Relationship of Suspect to Victim, Canada, 1961-74

Relationship of suspect to victim		Age and sex of victim											
		Under 1 year		1-6 years		7-10 years		11-15 years		16-19 years		20-29 years	
		M	F	M	F	M	F	M	F	M	F	M	F
Domestic relationship, total	No.	45	32	94	84	31	35	32	25	32	42	109	248
	%	90.0	88.9	79.7	80.0	62.0	60.3	58.2	35.2	18.0	24.0	17.2	56.0
Immediate family	No.	44	29	83	72	26	31	28	19	18	29	66	170
	%	88.0	80.5	70.4	68.6	52.0	53.4	50.9	26.8	10.1	16.6	10.4	38.4
Other kinship	No.	—	2	6	6	5	4	4	3	14	—	29	9
	%		5.6	5.1	5.7	10.0	6.9	7.3	4.2	7.9		4.6	2.0
Common-law family	No.	1	1	5	6	—	—	—	3	—	13	14	69
	%	2.0	2.8	4.2	5.7				4.2		7.4	2.2	15.6
Social or business relationship	No.	4	1	11	12	6	6	10	6	85	58	280	92
	%	8.0	2.8	9.3	11.4	12.0	10.3	18.2	8.5	47.7	33.2	44.1	20.8
During commission of other Criminal Act	No.	—	—	5	5	7	11	6	25	16	30	61	32
	%			4.2	4.8	14.0	19.0	10.9	35.2	9.0	17.1	9.6	7.2
No known relationship	No.	—	—	6	1	4	4	3	4	30	8	81	15
	%			5.1	1.0	8.0	6.9	5.4	1.6	16.9	4.6	12.7	3.4
Unsolved	No.	1	3	2	3	2	2	4	11	15	37	104	56
	%	2.0	8.3	1.7	2.8	4.0	3.5	7.3	15.5	8.4	21.1	16.4	12.6
Total	No.	50	36	118	105	50	58	55	71	178	175	635	443
	%	100.0	100.0	100.0	100.0	100.0	100.0	100.0	100.0	100.0	100.0	100.0	100.0

		30-39 years		40-49 years		50-59 years		60-69 years		70 years and over		All ages		
		M	F	M	F	M	F	M	F	M	F	M	F	Total
Domestic relationship, total	No.	132	232	132	208	81	111	27	44	37	27	753[1]	1,089[1]	1,842
	%	23.7	72.5	27.8	76.5	24.5	62.7	15.0	53.0	20.2	28.5	26.8	59.2	39.6
Immediate family	No.	69	157	76	140	59	79	15	37	70	22	504	786[1]	1,290
	%	12.4	49.0	16.0	51.5	17.9	44.6	8.4	44.6	10.9	23.2	17.9	42.7	27.7
Other kinship	No.	34	5	30	9	16	7	6	5	17	5	162[1]	55	217
	%	6.1	1.6	6.3	3.3	4.8	4.0	3.3	6.0	9.3	5.3	5.8	3.0	4.7
Common-law family	No.	29	70	26	59	6	25	6	2	—	—	87	248	335
	%	5.2	21.9	5.5	21.7	1.8	14.1	3.3	2.4	—	—	3.1	13.5	7.2
Social or business relationship	No.	232	45	171	33	123	32	67	14	39	19	1,028	318	1,346
	%	41.7	14.1	36.0	12.1	37.3	18.1	37.3	16.9	21.3	20.0	36.5	17.3	28.9
During commission of other Criminal Act	No.	48	16	51	13	49	14	51	14	71	31	367[2]	192[1]	559
	%	8.7	5.0	10.7	4.8	14.8	7.9	28.3	16.9	38.8	32.6	13.0	10.4	12.0
No known relationship	No.	59	3	55	4	25	4	15	4	15	2	293	49	342
	%	10.6	0.9	11.6	1.5	7.6	2.3	8.3	4.8	8.2	2.1	10.4	2.7	7.3
Unsolved	No.	85	24	66	14	52	16	20	7	21	16	376[3]	191[2]	569[4]
	%	15.3	7.5	13.9	5.1	15.8	9.0	11.1	8.4	11.5	16.8	13.3	10.4	12.2
Total	No.	556	320	475	272	330	177	180	83	183	95	2,817[5]	1,839[3]	4,658[4]
	%	100.0	100.0	100.0	100.0	100.0	100.0	100.0	100.0	100.0	100.0	100.0	100.0	100.0

[1] Includes one victim of unknown age.
[2] Includes two victims of unknown age.
[3] Includes four victims of unknown age.
[4] Includes two victims of unknown age and sex.
[5] Includes seven victims of unknown age.

35.4% in 1968-74. The percentage of suspects in the 16-19 year-old group has increased significantly, too, especially for females.

In all other age categories, males have declined in their proportions of all homicide suspects, and females have increased.

The growth of the 16-19 and 20-29 year-old groups is partly a product of the post-war "baby boom." As the large numbers of persons born immediately after World War II move into their late teens and twenties, there would naturally be an increase in the proportion of all homicide suspects who are between 16 and 29 years of age because of the enlarged population of potential offenders.

LEGAL PROCEEDINGS AND COURT DISPOSITIONS OF PERSONS CHARGED WITH MURDER

What happens to persons charged with murder? How many are sent to trial? What proportion are ultimately found guilty of murder? What kinds of sentences are imposed by the courts on these convicted murderers? And what happens to the others who are not convicted of murder?

The answers to these and other related questions are important for what they tell us about the manner in which Canada's justice system responds to incidents of homicide. And since only courts may specify whether a killing was a murder, a manslaughter, or neither, some of these answers are strategic for the statistical purpose of estimating the rate of murder in particular and homicide in general.

In the fourteen years between 1961 and 1974, 4,606 persons in Canada were reported by police as having been killed by another person in 4,140 separate incidents.

Four thousand two hundred and thirty-five adults and juveniles were suspected by police of having committed these murders. Of these, 83.2% were adult males, 11.0% were adult females, 5.3% juvenile males and 0.5% juvenile females.

By far the largest proportion of adult suspects* was cleared by charge—88.6%. The remaining 11.4% of adult suspects were cleared otherwise or by suicide before being charged.

By the end of December 31, 1974, of the total number of adults charged with murder, 6.1% were awaiting their preliminary hearing, 0.4% never reached the preliminary hearing stage, and 93.5% had completed their preliminary hearing.

What happened after the preliminary hearing? Seven point four per cent of the adults were not sent to trial or had no result of the preliminary hearing known for them and 92.6% were bound over for trial.

Figure 5

Incidents, Victims and Legal Status of Murder Suspects Prior to and After
Preliminary Hearing, Canada, 1961-1974

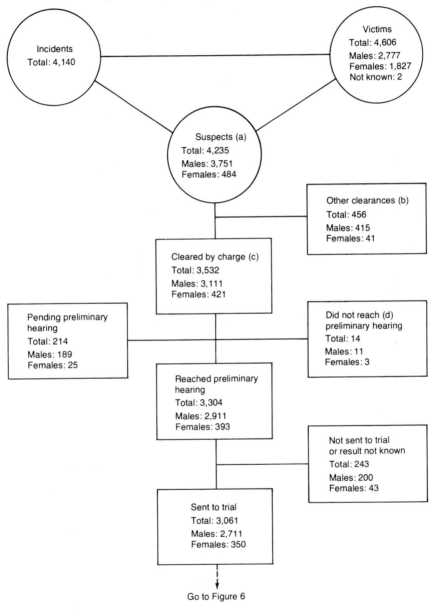

Go to Figure 6

(a) Includes 3,988 adult and 247 juvenile suspects.
(b) Includes only adult suspects who were cleared otherwise or who committed suicide after the offence.
(c) All subsequent figures will pertain only to adult suspects.
(d) Includes those adult suspects who committed suicide after being charged, who died of natural causes after being charged, as well as those who had their charge(s) withdrawn before preliminary hearing.

Figure 6
Legal Status of Adult Suspects Originally Charged with Murder and
Sent to Trial, Canada, 1961-1974

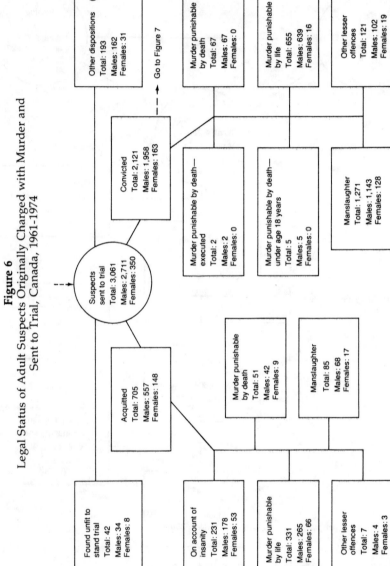

Figure 6 indicates the outcome of court proceedings for adults originally charged with murder who were sent to trial. (Note, though, that their original charge may have been reduced before going to trial, so not all were tried for murder.)

One point four per cent of all adult suspects were found unfit to stand trial, while 23.0% were acquitted and 69.3% were convicted.

Of the 705 adults who were acquitted, 54.2% were acquitted of murder (either punishable by death or punishable by life imprisonment). Almost 33% of the suspects were acquitted on account of insanity and 13% were acquitted of a reduced charge of manslaughter or of some lesser offence.

Of those adults convicted between 1961 and 1974, 60% were convicted of a reduced charge of manslaughter. Only 34.4% of the suspects were convicted of murder.

What kinds of final sentences were given to those adults who were convicted? While 64 adults were sentenced to death (3% of all convicted adults), only two were actually executed and most of the others had had their death sentences commuted to life imprisonment by the end of December 1974.

Overall, 30.9% of the convicted adults received a sentence of life imprisonment, 15.1% received a sentence of ten years or longer, 21.5% received a sentence of between five and under ten years, and 14.9% received a sentence of between two years and under five years.

It has been noted repeatedly throughout this report that only courts are empowered to decide positively whether a death reported as a murder was a murder or a manslaughter or neither. These summary statistics show that a diminishing proportion of deaths initially reported by police to be murder offences (and a consequent diminishing proportion of murder charges) are ultimately specified by the courts (in a murder conviction) to have been murder; an increasing proportion of reported murders, however, are ultimately defined to have been some kind of homicide (through a conviction for either murder or manslaughter). It is clear, too, that when final court dispositions are taken as the most stringent measure of the number of murders and used as the basis for calculating the rate of murder, this murder conviction rate has shown a much smaller increase in recent years than has the rate of police-reported murders; while the average murder conviction rate during the 1968-73 period was 34.8% greater than during the 1961-67 period, the corresponding increase in the police-reported murder rate was 64.1%. The actual change in the true rate of murder lies somewhere between these two extremes, since the police-reported rate of murder is higher than the true murder rate, and the rate based on court convictions is almost certainly lower than the true murder rate.

Figure 7
Final Sentence of Adult Suspects Sent to Trial, Canada, 1961-1974

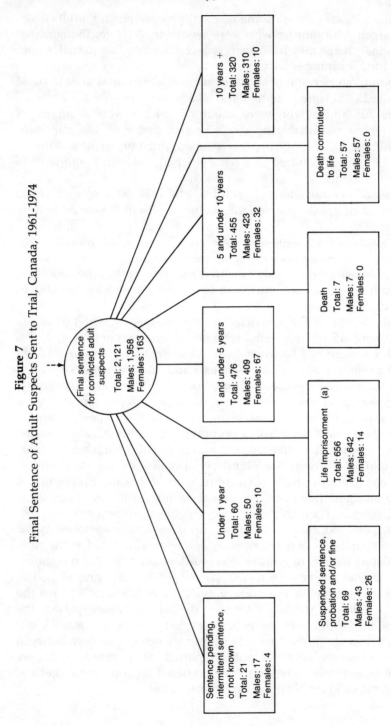

Final sentence for convicted adult suspects

Total: 2,121
Males: 1,958
Females: 163

10 years +
Total: 320
Males: 310
Females: 10

5 and under 10 years
Total: 455
Males: 423
Females: 32

Death commuted to life
Total: 57
Males: 57
Females: 0

1 and under 5 years
Total: 476
Males: 409
Females: 67

Death
Total: 7
Males: 7
Females: 0

Under 1 year
Total: 60
Males: 50
Females: 10

Life Imprisonment (a)
Total: 656
Males: 642
Females: 14

Suspended sentence, probation and/or fine
Total: 69
Males: 43
Females: 26

Sentence pending, intermittent sentence, or not known
Total: 21
Males: 17
Females: 4

(a) Total includes 5 males under age 18 years who were convicted of murder punishable by death and received automatic life sentences.

Table 6
Summary Statistics on Convictions Arising Out of Murder Charges in Canada, by Year, 1961-73

Year	Total convictions[1]		Convictions for murder				
	Number	Per cent of persons tried	Number	Per cent of reported murder offences	Per cent of persons charged	Per cent of persons tried	Per cent of total convictions
1961	80	58.0	31	16.8	21.2	22.5	38.8
1962	88	66.7	42	19.4	28.8	31.8	47.7
1963	111	64.5	46	21.4	23.5	26.7	41.4
1964	118	73.8	53	24.3	29.9	33.1	44.9
1965	129	75.9	54	22.2	28.0	31.8	41.9
1966	120	63.2	41	18.5	19.9	21.6	34.2
1967	136	73.9	42	14.9	21.5	22.8	30.9
1968	171	69.8	36	11.4	13.2	14.7	21.1
1969	200	74.1	60	17.3	21.0	22.2	30.0
1970	214	71.8	59	13.6	18.1	19.8	27.6
1971	252	75.4	83	19.5	22.6	24.9	32.9
1972	259	74.9	78	16.3	19.8	22.5	30.1
1973	250	73.1	82	17.1	19.7	24.0	32.8
1961-73	2,128	71.4	707	17.4	21.3	23.7	33.2
1961-67	782	68.2	309	19.5	24.5	27.0	39.5
1968-73	1,346	73.4	398	16.1	19.3	21.7	29.6

Year	Convictions for manslaughter			Homicide[2] convictions		Conviction rates[3] for murder and homicide[2]		Convictions for other lesser offences	
	Number	Per cent of persons tried	Per cent of total convic-tions	Number	Per cent of persons tried	Murder	Homi-cide[2]	Number	Per cent of total convic-tions
1961	42	30.4	52.5	73	52.9	0.17	0.40	5	6.3
1962	43	32.6	48.9	85	64.4	0.23	0.46	1	1.1
1963	58	33.7	52.3	104	60.5	0.24	0.55	4	3.6
1964	60	37.5	50.9	113	70.6	0.28	0.59	4	3.4
1965	62	36.5	48.1	116	68.2	0.28	0.59	8	6.2
1966	68	35.8	56.7	109	57.4	0.21	0.55	10	8.3
1967	86	46.7	63.2	128	69.6	0.21	0.63	6	4.4
1968	111	45.3	64.9	147	60.0	0.17	0.71	14	8.2
1969	124	45.9	62.0	184	68.1	0.29	0.88	8	4.0
1970	131	44.0	61.2	190	63.8	0.28	0.89	14	6.5
1971	149	44.6	59.1	232	69.5	0.39	1.08	17	6.8
1972	166	48.0	64.1	244	70.5	0.36	1.12	9	3.5
1973	149	43.6	59.6	231	67.5	0.37	1.05	16	6.4
1961-73	1,249	41.9	58.7	1,956	65.6	0.27	0.74	116	5.5
1961-67	419	36.6	53.6	728	63.5	0.23	0.54	38	4.9
1968-73	830	45.2	61.7	1,228	66.9	0.31	0.96	78	5.8

[1] "Total convictions" includes all convictions for murder, for manslaughter, and for other lesser offences, in cases of persons originally charged with murder. This total includes some juveniles for whom Statistics Canada does not have information on the particular type of conviction they received. Thus, in some years the "Total convictions" figure may not equal the sum of the specific types of conviction.

[2] Homicide here refers to murder and manslaughter together but does not include infanticide.

[3] Per 100,000 population.

SUMMARY

1. Increases in the rate of murder and other kinds of homicide in recent years have been moderate in comparison with increases in some other types of violent crime. The murder rate in 1974, for example, was 2.4 offences per 100,000 population, an increase of 9% over 1973, whereas the rate of wounding increased 10.7% and the rate of reported rape increased 13%. While there has clearly been a real increase in the incidence of homicide, increases in the murder rate appear to be due in part to changes in the manner in which police lay charges in cases involving killing. (These changes in the charging practices of police may be associated with changes in the law pertaining to murder.) The use of the charge of manslaughter by police has decreased considerably and murder charges are increasingly more likely to be laid initially but subsequently reduced before or during trial. A large and rising proportion of killings initially considered by police to be murders are thus ultimately found by the courts to be manslaughters or some other type of lesser criminal offence; the percentage of murder charges resulting in convictions for murder has actually been declining, whereas the percentage of murder charges resulting in manslaughter convictions is increasing. (Overall, the rate of conviction for murder and manslaughter together is rising.) The rate of reported murders is therefore an incomplete and imperfect indicator of the true extent of *murder*; it is nonetheless a reasonably reliable indicator of the rate of *homicide* in Canada.

2. Throughout the 1961-74 period, there has been great consistency in the proportion of all homicide incidents represented by each of the suspect-victim relationship types, with two exceptions. Unsolved murder incidents have increased disproportionately and the proportion of immediate family murder incidents has declined significantly. On average, domestic homicide incidents of all kinds make up 39.3% of all incidents, social or business relationship homicide incidents constitute 30.1%, homicide incidents occurring during the commission of another criminal act account for 10.7%, and homicides involving no known relationship between suspect and victim account for 7.1%. Unsolved homicide incidents represent 12.7% of the total. Other circumstantial factors such as the method of commission exhibit a similar consistency.

3. There appears to be a trend away from homicide being concentrated in Canada's largest urban centers (where formerly the great majority of homicides occurred) toward a greater dispersion of homicide across the country in urban and rural areas. This is particularly true for murder occurring during commission of another criminal act. Montreal remains an exception to this trend.

4. Fewer than one of every ten victims in solved homicide incidents

since 1961 have been uninvolved and probably innocent strangers and this percentage is declining.

	Number of incidents involving no known suspect-victim relationship	Percentage of total incidents
1961-67	143	10.06
1968-74	264	9.70
1961-74	407	9.83

The proportion of solved homicide incidents in which the suspect and victim had a previously established social relationship of some kind has remained consistently high; more than 90% of all homicide victims in solved incidents were related to or acquainted with their killer.

Since in 1974 the chances of a person in Canada being killed by an act of criminal homicide were approximately 24 in a million, the chances of being killed by a stranger were about two in a million.

5. Shooting is by far the most prevalent method of killing in homicide incidents—in 43.7% of all incidents since 1961. It occurred most frequently in murder incidents where the suspect and victim were linked in a domestic or social relationship. Beating was the method of commission in 22.3% of all homicide cases, and stabbing was the method in 18.3% of all cases.

6. Alcohol use is especially prevalent as a factor in homicides involving a domestic or social relationship. The use of other drugs as a factor in homicide incidents remains relatively rare.

7. Domestic or family killings are an especially distinct type of homicide. The majority of multiple-victim and murder-suicide homicide incidents take place in the context of a domestic relationship, for example.

8. Part of the rise in homicides is due to individuals establishing or entering a set of social and physical circumstances which unwittingly lead to a violent end. There are two major examples of this. First, there are those persons who consume alcohol and/or other drugs which reduce their ability to control aggressive behaviour, and in this same situation their alcohol/drug-modified behaviour appears to produce a heightened level of conflict with other persons nearby; this conflict prompts, in the absence of normal self-control of behaviour, a high incidence of violent aggression. This aggression is frequently facilitated by the availability of a lethal weapon such as a gun, or to a lesser extent a knife. The second example consists of cases in which an individual sets out to commit a property/monetary crime (breaking and entry, or robbery and thereby involves himself in a sequence of events which he is unable to anticipate or control (such as being caught in the act or

attacked by the victim); his response to these events is one of panicky, uncontrolled aggression, he (typically) attempts to shoot or fight his way out of the situation. The rise in the rate of homicides committed in the course of a property/monetary crime could be the product, to a substantial degree, of the rising rate of property/monetary crimes in general.

There is other evidence which suggests that the rise in homicides committed during commission of another criminal act is the result of an "overflow" from or a partial consequence of the increase in other types of criminal offences. Property/monetary crime-related homicides manifest the following features: (i) The majority of suspects in such cases are young and the trend indicates that they are getting younger; 78% of suspects in these cases are under 30 years of age and 28% are under 20; (ii) in approximately 50% of robbery homicides the suspect panics or is attacked or resisted by the victim; (iii) the type of victim or establishment robbed is not of the same kind as that robbed by the professional criminal; (typically it is cab drivers and small stores); (iv) in 90.4% of homicides which occurred during the breaking and entry of homes or businesses, the suspect was surprised or discovered by the victim and used whatever was available as a weapon to kill the victim.

In only a small proportion of these incidents was the weapon brought onto the premises by the suspect and in only one incident was the victim killed while sleeping and therefore uninvolved.

The rise in sexual assault killings of adults also appears to be a product or overflow of the large increase in rape and other sexual assault cases in Canada, particularly in the most recent seven-year period (1968-74). Two further points are noteworthy: first, in 62.7% of the sexual assault homicides of adults, the suspect and victim knew each other prior to the incident and were involved socially at the time of the incident; second, the consumption of alcohol has been a factor in a rather large proportion of such cases in recent years, 45.5% of the cases in the 1968-74 period. Homicide incidents of this type exhibit considerable similarity (in circumstances) to incidents of the social relationship types, "close acquaintances" and "casual acquaintances."

9. A small but growing factor in homicide incidents is the trend toward more Canadians acting aggressively or violently to protect themselves when attacked or intruded upon.

10. Homicides defined by the police as "gangland" killings represent a small proportion of all homicide incidents; 185 of 4,140 murder incidents (or 4.5%) between 1961 and 1974. However, this type of murder incident is increasing rapidly, primarily in Quebec and to a lesser degree in British Columbia. The percentage of murder incidents defined as "gangland" which are unsolved is exceptionally high, averaging approximately 80%. The per cent increase in this type of murder inci-

dent is a significant contributing factor to the doubling of the average percentage of murder incidents unsolved in Canada in 1968-74 compared to 1961-67. In the latter period 29.9% of unsolved incidents were labelled "gangland" compared to 19.3% of unsolved murder incidents in the 1961-67 period.

11. The incidence of murder of policemen and prison guards in Canada has not kept pace with the general increase in murder or homicide incidents, but has instead remained quite stable over the 14-year period from 1961 to 1974. Stated differently, the ratio of policemen and prison employee victims to all homicide victims has decreased slightly over this 14-year period.

12. Suspects in homicides are males by a wide margin. In all solved incidents other than immediate family and common-law family homicides, males are suspects in over 90% of the incidents. In these two family types, males are suspects in more than 75% of the incidents.

13. Suspects are mostly young (under 30 years of age) and the trend is toward a growing proportion of all suspects being even younger. The age groups which have shown disproportionate increases are 20-29 years and 16-19 years. Suspects in these age groups are more likely than other suspects to be convicted of murder.

14. Sixty per cent of all persons (adults and juveniles) charged with murder between 1961 and 1974 were eventually convicted of some offence as of December 31, 1974.

15. More than three-quarters of all suspects in solved homicide incidents initially defined by the police (i.e., in terms of the initial charge laid) as murder were *not* found by the courts to have been guilty of murder. Of all persons charged with murder in the years 1961-74, only 20% were convicted of murder, whereas 35% were convicted of manslaughter and 3% of another lesser offence. (Two per cent of suspects were juveniles adjudged in juvenile court to be delinquent.) This ratio of murder cases to manslaughter cases remains relatively constant when only convicted persons (rather than all persons charged) are considered. Of all persons charged with murder and convicted of some offence committed between 1961 and 1974, 34% were convicted of murder, 58% were convicted of manslaughter, 6% of another lesser offence and 2% were adjudged to be delinquent.

16. Court dispositions, verdicts and sentences, vary widely for different types and circumstances of homicide incidents. Forty-four per cent of suspects charged with a murder (between 1961 and 1974) which occurred during commission of another criminal act were convicted of murder and sentenced to death or life imprisonment. Cases of this type

account for a disproportionately high percentage of all convictions for murder; as shown in the following table, the proportion of persons suspected of "during commission" murders who are convicted is more than twice that of any other relationship category. In cases where there was a prior social or business relationship between suspect(s) and victim(s), 17% of the suspects were convicted of murder, but this figure drops to 11% for suspects in domestic homicides.

A comparison of court dispositions for sexual assault murders of adults with dispositions for victim-precipitated murders involving no known suspect-victim relationship illustrates the variability of court dispositions for two types of homicide. Seventy-four per cent of suspects charged with sexual assault murders were convicted of some offence and imprisoned, compared to 51% of suspects in victim-precipitated (no known relationship) cases. A closer examination reveals that such dispositions as "adjudged insane" are given to a greater proportion of suspects not sent to prison for sexual assault murders, and that persons convicted of sexual assault murders receive much harsher sentences than those persons convicted of some offence as a result of a "no known relationship", victim-precipitated killing.

1961-1974

Type	Percentage of total suspects charged with murder	Percentage of all convictions for some offence	Percentage of convictions for murder	Percentage of convictions for man-slaughter
Domestic	34.9	32.6	19.8	39.6
Social and business	36.4	37.7	31.4	41.8
During commission of another Criminal Act	17.8	20.1	39.0	10.1

17. It appears that in general the more distant the suspect-victim relationship is, the more severe will be the sentence.

18. When charged with murder, males receive different court dispositions and sentences than females. For example, females have a disproportionately higher likelihood of being adjudged insane, of being acquitted, or if convicted, of being convicted of manslaughter or a lesser offence. Males have a higher probability of being convicted of murder, and of receiving a more severe sentence.

19. Compared to adult suspects, a higher proportion of juvenile suspects (tried in adult court) receive life sentences.

20. A very high rate of success on parole has been exhibited by persons convicted of murder punishable by death and murder punishable by life

imprisonment. Since 1920 only one person convicted of murder and subsequently paroled was involved in a new murder for which he was convicted. Since 1920, only ten persons convicted of murder who were paroled were involved in other crimes "against the person" while on parole. Of the large number of persons convicted of manslaughter and paroled between 1961 and 1974, only three were implicated (two convicted of manslaughter, one pending trial) in another homicide while on parole.

21. Between 1961 and 1974, five persons once convicted of murder were again involved in and convicted of some offence for a new subsequent homicide. Three of the second homicides occurred in prison (with fellow prisoners as the victims) and two occurred while the murderer was at large after escaping custody (one of these victims was a criminal partner of the murderer).

During this same period seven persons once convicted of manslaughter were again involved in and convicted of some offence for a new subsequent homicide. One of the second homicides occurred in prison (a fellow prisoner was the victim), one occurred while the accused was at large after escaping custody (the victim was an acquaintance), three occurred after the expiration of the initial sentence of the accused and two occurred while the accused was on parole for the initial manslaughter conviction.

Of the total of four persons implicated in a second homicide which occurred while they were in prison, three were implicated in the killing of a convicted sex offender during the riot in Kingston penitentiary in 1971.

22. The other group of suspects involved in more than one murder incident, those persons who kill on more than one occasion before being apprehended, exhibited clearly pathological behaviour. While their total number is small (31 out of 4,235 suspects between 1961 and 1974), the evidence of consistent pathological character is strong. Out of the 31 cases, eight suspects were involved exclusively in sex-related homicides, another eight suspects were adjudged insane, while in a further eight cases the suspects were involved solely in gangland murders of persons involved in some way in criminal activities.

APPENDIX

Definitions:

Homicide: A general category which includes any act in which the life of one person is lost at the hands of another person. Includes capital murder, non capital murder, murder-type not specified, manslaughter, and infanticide as defined and reported by the police.

Manslaughter:	Manslaughter is culpable homicide that is not murder, infanticide, or death caused by criminal negligence.
Murder:	Prior to September 1961, all murder was considered capital and the only possible sentence was the death penalty. After September 1961, it was divided into capital and non-capital murder. Capital murder was premeditated murder or the murder of a police officer, prison guard, etc., or murder during the commission of another criminal act. The penalty was death. All other types of murder were considered non-capital, and were punished by mandatory life imprisonment. In December 1967, the Criminal Code sections dealing with murder were amended again, this time for a five-year trial period. Capital murder then referred only to the murder of a "law officer, warden," etc. The required penalty was death. Non-capital murder referred to all other kinds. Life imprisonment is the minimum penalty. This trial period was extended for another five years in 1973 and the legal terms "capital murder" and "non-capital murder" were changed to "murder punishable by death" and "murder punishable by life imprisonment" respectively.

"Murder, type not specified", indicates that in some cases the type of murder is not specified because the police for a number of reasons are unable to charge (or occasionally to apprehend) the suspected offender(s). Nearly all of these "murder, type not specified" cases involve suspects who committed suicide before being charged.

NOTES

* Because juvenile suspects in murder incidents are treated differently under Canadian law than adult suspects and because juvenile suspects in this study were relatively few in number, the analysis here is concerned almost exclusively with adults.

PART FOUR

VIOLENCE AND THE MEDIA

Chapter 12

THE VIOLENCE
OF THE MEDIA

Marshall McLuhan

If one is to understand McLuhan with any clarity, the propensity to relate cause and effect must be reshaped, or perhaps set aside. The avoidance of theoretical preconceptions is the key to overcoming statics and moving on to the simultaneous effect of process and pattern. McLuhanism will not fit neatly into any established theoretical construct and for purposes of academic discussion his approach has come to be known as "The McLuhan System."[1]

The violence of television is the violence of all electric media. It is the invasion of privacy and theft of personal identity. For him, content has nothing to do with the activity of the media and quantitative analysis cannot study change. The views of Canada's heavyweight intellectual contrast sharply with both his predecessors and followers. A philosopher of popular culture, he believes that television for the unready is a psychic disaster comparable to giving rum to primitives.[2] "Television action reverses the age-old pattern of American life by which we go outside to be alone and inside to be with people. (Every other culture in the world goes outside to be with people—to enjoy community—and inside to be alone."[3])

He is interested not in the manner in which the media transmits, but in the manner in which it transforms, for communication is transformation, not transportation. He is looking for an understanding of the real questions, not for answers. As he once stated, "I don't explain, I explore."

"The Kingdom of Heaven suffereth violence." Violence against the Kingdom of Heaven proceeds by prayer and petition, prayer being one of the more extreme forms of violence, since it is conducted by superhuman force. It should not be surprising, therefore, that the ages of the utmost physical violence have also produced the greatest exemplars of heroic sanctity, as in the sixteenth century, and also today. Violence means the violation of territories, whether political or psychic, physical or moral. *The Listener* (December 75/January 76) records a discussion on pornographic violence under the head "No victim, no pornography":

* This paper is reprinted with permission of the author and *The Canadian Forum*. It was originally written for *The Canadian Forum*, September, 1976, Vol. LV1, No. 664, p. 9.

. . . How, in the age of Marxism, socialism, liberation, have we all come to be landed with de Sade? There's another very important thing to say here. To you and me, sexual meaning is meeting and entering the body of another person in the closest creative intimacy. The pervert—that is, the person to whom this has no meaning, who needs pornography—doesn't understand the meaning of sexuality. He needs to penetrate the body of the other person in order to find whether there is any meaning in there, just like a child sticking its needle in a teddy bear.

To invade the private person, or to invade a group with teaching, with doctrines, with entertainment, all these are alike forms of violence. To assume the right to program the sensibilities or thoughts and fantasies of individuals or groups, has long been taken for granted as a viable form of personal or social action. The private educator as much as the college of propaganda in Rome, assumes a mandate to shape individuals and societies in any age.

Today, however, there is a new dimension in all of these activities. Electric media move information and people at the speed of light. It is this instant and total quality that constitutes the condition of mass man and the mass society, an effect that occurs not so much by virtue of size as speed of involvement and inclusiveness. Moreover, the hidden dimension in all electric media, whether the telephone, TV, or radio, is that *the sender is sent*. When you are on the phone, or on the air, you can be anywhere and everywhere at the same moment.

The violence that all electric media inflict on their users is that they are instantly invaded and deprived of their physical bodies and are merged in a network of extensions of their own nervous systems. As if this were not sufficient violence or invasion of individual rights, the elimination of the physical bodies of the electric media users also deprives them of the means of relating the program experience to their private individual selves, even as instant involvement suppresses private identity.

The loss of individual and personal meaning via the electronic media ensures a corresponding and reciprocal violence from those so deprived of their identities; for violence, whether spiritual or physical, is a quest for identity and the meaningful. The less identity, the more violence. Violence exerted by private individuals tends to have limited results, whereas the violence exerted by groups knows no bounds. Media are always and necessarily corporate or group activities, whether they are the mother tongues or the father images of big corporations. With the proliferation of multi-media in our time, there is a new consensus that some manner of media ecology and control be put into action; but against this proposal there is a negative and hidden factor in the Western world. Edward Hall, the anthropologist, has drawn attention to this negative attitude in the Western world in a recent study, *The Fourth Dimension in Architecture: The Impact of Building on Man's Behaviour:*

The most pervasive and important assumption, a cornerstone in the edifice of Western thought, is one that lies hidden from our consciousness and has to do with man's relationship to his environment. Quite simply the Western view is that human processes, particularly behaviour, are independent of environmental controls and influence.

The obsessional concern of Western man with "content" and the correlative indifference to hidden environmental or side effects, stems from the very character of Western literacy. This is easy to observe by contrasting our scepticism about general or environmental effects with the attitudes of preliterate or non-literate societies of the Third World. In his *The Savage Mind* Levi-Strauss discusses the pervasive feeling of non-visual cultures that every kind of change effects everything else, adding that this kind of awareness is pure paranoia. Literate, or visual man, in contrast, has to be *shown* every kind of relationship. Visuality favours quantification and exact measurement and is not inclined to listen to the protests of the Chinese that telephone poles deeply disturb their entire psychic balance. It is true that Plato at the end of *The Republic* mentions that any change in musical rhythms could cause a political revolution: but jazz and Rock and jets are accepted as natural phenomena which could not disturb the psyche or sanity of a literate man. The "content" of any work, philosophical or physical, is the *efficient* cause in the situation. The *formal* cause concerns the effects proceeding from the total structure of the situation, which includes the public and the users. It is the *formal* cause which constitutes the environmental violence, the side effects of the media.

Harold Innis was one of the very few people since Plato to show serious interest in formal causes and the effects that result from the formal structures of total situations. The numerous commissions on violence that have marked our violent time have, without exception, paid attention only to the *efficient* cause, the program content of the media. The effects of the media themselves represent a form of violence so vast as to be unnoticed. It is a situation not unlike that in the old rhyme:

> You hang the thief
> Who steals the goose
>   from off the common,
> But leave the larger felon loose
> Who steals the common
>   from the goose.

In *Identity, Youth and Crisis* Erik H. Erikson observes:

> In Jung's "persona" a weak ego seems to sell out to a compelling social prototype. A fake ego identity is established which suppresses rather than synthesizes those experiences and functions which endanger the "front".

In *The Nuremberg Mind*, F. R. Miale and Michael Selzer, in search of understanding how the Nazi leaders could seem to be ordinary, well-intentioned people, encountered the fact that:

> . . . values, and behaviour of individuals are shaped by social forces beyond our control—and often, indeed, beyond our recognition.

The forces which are typically "beyond our recognition" are the environmental or diffused forces, what we ordinarily take for granted as the existing social services of the media, whether they be highways or airways. Since visual, rational man can find no "connection" between such forces and their victims, he throws up his hands in mystification. Radio had a fantastic and profound effect in retrieving the ordinary tribal consciousness of Germany in the 1920s and 1930s. TV, which is an addictive inner trip (regardless of program), sent American youth in pursuit of the occult and group awareness. Since there are no visual or quantifiable *connections* between radio and TV and their effects, Western man humbly and dumbly submits to their magic. What Miale and Selzer found by way of analogue for the monstrous behaviour of the Nazi leaders relates to the case of the psychological study at Yale undertaken by Stanley Milgram who "sought to discover the extent to which human beings will obey commands which come increasingly into conflict with their consciences." The teachers chosen for the job proceeded to demonstrate experimental shocks to subjects as part of a memory test:

> Sweating, trembling, and in other ways indicating their extreme reluctance to continue administering the punishments, 65 percent of the teachers nevertheless obeyed orders all the way to the end of the scale on the shock generator! Not a single teacher disobeyed the experimenter's orders before reaching 300 volts—marked INTENSE SHOCK—and only 12.5 percent of them stopped at this point.

Milgram concluded:

> When the individual is on his own, conscience is brought into play. But when he functions in an organized mode, directions that come from the higher level component are not assessed against the internal standards of moral judgment. . . . The psychology of obedience does not depend on the placement within the larger hierarchy: . . . The social psychology of this century reveals a major lesson: often, it is not so much the kind of person a man is as the kind of situation in which he finds himself that determines how he will act.

Since the kind of situations in which twentieth century man exists are almost entirely products of the mass media, we have to face the further fact that these situations are beyond the ken of Western awareness. Western literate man is easily inclined to make moral protests, but is seemingly incapable of recognizing the *formal* or "acoustic" structure of situations which are disturbing and destroying him.

The group, or the crowd, has minimal identity and exists in a state of paranoic anxiety about any threats to its precarious pattern. In his classic work *Crowds and Power* Elias Canetti explains that all kinds of crowds experience a need to get bigger, and also fear that they are getting smaller. This passion can extend to money (one kind of crowd), as much as to the mindless group. The formal effects of the electric media in invading individuals and groups are in no way limited by the content or the programs so purveyed. The effects of the car are felt in the highways, factories and oil companies, or the service environment. The service environment constituted by electric networks acts as a kind of *formal* cause, or hidden *ground*. That which appears or is noticed is only the efficient cause. The Greeks gave no heed to the effects of the phonetic alphabet which transformed their inner and outer lives, ending the bardic colleges which had long served as their educational establishment. Like ourselves, the Greeks had a strong visual bias toward efficient causality and ethics and applied knowledge. Efficient causality is the world of logic and connectedness, and of specific goals and directions. In a word, it is the province of visual man. Until visual man, or alphabetic man, the pre-Socratics lived and thought in the acoustic or multi-directional world.

Today, the Third World, which is eager to resemble and to surpass the First World, is still in the elder province of intuitive experience which precedes the advent of phonetically literate or visual man. From his beginnings, phonetically literate man assumed it was his right to invade other cultures and to impose his discoveries wherever possible. Whereas the Graeco/Roman world, constituted by the phonetic alphabet and by techniques of visually applied knowledge, assumed a mission to extend itself and its institutions to the "lesser breeds," electronic man, on the other hand, has re-entered the world of acoustic experience, thereby losing all confidence in his right to impose the old visual culture of the West on people who have not yet been invaded by the phonetic alphabet. From the first, identified with the Graeco/Roman culture, Christianity had at the same time brought the hidden Word and the new visual culture to the "lesser breeds." Today, a crisis in Christianity emerges with the possibility of propagating the hidden Word directly without the benefit of the written word, or Graeco/Roman culture. The patterns of Western civilization are as incompatible with simultaneous or acoustic culture as the pre-Socratic Logos was incompatible with the alphabetic innovation.

The violence of dominant culture consists in the assumption of the right to invade and to shape groups and individuals with the preferred norms of one's choice. In the electronic world we now take for granted the co-existence of all cultures and their immediacy of access, while sheer diversity and range of cultural choice daily brings into doubt the rights of any one culture to impose itself on another. We have begun to doubt our own rights to mould and shape our own children. Women's Lib is by comparison a side issue, yet one that is essentially electronic in offering power to all participants.

Without exception, then, the activity of media, old and new, as invaders of both public and private space, raises the question and image of violence at every turn. At the speed of light, American political institutions are trembling and quailing in this bi-centennial year. Writing on "Pre-election blues" in the *Globe and Mail* on March 16, 1976, James Reston observed:

> The more this capital fusses and agonizes over the election, the more it seems to long for fundamental change. It would never admit as much in public, but the truth comes out in private: from the top of the Administration and the Congress to the critical levels of the civil service, it is almost yearning for new faces and new beginnings. This may not be logical or even rational, for all the devilishly complicated problems will remain after the election, but there it is—an intuitive feeling that something is deeply wrong here and probably won't be corrected by the old cast of characters or the old ideological arguments of either party.

He adds that:

> This is not a partisan but a general feeling that Washington is not at the beginning of something but at the end of something.

In the February issue of *Atlantic*, David Halberstam has some observations on TV and politics:

> Television not only changed the balance of power, but it became a vital part of the new balance of power. Presidents knew the advantage they had in gaining access to the air and the difficulties any competing politician or institution had. Presidents had used or suffered press conferences for a variety of reasons, including a chance to listen to the country. Kennedy seized on live television as an opportunity for political theater. He used reporters as pawns to help make him look better, smarter, shrewder, more capable, and in control. Indeed, mastery of the press conference became a kind of substitute for mastery of the political scene.

He continues:

> In that sense John Kennedy changed the presidency more than any recent predecessor with the exception of Franklin Roosevelt, who had slipped so naturally into the radio presidency. Kennedy's ascendancy, like Roosevelt's, was a confluence of a man and a technology, of a new political force and a politician with the skills and instincts to exploit it. The television audiences were acutely aware of style now. The President came not just into their towns but into their homes.

The last sentence points to the violent invasive character of radio and television. Representative government had belonged to a period of communication by rail, when the representatives were at a considerable distance from the home. Both radio and TV restored the character of the tribal chieftain:

> At the same time that television was granting immense and almost unchallenged power to the President, it was granting less and less power to anyone else, particularly its own people. The role of reporter and commentator was diminishing. There was less time for serious analysis, and fewer explanations of complicated stories. As the role of the reporter diminished, the role of technology grew.

As the primacy of the image increases, the role of parties and policies recedes, as is the case with all media "content." This is not to say that content and program have no function on TV. Indeed, their function is to assure that TV will be turned on so that it can perform its work of obliterating all individuality and all privacy. Mr. Eliot observed long ago that the chief use of the content of a poem is "to satisfy one habit of the reader, to keep his mind diverted and quiet, while the poem does its work upon him: much as the imaginary burglar is always provided with a bit of nice meat for the house-dog." Likewise, the function of a program is to keep the users occupied by some diversion while the medium itself does its work upon him.

NOTES

[1] Further analysis of "The McLuhan System" can be found in *Marshall McLuhan*, by Dennis Duffy, Canadian Writers New Canadian Library Original, McClelland and Stewart, Toronto, 1969. For an interesting application of theory evoked from this system, see, "Hot and Cool Sex: Fidelity in Marriage," by Robert T. Francoeur and Anna K. Francoeur, in *Marriage and Alternatives: Exploring Intimate Relationships*, Roger W. Libby and Robert N. Whitehurst (eds.), Scott, Foresman and Company, Glenview, Illinois, 1977.
[2] *Globe and Mail*, November 25, 1974, "The Informal Mr. McLuhan," by June Callwood.
[3] *Globe and Mail*, September 10, 1973, "Understanding McLuhan—and Fie on any Who Don't," by Marshall McLuhan.

Chapter 13

REPORT OF THE ROYAL COMMISSION ON VIOLENCE IN THE COMMUNICATIONS INDUSTRY

J. C. Thatcher, Queen's Printer for Ontario

For purposes of its report, the Royal Commission on Violence in the Communications Industry has taken a broad definitional base, defining violence as "action which intrudes painfully or harmfully into the physical, psychological or social well-being of persons or groups." For purposes of this brief summary, suffice it to say that the most important outcome can be found in the portion of the study concerned with the cause and effect relationship between violence in the media and its incidence in Canadian society. Because this report seeks to provide a base for governmental action which will affect most Canadian citizens, it will take its place in the history of the development of Canada and likely will generate research in the years to come. The following excerpt on collective conflict in Canada found no direct causal relationship between the media and violence. The presence of the media, however, posed fundamental problems in police-press relations. There are no simple answers to the effect of the media on violence in Canada. Rather, a complexity of relationships between the media and general political behaviour is indicated.

CONJECTURES AND PROBLEMS IN THE LITERATURE

Adult Canadians have all witnessed incidents of collective conflict and violence, such as the student protests of the 1960s and the war in Vietnam. Extremely few, however, have witnessed these or similar events in reality. The vast majority watched them on the radio, read about them in the newspapers, or were informed by their friends and acquaintances. Clearly, most of our information about such violence is received from an intermediary body—be it acquaintances or the media—and it is likely that our personal contacts will have received their knowledge from the media.

The effects of such communications on individuals and society have long been recognized as significant for the political system. While specific consequences are difficult to isolate in the web of other social

---

* This paper is reprinted from The Report of the Royal Commission on Violence in the Communications Industry, Vol. 5, *Learning from the Media* with the permission of J. C. Thatcher, Queen's Printer for Ontario.

events, it is certain that most citizens rely heavily on the mass media for their information about Canada and the world. Richard R. Fagen, author of *Politics and Communication*, shows how a bizarre hoax to convince Americans that the President was dead could be carried out successfully by only 2,000 mass media personnel.[1]

In Canada we only need to recall the "communication war" between the *Front de libération du Québec* and Prime Minister Pierre Trudeau over the Cross and Laporte kidnappings to realize how we experience such important events.

A less contentious example may be drawn from the work of a foremost student of the media. Walter Lippman's *Public Opinion* reads:

> There is an island in the ocean where in 1914 a few Englishmen, Frenchmen, and Germans lived. No cable reached that island, and the British mail steamer comes but once in sixty days. In September it had not yet come, and the islanders were still talking about the latest newspaper which told them about the approaching trial of Madame Caillaux for the shooting of Gaston Calmette. It was, therefore, with more than usual eagerness that the whole colony assembled at the quay on a day in mid-September to hear from the captain what the verdict had been. They learned that for over six weeks now those of them who were English and those of them who were French had been fighting on behalf of the sanctity of treaties against those of them who were Germans. For six strange weeks they had acted as if they were friends when in fact they were enemies.[2]

The actual effects of the media on Canadian society may not be easy to determine, but the circumstantial evidence for their importance in collective conflict and violence is great. The Special Senate Committee on Mass Media, chaired by Senator Keith Davey, found that adult Canadians spend 30 to 40 minutes daily reading their newspapers and that eight out of every ten of them use all three media—newspapers, radio, and television—on a daily basis.[3] Of course, these surveys mask different levels of interest and concern across the population. As T. Joseph Scanlon put it: " . . . that some persons watch a truly staggering 53.9 hours of television a week should not obscure the fact that others average only 4.8 hours."[4] Collective conflict events in particular are normally experienced only vicariously through the mass media. Regional studies have confirmed this contention. An Ottawa-Hull survey showed that four-fifths of the population learned about the murder of former Quebec Labour Minister Pierre Laporte in 1970 directly from the media.[5] Carleton University journalism students found that two-thirds of their sample population in Kingston learned directly from the media that kidnapped British diplomat James Cross had been found.[6]

To assert that the media are important to society is now, however, to determine in what way there are relationships between them. It is difficult to establish in a convincing fashion exactly how the mass media shape behaviour. Most scholarly work in political science indicates the complexity of relationships between the media and general political behaviour.[7] And, in a similar manner, communications literature shows a complex interactive pattern between the mass media and its effects.[8] Modern mass media have not displaced personal contacts, face-to-face communications, or other channels of communication, but they have provided new links to existing networks and offered independent forms of communication. Therefore, to single out the effects of the media on collective conflict and violence is going to require the skills of social scientists for generations and early definitive success cannot be expected.

THE MEDIA AND VIOLENCE

Complex social reality is unlikely to be "explained" by any single factor such as the media. The allegation that the Commission cannot establish that the media are the cause of violence is really rather premature.[9] The 1972 report of the United States Surgeon General's Scientific Advisory Committee, based on 60 reports and a million dollar expenditure, was not able to do that either.[10] But that report and others,[11] undertaken independently or on government contract, have provided insightful hypotheses and have established a basis for the need to continue probing into such relationships. If public policy is to be based on the best social science available at any given time, then despair about the difficulties of discovering ironclad relations between violence and the media cannot be allowed to prevent efforts to establish tentative generalizations.

The study of violence itself is replete with theoretical, philosophical, and political difficulties. If causal relations ever were established between media output and violence in society, it would have immediate policy consequences. Benjamin D. Singer put it this way: "Some would have argued that reportage of such events, particularly the dramatized reportage so prevalent on television, is a determinant of such events as air hijacking, arson, bombings, mass murders, campus disturbances, and urban riots. The policy implications of this question are enormous and ultimately become matters of political philosophy."[12] However, even if causal relations are not established in a conclusive, scientific manner, the issue is already part of public discussion as the Commission has shown through its public hearings. Contrary to the views of some scholars, negative findings in this field will also have policy implications. Research grants may vanish, but the policy considerations do not disappear merely because social scientists find no positive correlations.

The Commission has taken a rather broad definition of violence in order to make their scope as comprehensive as possible. They have taken as their definition the following:

Violence is action which intrudes painfully or harmfully into the physical, psychological or social well-being of persons or groups.

Violence or its effects may range from trivial to catastrophic.

Violence may be obvious or subtle.

It may arise naturally or by human design.

Violence may take place against persons or against property.

It may be justified or unjustified, or justified by some standards and not by others.

It may be real or symbolic.

Violence may be sudden or gradual.[13]

Such a broad concern is justified in order to provide an exhaustive treatment of the subject, but it must be restricted for specific research purposes. Social science requires that definitions be operationalized so that empirical referents can be determined. Moreover, many definitions tend to assume that violence is not part of the normal fabric of society. Collective conflict and violence occur with such frequency that they cannot be regarded as aberrations. Disorder may not be the norm of Canadian society, but neither is it rare in political systems. H. L. Nieburg, in his volume *Political Violence: The Behavioural Process*, argued:

> Extreme and violent political behaviour cannot be dismissed as erratic, exceptional, and meaningless. To set it apart from the processes that are characteristic of society is to ignore the continuum that exists between peaceable and disruptive behaviour; it is to deny the role of violence in creating and testing political legitimacy and in conditioning the terms of all social bargaining and adjustment. Violence in all its forms, up to and including assassination, is a natural form of political behaviour.[14]

One does not need to accept the contentious judgment of the author of this quotation to understand that there is some merit to the argument that the role of violence in society may be considered "good" or "bad" depending on the ideology, the motives, and even the success of the perpetrators. Crime, itself, is a political concept according to many writers.[15] However, even if definitions are coloured by ideology, public officials must learn to deal with the short-run interference in democratic processes and the personal harm that emanate from violence. One instrumental approach to the philosophical problem is to restrict the definition to harmful violence. Nieburg, for example, who wishes to show that violence is merely another instrument in politics, defines it as:

> acts of disruption, destruction, injury whose purpose, choice of targets or victims, surrounding circumstances, implementation, and/or effects have political significance, that is, tend to modify the behaviour of others in a bargaining situation that has consequences for the social system.[16]

While this type of definition is helpful for making the concept of violence as wide as possible and for diminishing the use of the term to depict only erratic or deviant behaviour, it is not very useful either for the science of violent behaviour or for public policy debate. There is simply no way that we have found to operationalize this definition to provide measures of collective conflict and violence in order to carry out empirical research. Moreover, in this report we wish to steer the discussion away from whether such behaviour is beneficial or harmful in the long term, but to ascertain what relations exist between the media and this phenomenon. Thus, while this report will initially focus on the relationship between the media and the phenomenon of collective conflict in general, it is our ultimate intention to concentrate on the violent aspects of conflict. Conflict is used here as a generic term to connote the entire spectrum of confrontation politics. It may be legal or illegal, violent or non-violent, but it always implies the threat or use of physical force. Violence, on the other hand, entails the actual use of physical force.

COLLECTIVE CONFLICT IN CANADA

The myth of the "peaceable kingdom" has been one of the most durable themes in Canadian political culture.[17] The assumption that pervades this idea is that Canadians have traditionally been, and remain, a thoroughly non-violent people. It has been noted by one prominent historian that practically all Canadian textbooks in history, political science, and sociology presume that Canada has always been a tranquil and pacific society—one that evolved from colony to responsible government to independence by peaceful debate.[18] Or, as Joseph Howe characterized the advent of responsible government in Nova Scotia, "without the breaking of a pane of glass."[19] Implicit in the optimistic parochialism of this myth is the further suggestion that Canadian history has been relatively free of the violence and extremism that have characterized the growth and development of the United States. It is, thus, a general point of consensus that not only was Canadian Confederation bloodless in contrast to the revolutionary origin of the United States, but also that our history has been virtually free of the lawlessness and violence that characterized the American frontier experience. The Hollywood image of the rugged, individualistic gunman or the roving bands of the night riders to which we are exposed by the American media is thought to have no parallel in Canadian history, where the West was secured by a law-enforcement agency—the RCMP. Moreover, it is also a fundamental supposition in the peaceable kingdom myth that Canada has experienced substantially less radical and criminal violence than has occurred in the United States. While the occurrence of a few

comic-opera rebellions and some rather bothersome strikes are acknowledged, citizens assume complacently that resorting to violence has been
atypical of the Canadian experience.

Unfortunately, the uncritical acceptance of this thesis has caused
misjudgments about the degree of abnormality represented by conflict
behaviour in this country and posed obstacles to its understanding.
Largely as a result, domestic conflict has been neglected for some time as
a field worthy of serious research. The conscious and unconscious
perpetuation of the peaceable kingdom myth also accounts to a large
extent, for the current tendency in private, political, and academic
circles to react to contemporary expressions of conflict with a good deal
of shock. It has also led to the acceptance of certain misplaced conclusions about the undercurrents present in our own society, as seen in the
attempt of many politicians to attribute the "contretemps" of the sixties
to the fall-out of American violence or to various imaginary conspira-
cies.

Although it is not incorrect to assume that social strife in this country
has never reached the quantity or the intensity of American violence,
such a comparison is both insidious and irrelevant. The fact that there
has been appreciably less violence in Canada over the past two centuries
than has occurred in the United States should not be construed to mean
that civil conflict has been adventitious to the development of Canadian
society. The fact is that there has been appreciably more violent conflict
in the past than most of us are aware of. It has been less dramatic and
less well-publicized than in the United States, but it has nonetheless
been an integral part of the Canadian political process.[20]

Even a selective review of some violent incidents in Canadian history
seems to bear out this contention. First of all, while the lack of blood-
shed over Confederation is something of a moot point, neither the pre-
nor-post Confederation period was totally calm or serene. Until 1867,
Canada gave the image of a relatively disorderly country in which overt
conflict was frequent between whites and Indians, French and English,
Canadians and Americans, different fur-trading interests, and rebels
supporting Papineau and Mackenzie versus the Tory establishment.[21]
Neither was the Canadian experience with manifest destiny as tranquil
as it has usually been portrayed. Social disorder was generally characteristic of the Canadian frontier, due to the highly competitive nature of
frontier economics which centred on the timber and fur trades.

There are two recurrent themes in the later history of Canadian collective conflict—religion and race. Sectarian violence was especially prominent in this country during the late nineteenth and early twentieth
centuries. Violent encounters between Orangemen and Irish reached
such ritualistic dimensions that every March 17 and July 12 brought with
it a call to arms.[22] The nineteenth century also witnessed a number of
small-scale civil wars with serious racial overtones. Undoubtedly the

pre-eminent among these was the Riel Rebellion in the West.[23] There was also what has been called the Shiners War, involving the Irish and other ethnic groups, which raged in Ottawa (then Bytown) between 1837 and 1845.[24] While now something of a curio of Canadian history, this struggle for recognition and economic security epitomized the social disorder in Ontario during the period.

There have also been some very substantial outbreaks of election violence during the last hundred-odd years. Intimidation and "Teddy Boy" tactics were at one time an almost integral part of political campaigning in this country. Again, this was frequently due to the sectarian nature of the competing political parties. Whatever the reason, most election days were, as one prominent Orangeman characterized them, "days of blood and fire."[25] During the mid and late nineteenth century, campaign slogans such as "No Popery, No Surrender" or "Vote Conservative or your barns burn" were quite prevalent.[26] Often they had significantly more impact than more recent electioneering practices. While the present century has been quite tranquil in comparison, it too has witnessed some very violent elections. The federal election in 1911 over the reciprocity treaty occasioned numerous incidents of mob-rioting and street-fighting.[27] The federal election of 1935 was highlighted by a series of sectarian incidents which assumed, according to one historian, the dimensions of a small war.[28] More recently, a rather substantial riot broke out in Montreal on the eve of the 1968 federal election when militant separatists confronted Prime Minister Pierre Trudeau on the reviewing stand of the Saint-Jean Baptiste parade.

With the exception of the 1960s which are examined below, most of the major violence of the present century, with certain notable exceptions (for example, election violence, the conscription riots in Quebec in 1918, the VE-and the VJ-day rioting, and various episodes of Doukhobor violence) has been labour-related.[29] Such conflict has been extensive and often quite bitter, as much of it involved the fundamental question of the right to unionize. Between 1910 and 1966, Canada had 227 strikes marked by explosions of violence.[30] Many of these incidents, moreover, had significant political implications and federal troops and the RCMP were frequently used to suppress them.[31]

While none of the incidents of Canadian economic violence was comparable to the Ludlow Massacre in Colorado in 1914 or the 1937 Memorial Day massacre during the Little Steel strike in Chicago, some of them were incredibly vicious. One of these incidents, the Winnipeg General Strike, has been called one of the most significant violent occurrences in Canadian history.[32] Others, such as the strikes at Murdochville and Asbestos, have also had significant societal repercussion. The history of labour violence in the twentieth century rings like a litany of the major industrial and railway centres in Canada. While many of these incidents are not as well known as those mentioned above, they have nevertheless had a significant impact on the economic structure of our society and, to an extent, also on the political structure due to the frequent interventions of various levels of government.

This cursory review of Canadian history should serve to implant some doubts about the unrealistic tranquility and rationality that is often attributed to our society. While it is not necessary to assume that violent conflict is endemic to Canadian society, there do seem to have been some significant antagonisms in the social fabric. Awareness of this fact may permit a better perspective from which to judge the degree of extranormality of contemporary expressions of violence and their causes.

CONTEMPORARY COLLECTIVE CONFLICT IN CANADA IN A COMPARATIVE PERSPECTIVE

During the 1960s disorder in Canada seemed part of a global epidemic. For some time the list seemed endless—Paris, London, Rome, Montreal, Chicago, Warsaw, Peking. No country appeared to escape unscathed. Civil conflict was so pervasive that one Canadian psychiatrist referred to the sixties as the age of the psychopath.[33]

According to the data used in cross-national analysis, Canada experienced, during the period of 1955 to 1965, 24 anti-government demonstrations, 19 riots, one political strike, ten pro-government demonstrations, 92 armed attacks, and eight conflict-related deaths. A time profile showing the occurrence of these incidents is provided in the following figure. It indicates that almost 85 per cent of these incidents took place between the years 1962 and 1965.[34] In light of the previous discussion about the recurrence of racial conflict in this country, it should be noted that most of the incidents recorded here, specifically the armed attacks and the conflict-related deaths, may be attributed to two ethno-political groups—the Sons of Freedom Doukhobors sect and the *Front de libération du Québec*. The violence of the Sons of Freedom reached its apogee in 1962 and little has been heard from this group since.[35] From 1963 onward, most of the violence can be attributed to the FLQ and separatist unrest in Quebec. Moreover, four of the eight deaths resulting from domestic unrest can be attributed directly to this organization.

CASE STUDIES AND ILLUSTRATIONS

As a means of deriving additional insights about news reporting of violence and some of the problems newsmen both engender and encounter, a case-study approach was adopted. This method of research opened up a number of new avenues of inquiry.

Figure 1
Time Profile of Canadian Collective Conflict, 1955-1965

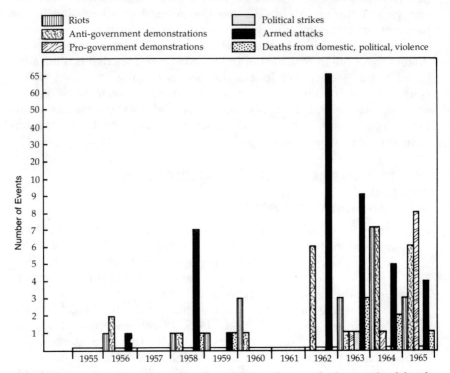

To a large extent, the Canadian experience with disorder over the last couple of decades has not been markedly dissimilar from that of many other countries. An analysis of various data sets using different conflict measures, different time frames, and different samples of nations all seem to indicate that although Canada had a relatively low level of intro-social conflict, it was somewhere around the median for advanced industrialized nations.

An incident of collective violence is a complex and dynamic phenomenon. The case-study method seeks to explore the "how" and "why" aspects of such situations in virtually the only way that such questions can be answered. While no claim is made here of scientific validity, nonetheless an attempt has been made to explore a wide variety of cases with apparent clinical potential. The particular advantage of the case study is that it allows observation in great depth and from a variety of perspectives. The case-study method is not without its limitations and drawbacks, but was judged to be of value given the particular interests of this study.

A selection of six case studies was made from the list of collective violence events in Ontario from 1965 to 1975. A seventh case study, an instance of individual political violence, was added, as it was closely related to one of the collective cases and provided a somewhat different perspective. The seven case studies selected were the following: an anti-Nazi demonstration in Toronto in 1965; a hippie protest in the Yorkville section of Toronto in 1967; an anti-Vietnam demonstration in front of the American consulate in Toronto in 1970; a labour strike at the Texpack plant in Brantford during the late summer of 1971; a personal assault on Premier Kosygin of the USSR during his tour of Parliament Hill in Ottawa in 1971; an anti-Soviet demonstration protesting Premier Kosygin's visit to Toronto in 1971; and a clash between Indians and the RCMP on Parliament Hill in 1974.

The seven were chosen because of the extensive media coverage that they received and also because they seemed to be reasonably representative of the data set as a whole in terms of form, issue and location. Five of the incidents were demonstrations, one was a strike, and one was an act of individual political violence. Three of the cases involved foreign political issues, three were occasioned by domestic political issues, and one was labour-related. Four of the incidents took place in Toronto, two in Ottawa, and one occurred in Brantford.

At the outset, each case study was meticulously researched from the newspapers and other available sources. For example, the anti-Kosygin demonstration in Toronto had resulted in an Ontario Royal Commission Investigation (the Vannini Report), while the Yorkville case had been captured in two National Film Board features: *Flowers on a One-Way Street* and *Christopher's Movie Matinee*. A number of briefs were also collected from such organizations as the Canadian Federation of Civil Liberties, the Canadian Association of Broadcasters, the Canadian Broadcasting Corporation, and other news sources. As a means of providing an additional body of data with which to evaluate the case studies, an extensive interviewing project was undertaken. A master list of all individuals mentioned in the *Globe and Mail*'s coverage of each case was developed. The list for each incident was broken down into three broad categories: participants, authorities, and media.[36] The term "participants" refers to those who were spokesmen for particular organizations or who were bystanders in a position to make some meaningful observations. It should be clearly stated that the term "participants" is in no way meant to imply that the individual was directly involved in an act of violence.

The term "authorities" refers to those members of the various police forces who were responsible for security at the site of the respective incidents of collective violence. "Media" were those reporters and photographers who were actually on the scene covering the events. A questionnaire specially designed for each of these three general categories was developed, from which a considerable body of interview testimony was generated.[37]

The questionnaire sought to focus on a number of the major controversies regarding the rights and responsibilities of these three general groups. Of particular interest was the nature of the relationship between police and media. As a means of providing the reader with a degree of perspective regarding the seven case studies, there follows a series of brief narratives describing the chronology and major features of each.

REPORTED CASE STUDY NARRATIVES[38]

Anti-Nazi Rally

On Sunday afternoon, May 30, 1965, about five thousand people, most of them middle-aged and many of them Eastern European or members of various Jewish organizations, gathered to protest against the holding of a Nazi rally at Allan Gardens. Many of these people had been brought out by the continuous and inaccurate publicity (it was reported that the Nazis had a permit when in fact they did not) that the media had given this event during the preceding week. The protest developed into a near-riot when a mob of about five hundred people, many carrying sticks and clubs, made several attacks on youths believed to be members of a Toronto Nazi group. The mob, which was described by news sources as being in an hysterical frenzy, screamed "Kill! Kill! Kill!" as they chased and clubbed the eight victims, all but one of whom were later reported to be innocent passers-by, to the ground, where they were beaten with fists and battered with hunks of wood and tree branches. The incident was broken up within 15 minutes when an estimated fifty police on foot, motorcycle, and horseback fought their way into the mob and dispersed it. Eight members of the crowd and William J. Beattie, self-styled Toronto Nazi leader, were arrested.

Yorkville Demonstration

Yorkville, the then coffee-house (and discothèque) district of Toronto, erupted into violence on the evening of August 20, 1967, during what various reports characterized as the worse outbreak of rowdyism in the village's history. A series of skirmishes began when a crowd estimated at between three and five thousand "hippies" congregated in a one-block section of Yorkville Avenue and attempted to hold a sit-in to protest the city's failure to close the street to traffic as they had requested. In an attempt to break up the sit-in, police waded into the crowd and were reported to have "slapped," "kicked," "punched," and "clubbed" the protestors. There were fifty arrests as a result of this incident, and several people reported injuries, including a number of broken bones. A few days subsequent to this event, a serious controversy arose concerning the participation of a National Film Board crew in some of the incidents, including an individual who had trained the hippies in passive resistance. Some Film Board officials were also reported to have admitted that they had helped manoeuvre some of the Yorkville events previous to the sit-in.

Demonstration at the American Consulate

On Saturday, May 9, 1970, eight days after the American invasion of Cambodia and five days after the killing of four students at Kent State University in Ohio, a protest in front of the American Consulate General in Toronto erupted into what was described as one of the most violent demonstrations in that city since the protests of the unemployed at Queen's Park in the 1930s. This protest at the consulate had been preceded during the week by two smaller demonstrations in which about a dozen demonstrators were reported to have been arrested. At this Saturday protest, about five thousand people variously affiliated with the Vietnam Mobilization Committee, the Canadian Party of Labour, and the May 4th Movement were directly in front of the consulate. The protest escalated to violence when mounted police rode into the crowd in an attempt to disperse it. At this point, fights broke out and earth from flower-beds, bricks, stones, and firecrackers rained down on the 250 police officers. After the mounted-police charge forced demonstrators away from the consulate, several hundred people streamed through downtown Toronto smashing windows in several department stores and causing about $7,000 worth of damage. Ninety-one arrests resulted from this incident and several injuries were reported, including six to police.

Texpack Strike

A lengthy strike by workers of the Texpack plant in Brantford led to a series of five episodes of collective violence in the late summer of 1971. The strike at Texpack, a manufacturer of hospital bandages, began following a walk-out on July 16. On August 12, the Ontario Supreme Court issued an injunction limiting the number of pickets to seven. Efforts by Texpack officials to replace striking workers with scabs bussed in from Hamilton and other nearby communities, led to an angry confrontation on August 25. Police and firemen were attacked by strikers, and a considerable degree of vandalism ensued. In September, the Texpack strikers were joined by representatives of other unions and by members of the Waffle group of the New Democratic Party. During the course of the dispute, an attempt was made to relocate the Texpack operation in Rexdale. While the immediate issue of the strike was a demand for a wage increase of 65 cents per hour, the tactics of the American-based company generated substantial support for the strikers. On

September 14, two York University professors were injured by a bus carrying a large number of non-union workers. The tension at the Texpack plant continued until October 18 when a compromise was reached between union and management that granted a 44-cent increase over a two-year contract. During the prolonged strike, 65 people were arrested on some hundred charges.

Incidents Related to the Kosygin Visit

On October 18, 1971, a lone attacker broke through the rear of a crowd and attacked Soviet Premier Alexei Kosygin as he walked with Prime Minister Pierre Trudeau just outside the East Block of Parliament. Geza Matrai, a 27-year-old Hungarian refugee, Toronto, member of the Edmund Burke Society, and provincial Social Credit candidate, burst out of a crowd of two to three hundred Jewish and Latvian demonstrators, leaped a wooden barricade, and butted through reporters, cameramen, and plain-clothes security police. Shouting "Freedom for Hungary!", Matrai jumped on Kosygin's back and got a forearm around his neck, almost dragging him to the ground. He was torn away and pinned to the ground by half a dozen RCMP officers. Kosygin was shaken but unhurt, and Matrai was carried away and charged with common assault.

Eight days after the incident in Ottawa, Soviet Premier Kosygin was the object of another violent protest in Toronto. On the evening of October 25, 1971, an estimated fourteen thousand demonstrators were protesting in the vicinity of the Ontario Science Centre where the Soviet Premier was attending a dinner given by the Canadian Manufacturers Association. Directly across from the Centre were about three to six thousand people, members of various Ukranian, Bulgarian, Lithuanian, and Latvian groups. There were also reported to be a number of members of the Edmund Burke Society in the crowd. As demonstrators began pressing against police-security lines, some in the crowd began to hurl debris at police. After a short time, mounted policemen charged into the chanting crowd to restrain them. This manoeuvre was repeated several times, with a full-scale confrontation ensuing as police began to beat protestors with clubs and riding crops. The confrontation lasted about 20 minutes and resulted in twenty arrests and injuries to eleven people, including five policemen. A Royal Commission investigation was initiated to look into the conduct of the public and the tactics used by the police in dispersing the crowd.

Indian Demonstration

On September 30, 1974, in an incident designated by the media as the "Battle of Parliament Hill" the RCMP put down attempts by several hundred Indians to enter the Centre Block of Parliament. The Indians, most of whom were members of the Native Peoples Caravan, coming from as far away as Vancouver, had assembled on the Hill to demonstrate for improved social and medical services and the settlement of territorial claims. They were joined on the Hill by several members of the Communist Party of Canada (Marxist-Leninist). There they were confronted by unarmed Mounties and a hundred-man Canadian Forces Honour Guard, present for the opening ceremonies of the Thirtieth Parliament. As the Indians marched towards the Centre Block, about two hundred of them charged the police barricade and began scuffling with the RCMP. Others in the crowd were reportedly flinging heavy stones, sticks, and broken bottles, and setting fire to the shrubbery below the steps of the Centre Block. Busloads of RCMP reserves, including a riot squad with helmets, shields, and clubs, were called in as reinforcements and forced the demonstrators back to the main lawn in front of the Parliament Buildings. In the "battle" that continued sporadically for three hours, 15 people were arrested and 20 injured, including 10 members of the RCMP.

CASE-STUDY TESTIMONY

While this study has not uncovered any evidence of a relationship between the media and collective conflict and violence in terms of a direct causal sequence, there nevertheless remains a number of other ways in which the media have been seen to affect civil unrest. As illustrated earlier in this report, the Eisenhower and Kerner commissions as well as the Surgeon General's report all offer some evidence that although the media may not actually cause violence in an etiological sense, they might in some instances aggravate or exacerbate certain aspects of conflict. For example, it was suggested that the very presence of the media at the scene of a demonstration or strike could become a factor in the dynamics of the conflict situation. The presence of large number of media representatives—in particular, camera crews with their lights, cables, and other equipment—in a crowd of protestors has frequently been found to complicate crowd control and sometimes adds to the general confusion and chaos. Evidence uncovered by the Royal Commission of Inquiry in Relation to the Conduct of the Public and the Metro Toronto Police in the Kosygin affair relates directly to this problem. In the opinion of the author, the media—especially television crews—stimulated and added to some of the turmoil and confusion during the riot in front of the Ontario Science Centre.[39]

In another, yet related, sense, it has also been proposed that the presence of the media may have a tendency to transform the character of an incident, because strikers and demonstrators attempt to manipulate the press to obtain headlines. The event becomes a sort of stage drama with the protestors playing to the cameras.

Possibly a much more polemical and problematical aspect of the media-civil unrest relationship begs the question of what news is. A fundamental question arises as to whether the newsworthiness of an incident of conflict is based exclusively on the occurrence of violence, or whether the media have a further obligation to inform the public by conveying the message that the protestors, or even the authorities, are attempting to present. More directly—can the form that a protest takes be isolated from the content of the protest? Understandably this is a very contentious issue. It would appear, however, that the tendency of media to give prominence to the violent aspects of a dispute while at the same time providing inadequate discussion of the issues can essentially lead beyond the reporting of news to the actual creation of news. This can both misrepresent the event and mislead the public. While the concept of censorship is anathema to most journalists, this pre-selection of news may in itself be seen as constituting a form of censorship. To the extent that demonstrations and other forms of protest are generally directed at the public via the media, the societal implications of this practice are profound.

An attempt to examine these various controversies was made through a series of interviews based on the seven case studies. A general list of names was compiled from various newspaper reports of the incidents. Several additional names were obtained in the course of some of the initial contacts.

The sample of interviewees was divided into three groups—participants, media representatives, and authorities. All individuals interviewed in each of the three categories were either involved in one of the events or were in a position to make informed observations.

A specific questionnaire was administered to each group. There was some overlap among the three questionnaires, which consisted of several general media-violence questions and a series of questions relating to the particular incident with which the respondent was associated. Generally, each of these interviews attempted to focus on some of the controversies outlined above or discussed in earlier (sections). Particular emphasis was placed on questions of police-press and participant-press interaction at the scene of a disturbance, and also on the form-content or the violence-versus-issue dispute. The following . . . therefore, make(s) no attempt to seek an objective appraisal of the events themselves, but constitute a survey of opinions on media-violence relations.

PARTICIPANTS

Interviews were conducted with seventeen individuals who had participated in one of the seven incidents either directly or as unofficial observers. At least one participant was interviewed for each of the case studies with the single exception of the Kosygin assault incident in Ottawa. Unfortunately, none of the principals involved in this particular incident was accessible. The interviews conducted with the participants attempted to focus on several general topics, including their perception of the function of the demonstrations and the tactical uses of violence, confrontation, and escalation with respect to media coverage. Consideration was also given to whether the media coverage of the incident gave undue prominence to its violent aspects.

With respect to the function of demonstrations, most of the participants interviewed considered their protest activity to have been a conscious exercise in media manipulation. Their ultimate objective was not only to manifest discontent but, according to most of the respondents, to gain recognition, sympathy, and a wider audience.

> In any demonstration there's no purpose in being out demonstrating if you're not going to get media coverage . . . If you have a demonstration and no one (the media) shows up, it's not worth having . . . If there's no media coverage, there's no effect from it. I've been involved in demonstrations in the prisons recently, over the last two summers, and what we've found is that, for instance, at Millhaven and the B.C. Pen a year and a bit ago, when they had a hunger strike nation-wide, and a reasonably effective one, there was no media coverage of it, and it put no pressure on the administration. This year's (strikes) received a little bit better media coverage. We're a little bit better at manipulating the media in relation to the demonstrations, and it put a little more pressure on the administration, brought a few more approving editorial comments. That to me is what demonstrating is all about; it's just solely an exercise in manipulating the media.

> It is only after something happens that the media is responsive and then only to a degree.

> That (to get media access) was the entire purpose of this thing (the Kosygin Demonstration).

While there may have been a consensus among most participants and observers concerning the generalities of the demonstration-media exposure strategy, the idea that violence was an integral part of this strategy was not accepted by the majority of those interviewed. It was the observation of a prominent civil libertarian, as well as of several of the demonstrators, that there were no deliberate attempts to incite violence to get media attention. Nor did these individuals perceive any attempt on the part of the demonstrators to play to the media. Nevertheless, there were a few individuals who did view confrontation politics as a useful tactic in gaining publicity. One respondent even considered it more a necessary than a useful tactic because of what he considered to be the media's ever-changing threshold of what constitutes news.

My general impression is that (playing to the media) isn't the way it happens. Undoubtedly, there are situations where that does happen, but I haven't been in any situation so far where I've seen someone deliberately try to engage in a violent act in order to get coverage.

It's hard to say—probably not. If a person was getting hassled by acop, and the cop was beating him up, then the person wouldn't have time to notice a cameraman in the midst, because he would be too worried about himself to put on an act for the camera.

. . . nobody was there to make a scene for the media. At least nobody that I know.

Create a confrontation and create an incident. What you say doesn't matter; you create the confrontation and get the publicity. It's an interesting trick. The press falls for it every time.

In my opinion what happened was that to get the same media coverage you had to put on a bigger extravaganza each time . . . You had to keep escalating your mode of demonstration to get the same media coverage. As I said, there's no purpose in having a demonstration unless you manage to communicate to people who aren't there that there are a significant number of people taking a particular position.

Conversely, there were several participants who offered the opinion that the media frequently played an active and even sinister role in the occurrence of violent conflict. This was seen to happen indirectly through the publicity and the projections of confrontation and violence that often emanate from the news media prior to an event. In a more direct sense, it has also been alleged that the media have indulged in the actual manipulation of the demonstrators, and the orchestration of the scenario, as was charged in the Yorkville incident.

It (Allan Gardens) became a major event. It was somewhat media-created by pre-publicity. . . . All the curiosity-seekers came. Radio reports that morning did build the crowd.

Starting two days prior, the media, and specifically in this case the radio stations, were putting on blurbs every 15 minutes about going to Allan Gardens.

I think it's very frustrating for a TV crew when they come out to a demonstration and everything is quiet. They call on people to arrange themselves in certain ways to make a more dramatic shot and this can spill over into creating news. This may or may not interfere with the public's right to protest and to make its protest heard, but it certainly interferes with the public's right to get an honest news story.

Despite these very different impressions about the relationship between the use of violence and media interest, the majority of those interviewed expressed considerable consternation at the way the news media covered their protest. Most of this displeasure centred around the perceived tendency of the media to concentrate exclusively on the dramatic and violent aspects of the incident at the expense of the issues and grievances that motivated the protest.

> I think they (the media) did emphasize these confrontations at the corner and the fact that there was an injunction. The media tried to portray the people who were supporting it as violent types who were interested in stirring up trouble. It wasn't so much that they were concerned about justice for the women at the plant.

> Generally, the press isn't interested in why it happened, just what happened. Allan Gardens was a one-day wonder. . . . The issues weren't discussed. They were totally downgraded in the report of violence.

> They (the "capitalist press") have generally used violence or focused on violence to avoid looking at real issues. They have generally avoided looking at the substance of why people are demonstrating. I think that's been a real failure of all the media here, certainly the newspapers.

> If an incident lasts for two hours and there are one-and-a-half minutes of yelling, screaming, and pushing, that's what gets on TV of course. The 98 minutes when nothing is happening does not get on.

> The real purpose of the demonstration was lost in the shuffle. The concentration was on the dramatic . . . There was more interest in trying to paint the people who had come there as violent than in trying to find out why they were there . . . In my opinion it was a question of selling newspapers.

> I think the press and the media dwell on the violent aspects. Of course sensationalism sells papers better than a cold recounting of issues or a reasoned discourse; this doesn't appeal to the reading public. But a lurid description of violence, and if you can get some pictures, that makes it easier to get readers to buy the paper. I think they do exploit violence unnecessarily for commercial gain.

> Sure (the media focused on the violence), that's all the media wants. They don't want anything that is even semi-intelligent. That doesn't sell newspapers . . . Most radio and TV shows assume that everyone in the country is an idiot and that the only thing they are interested in is somebody getting whacked on the head, somebody getting murdered, and all the details on how somebody chopped somebody up and so on. They figure this is what sells newspapers.

> There was no discussion of issues. The Canadian public is not too issue-oriented except when it comes to hockey games . . . The issues in this case were genuine, but they were overlooked completely.

> The content of the protest tended to get swallowed in the press coverage.

Moreover, in two specific instances individuals insisted that the news media focused intentionally and exclusively on the dramatic and sensational aspects of an incident, while evidencing little or no concern about why the discontent was expressed. Furthermore, in one of these cases, it was also suggested that the press consciously misrepresented the protest and the elements involved.

> Any time the Jewish Defense League came out with a statement it was all over the front page. Any time the Canadian Jewish Congress said something it was either not printed, or any time we sent them something it emerged in an obscure part of the paper. And what the JDL said at that time was in every case threatening violence. Even though the JDL represents an infinitesimally small segment of the Jewish population here . . . the JDL was given total attention. The impression was because some obscure group representing nobody makes a cock-eyed threat that Kosygin will not leave Canada alive, that Jews were out to kill Kosygin. This fanned the fire . . . the Jewish protest lost out in the face of violence. The press was only interested in the threats of the JDL and the riots at the Science Centre.
>
> There was the drama of two professors injured in the strike. But the press never interviewed me. They never tried to find out what happened . . . I was very embarrassed that I should have got the publicity that distracted attention from the way the women pickets were being treated, because not only were they suffering economically but, as always happens, people on the picket-lines were being roughed up at the very least.

Evidently most of those interviewed attributed the media's emphasis of the violent aspects of conflict to the intensity of the competition among the various media. There were several others, however, who attributed more insidious motives to the news media. A number contended that the practice of focusing on the violence is undoubtedly intended to discredit the validity of the issues and the legitimacy of the protest groups.

> Some of the media would concentrate on, or emphasize, violence as a means of discrediting the objective of the student movement in the sixties. If you portray the actions and outlook of a small percentage as being characteristic of the whole movement, you may convince people that the whole thing is rotten.
>
> Nobody in this country had really been accepted except the Anglos. This is where it starts. If you're not an Anglo, you're not accepted . . . Any time that any ethno-cultural group or anyone who is not Canadian (and Canadian means Anglo-Saxon 100 per cent) raises his head in any issue, whether it be a change in the educational system, electing a Member of Parliament, or he makes some kind of specific political demands—even though in almost all instances it is for the good of the whole country—it is looked upon as being unCanadian, and in this country protesting on the whole is looked upon as non-Canadian. But if it's done by a "non-Canadian group" even though you're born here, that's looked upon as un-Canadian, as meddling into someone else's business, et cetera, et cetera.

When there is this editorial line (re demonstrations due to long-haired American draft dodgers), the individual reporter is on notice that this is the way to get space. This slants stories. A large percentage of reporters are influenced by the editorial tone . . . The manner in which the press responded to the police action on this and other occasions was not a question of the time available for reflection but a question of not looking with honest eyes at what they saw. This was based on the knowledge of what would be acceptable to editors. . . . That introduces an element of prior slanting on the part of reporters.

AUTHORITIES

Seven interviews were conducted with representatives of various police forces in Ontario. These included one senior police officer in Brantford, five senior police officers in Toronto, and a representative of the Royal Canadian Mounted Police in Ottawa. These interviews focused on such concerns as how the media obtain information about violent events, police guidelines governing the dissemination of information, and the potential role of the media in stimulating and encouraging violence by their conduct on the scene. An examination was also made with respect to the suggestion of Vannini Royal Commission Report that some types of media equipment may exacerbate and complicate conflict situations.

In probing media coverage of violent demonstrations and strikes, the source of some of the basic information in the press is not always entirely clear. Most of the police officials interviewed maintained that there is an attempt to cooperate with the press and coordinate information. Some police forces have media-relations officers, but in general any cooperation is contingent on the senior officer at the scene of the event. This individual is usually the sole person empowered to talk to reporters. It may be interesting to note, however, that some of the police officials contended that in the final analysis, the newsman usually makes his own estimates.

We have a media-relations officer, first of all. He is usually kept aware of what is transpiring in a major operation. In addition to this, the commander of the major operation, who is usually a commissioned officer, is authorized to give certain general information to the media.

If they approach the senior officer who is in charge of the scene, and if it's convenient, that officer usually provides whatever information is necessary or required.

(They) ask officers in charge with respect to numbers involved, but will strictly take their own numbers in the end anyway. . . . The arrest figures come out of the station wherever arrests are processed.

There's a limit to what we can give them at the time—we have to do our job. Usually the commanding officer on the scene is empowered to release whatever information is available. They'll want to know estimates of the crowd, what the problems are. Generally we do tell them.

We had tried, although not in a concentrated effort, to have information officers. Unfortunately, they have the idea then that we're watering it down, and we're not giving them (the truth). So they want to go in and get their own facts.

Apart from this cooperation, there apparently exists no official structure or even a set of guidelines to govern the sharing of information between police and news reporters in Ontario. No indication about the existence of facilities providing direct access to police officials appeared in our interviews. Official police-press contacts are usually limited to *pro forma* exchanges of information, such as crime-occurrence sheets and prepared releases.

We make available to all members of the media information on crime that occurs daily in the metropolis. We prepare a 24-hour crime-occurrence sheet.

Yes, as I understand it, the press have a—what should I say—some facilities provided for them at police headquarters. Most information that comes to hand—where they might be interested—is provided generally through the facilities of the inspector on duty at the police headquarters. He, in fact, distributes the various information periodically throughout the day to all the media.

There's an open line at headquarters that's under the control of the deputy police chief of the CID, who looks after that end of it. Anything at all that comes through is given out to the press.

There appears to be an inherent distrust and animosity regarding the quantity and quality of press releases. The impression is given that the police, at their discretion, make available to the press only the most basic items of information. Obviously, the press for its part attempts to obtain whatever information it can and then reserves the right to decide which items should be made public knowledge. One police official pointed out that, because of this stance, the media, as the guardian of the public's right to know, do not have a great deal of credibility in police circles.

Their (reporters) apparent feeling is that they have a sacred duty to let the public know what's going on—unfortunately, they are not as objective as they might be in this regard.

As noted previously, one of the major controversies of police-press relations centres on whether the presence of media representatives at the scene of a confrontation makes the work of the police more difficult. A number of police officials suggested that newsmen sometimes interfere with policemen doing their duty, and frequently add to the confusion that often pervades the scene of a disturbance.

Generally you find most of them are very good in this regard. We had a fairly good working relationship with them. But again we have people who want to become "Number 1"—want to be a little more aggressive, et cetera.

If a reporter gets over-exuberant and becomes part of the crowd, he will be treated as one of them.

The police have the problem naturally of where, with all respect to them, quite frequently they (reporters) get in your way rather than be a help to you. When I use that term "get in your way" I mean they will insist on getting into the thick of it; and possibly you've got a problem you're trying to get squared away and they're on your tail. It's not always convenient.

Suppose there is an arrest being made—the photographers will flood to that area to try and photograph the arrest being made—each with his own interest in mind. Each wants to obtain the best possible photograph for his newspaper or television station—whatever the case may be. So they do interfere, to a certain extent, with police officers.

The presence of cumbersome media equipment was specifically pointed out as a difficulty facing the police. A number of those interviewed expressed the opinion that such equipment on the scene unnecessarily complicates and exacerbates the problem of crowd control. Television cameramen and still photographers were especially cited by policemen in this regard.

Yes, to a certain degree it is a problem. They have for the most part two men that operate a television camera—one carrying the sound and battery equipment and the other one carrying the actual camera. Just the fact of having two men moving through a crowd or moving through police lines with this type of cumbersome equipment is awkward for us.

It is as you might expect. When you've got a confrontation going on, you're dealing with four, five, six hundred, a thousand, two thousand people, and their cables and equipment sometimes can get in the way.

No, I never had a problem of a hindrance. There have been occasions where the people of the media has been bowled over, knocked down in melees—because they want to get where the action is.

It was also alleged that the presence of the media on the scene adds yet another element to the dynamics of the confrontation. Most of the police officials seemed generally aware of the interrelationship between public protest and the media. Yet many apparently feel that the presence of the media, albeit unavoidably, serves as a catalyst provoking the protestors to escalate their tactics to hold media interest.

An inactive crowd notices the presence of a camera. "Hey—here comes a camera, let's do something." I've personally seen that.

I couldn't give you a percentage, but it's quite apparent that some people will act up when they see the media there and they will act up when they see cameras focused on them. It's not a general thing, but it does happen.

Some of them do (play to the media), some of them don't. This will happen on occasion—more with the younger people. Particularly with the Anti-Vietnam War demonstration.

Oh, there's no question about the demonstrators playing to the media. That Kent State deal that you're referring to now—we know definitely—without any shadow of a doubt—that they notified the media. They were going to be there to get as much publicity as they possibly could and then went one step further. As soon as they had the media there—making use of the media to further their own ends—they conducted a show disturbance in order to be picked up by the police and put into a wagon—or put into a police car. They made sure the media was there to get the pictures—the media was all over. "Look, that's what the law enforcement agencies are doing to us." Now we know for a fact that happened down there on that instance. We know it definitely.

That is the whole purpose of a demonstration. Why do you think that people in Canada demonstrated against the Vietnam War? Just for the purpose of walking down in front of the consulate? No, they wanted media coverage. Canada wasn't at war with Vietnam, had nothing to do with Vietnam. Now what purpose would it serve for a person or a number of persons to take placards and walk up and down, if they don't get their message out?

Demonstrators always made a point to notify the media. We had suspicions that there was collusion beyond that point, very strong suspicions in some instances. . . .

Not only did most police officials suggest that the media can stimulate violence, but like the participants interviewed, several of them sensed a tendency on the part of the media to exploit this aspect of the protest. Once again, the media's focus on violence was attributed to the competitiveness of the profession. Many police officials expressed displeasure at being pawns in this game and felt that they were being manipulated by the media for their own ends.

The print medium, more than anything else, are so dependent on circulation that the purpose of their paper is to attract and sell. My experience with them, and I have had a fair bit of experience, has been that you never can get to the individual who has the responsibility for the item that appeared in the paper. I am talking to you as a reporter—by the time what I have said to you reaches the media or the printed word and is out on the street, it is distorted, taken out of context, it is changed so that the headline will attract.

Spectacular news sells newspapers. Ordinary routine news doesn't. I would assume the more spectacular the article the better—the more forcible it is for the newspaper.

> It appeared that that's (violence) what they were there to cover. They didn't miss anything. They had lots of coverage. Many cameras, photographers there. I thought (in the Yorkville case) they were more interested in what might happen in the way of confrontation.
>
> They are inclined at times to exaggerate. In other words, you help an old lady across the street—that's not news, but if you lock somebody up it is. So they dwell on the part of it (violence), and I am inclined to think at times—to glamorize it to the point of exaggerating a situation.

From the perspective of the police, their relationship with the media is at best awkward and difficult. The police resent what they consider to be press interference in the performance of their duties. They also seem concerned about the media's tendency to exploit a confrontation for their own advantage, rather than give the public a reasoned and objective account. Above all, however, a great deal of resentment appears to be based on the fact that the public's perception of the police can be determined by a source that is not necessarily free of bias.

> The media should respect the police and let them do their job before the reporter does his. Reporters should not get in the way.
>
> I am not adverse to an investigating or inquiring press, but I am adverse to one that will manipulate for its own designs and will not give the facts or give you the opportunity. We have no opportunity to tell the true story because we have to use their vehicle.
>
> You are (a policeman) not writing the scenario. You had nothing to do with the script, yet you have to direct it. Try it some time. It's a fine line between a hero and a bum in these situations. If things go right, you come out as a hero, but let one thing go wrong—that's the price of glory isn't it?

THE MEDIA

Ten interviews were conducted with representatives of the media. These included six newspaper reporters, one television reporter, two newspaper photographers, and a film director with the National Film Board. These interviews focused on such diverse concerns as newsmen's perceptions of consumer preferences for violence, and the guidelines and problems relating to the conduct of media personnel at the scene of a disturbance. Particular attention was devoted to exploring the journalist's view of press-police relations and the "violence versus issue" controversy.

One of the fundamental controversies underlying the question of violence in the media relates to the quandary over whether the consumer is presented with violence because he has an appetite for it, or whether the individual consumer has little interest in news alternatives and accepts what he is offered. If the newsmen interviewed here are representative of the journalistic profession as a whole, it would appear that the reader is given violence because that's what journalists think he desires and demands.

> I suppose to a certain type of reader stories of violence do have a certain excitement for them, perhaps not so much for the responsible reader. But keep in mind that the average newspaper reader, if there is such a thing, and always keeping in mind that this is very general, the average newspaper reader in the country has a Grade Eight education. That's why newspaper language is always written simply—it's written so that a person with a Grade Eight education can understand it. I think the reader gets a better kick out of it. I don't know why. I am not saying that you should gear your story to satisfy a reader. You do your story hopefully with a view that is going to be relatively accurate, but I think the reader gets a better kick out of that kind of thing.

> I would like to see less of it, but that's what people want.

> It's hard to come up with a general answer for that, but if there were a general black-and-white answer I am afraid it would have to be yes. . . . There does seem to be a strong appetite in a minority of the public I would guess.

In a different vein, we have already noted that there is also a great deal of controversy related to the perceived tendency of the media to stimulate or exacerbate conflict situations. Covering a riot, or any type of civil disturbance, is at best a hazardous endeavour. Nevertheless, despite these considerations few media agencies were found to have guidelines for reporters and photographers covering such incidents. Of the five news agencies contacted (*The Globe and Mail*, *The Toronto Star*, *The Ottawa Citizen*, *Canadian Press*, and the Canadian Broadcasting Corporation), only the CBC was found to have guidelines for personnel involved in reporting such incidents. The CBC guidelines, however, were both very general and very informal, suggesting only that:

> "the intrusion of cameras into a scene of riot or civil disorder raises complex problems, and places heavy responsibility on the broadcaster. There is every evidence that, in some situations, the presence of television cameras has had a moderating effect on violent incidents. In other cases it is clear that the presence of cameras has been a provocation to violence. Where plans are being made for coverage of events where civil violence may be expected, every precaution should be taken that the presence of CBC reporters and cameras is not used as a 'provocation.' "[40]

Generally, however, the opinion obtained from most of the reporters interviewed was that their conduct at the scene of a disturbance is a matter of news judgment and common sense, and as such has to be left to the discretion of the individual newsman.

Virtually none, he (a reporter) is his own man. To use the vernacular, he calls it as he sees it. He is the man on the spot and he is responsible to himself. That's chiefly it. . . . A reporter is sent on a job and he does the job with a minimum of instruction. He gets no guidelines from his editor at all.

From my own experience, I don't think there are any general ones established by the media. Editors don't hand out little forms that say should this occur you do this. If you get into a situation where there's a possibility of violence, you've got two things to think of. Firstly, your own skin, and secondly trying to observe what's going on in an objective way. It's pretty difficult. If you're saying, "Is there a criteria that can be applied?," I would say no. No two situations are similar.

There are no formal guidelines at *The Globe and Mail.* It's up to you how far into the crowd you want to get.

Concerning the question of the availability of information at the scene of a disturbance, several of the reporters indicated that the police were usually helpful with respect to crowd estimates and other such basic information. However, they indicated that in most cases such cooperation is contingent upon the pressure police are under and the restrictions imposed by the Police Act.[41]

It's very difficult to estimate the number in a crowd, so what we do is talk to the most senior officer on the scene and ask him for his estimate of the crowd and whatever he says we would attribute this estimate to him. . . . Police information is reasonably accurate, keeping in mind that police want to show themselves in the best light.

In an instance of a demonstration like that, the information that one is looking for is—how many men have they got there, arrests if any, casualties if any? It is generally kind of formal stuff that one would get from them in the general course of events anyway. But if you're thinking of more in terms of background stuff, like the police saying that we knew these people were full of Marxists, and it was going to be a bloody encounter to begin with so that we pulled in the riot squad way ahead—that's not the kind of stuff that you would get normally and you would have to generally depend on someone who had pretty good contacts with the police—someone who worked the police beat.

I always do my own counts, and then I'll look around for a senior police officer, and say what do you think the crowd is. This, of course, becomes part of a time-wasting question as far as they're concerned. If you're into a violent situation, they're up to their ears with their own work. . . . A lot of the difference in police information goes up and down with the individual officers involved. . . . Of course, the Police Act bars policemen from communicating with the press or public without permission of their superior officers.

A number of newsmen, particularly news photographers, did not seem to consider the police to be either helpful or cooperative. Two of the reporters interviewed offered some serious and detailed criticisms from the media perspective about police-press relations.

> They wouldn't give you the time of day.

> One of the major difficulties is the official obstruction of the press, such as authorities not allowing photographers admittance to a public place, or saying you can't stand there. . . . I don't know of any case where a photographer needs protection from a crowd.

> The relations between the press and the Metro police force are very limited, and in some cases it takes up to 24 hours before you even get information about something, and on the spot there's absolutely no information at all. Only certain senior officers are allowed to talk to you and that's from the rank of inspector and up. . . . They withhold the majority of information. That particular night (the Kosygin demonstration), I think the biggest rub against the police was that no one would say exactly what they did, how many did it, and the basis of it. . . . The police in Toronto have specific orders that they are not to talk to the press. They have been told that they can be charged under the Police Act. The only people that can talk to the press are the inspectors of each division during the day and then at night only the duty desk inspector . . . if he's available. On the scene, many police will talk to you because you don't quote them per se as an individual. They'll help you out, but they're awfully careful. The Chief had a senior officers' meeting, up to a year ago when I was closely associated with the police, every month, and he would read items from different newspapers and say how did they get this and how did they get that, and this shouldn't have been given out. . . . The result now is that even good stories about the police aren't coming out.

> Very often police have to be the source of official information. There's no alternative there and you have to take their word. . . . Anytime the police have to use force in a situation, then they're not cooperative, especially if you're carrying a camera, they're most uncooperative. They don't want pictures anywhere giving the impression, valid or otherwise, that they may be abusing the general public. . . . When it comes to police and press relations you're never going to change a great deal as long as you have police departments structured the way they are in this country. You take the current Metro police force and their police-press relations—I would say if anything they are minus two thousand and you'll never improve them. . . . The Maloney Report and the Morand Report supposedly dealt with problems concerning the police and what they in effect did was touch two pimples on a body that's covered with pimples. You have people running police departments today whose whole attitude is—secrecy must prevail. And you build up antagonisms with the media as a result of that, and you get the situation where the only kind of press coming out about the police is adverse. Very often it's just a case of damn sheer stupidity on the part of the police administration that they get that kind of publicity and only that kind of publicity. . . . Improve police-press relations? Police are always willing to cooperate with a reporter who allows himself to be co-opted. If he's willing to be co-opted then they'll always cooperate.

We have examples of it in this city, and this province. And when I say co-opted, I mean the reporter allows a cop to fix a ticket for him, so the cop is a good guy. Because just as cops work on the theory that you get something on the guy you work with and that protects you, they also work on the theory in dealing with the media. And what they've run into in the past five years or so is that they're not getting the kind of guys who are necessarily willing to be co-opted, and so you're creating all kinds of walls.

Most of the newsmen interviewed seemed well aware of the character of their relationship with the protestors, as well as the general relation between protest and the media. Almost all of them acknowledged that demonstrators frequently attempt to manipulate and play to the media and that some of the behaviour of demonstrators is attributable to media presence.

I've paraded with those people on several occasions up there, walking along, talking with them with their picket signs. They were completely orderly and completely responsible until somebody came along with a TV camera and then somebody handed them matches, they lit torches, they got into the whole bag. It's all part of pseudo-events and they are created a lot—on some occasions completely created by the media who want good pictures for their cameras.

Oh sure they would play to the gallery, very much so, and particularly if there was an empathy, or a sympathy and a rapport between the demonstrators and a specific newsman. . . . I certainly know—but I can't document them—I know of situations where reporters were friendly with people who always seemed to be involved in these demonstrations. Reporters who, for example, would know ahead of time when there was going to be a huge gathering and they would be preconditioned to report this particular happening when it did occur.

I would guess that a majority of demonstrations as such wouldn't happen if the media didn't cover them. A demonstration is designed not just to get the attention of the people on the street, it's to get publicity for some cause. And if the press weren't there, I would say a majority of demonstrations likely wouldn't happen.

It happens all the time. . . . A lot of these things shouldn't be covered at all—they should be ignored! For example, if the press had ignored the Nazi demonstration it would have subsided much more easily.

Demonstrations have become an art. People stage them for press coverage. Professional demonstrators are always trying to get photos in the paper. For example, a man is being led away by the police, he bends his arm back, throws back his head, rolls his eyes with a look of anguish, even though the policeman may be laughing. This happens with perpetual demonstrators—they try to put the media presence to good use.

Oh yes, sure, the Maoists and you name any other groups. Generally, they always make sure that they phone the press. Very few incidents would happen spontaneously without the press being there.

I suppose it's possible that it does have some effect. Look at the number of photographers who get bashed around for taking photographs of people at demonstrations. From that point of view, demonstrators aren't all that keen at having their photographs taken. . . . Large gatherings of people for various reasons create their own individual character. A crowd becomes an individual character with its own identity and its own reality. I suspect that there are a large number of things that go into the creating of a riot . . . and the presence of the media might well be one of those, but I wouldn't have thought that it was a major one. I would have thought the issues, the frustration, the size, the make-up of the crowd, the behaviour of the police, those would have been perhaps larger influences.

It was further suggested, however, that the media are not always an involuntary party in such manipulation.

One of the newsmen interviewed has alleged that the press did not necessarily play the role of impartial observer with respect to the controversy surrounding the Yorkville incident.

This is not the sort of thing that I would stand in the witness box and lay my hand on the Bible or my heart but it was the feeling at the time that a certain CBC crew (or crews) arranged (they really set it up) a situation which they knew damned fine the police couldn't walk away from—like kids lying across the street, for example, in order to get good footage on this. . . . The National Film Board didn't do themselves a lot of good at that time either. The particular situation, I just can't remember what it was . . . I think that there was not too much doubt that there was a certain amount of orchestration there.

While most of the reporters recognized the intention of the demonstrators to exploit the presence of the media, there seemed to be considerable disagreement over the extent to which the media should allow themselves to be used in this respect. Several of the newsmen interviewed conceived of demonstrations as an important outlet which should not be denied media coverage. Others, however, appeared to be much more cautious about how much assistance the media should give demonstrators and minority groups in articulating their grievances.

What are the odds that if you cut off the reporting on so-called violence events as we have them here that you aren't in effect going to deny the outlets that these people need for their frustrations and what the hell do you create then? You may create the very thing that does lead to real violence. . . . The media should be an outlet for them. The media should be an outlet for most people in society. It's not . . . a lot of the helpless, those who are looking for solutions to their particular problems, don't have a power base to manipulate the media . . . and so it's not accessible to them. Look at the cons . . . they've gotten sophisticated to the point where they can now say we're getting coverage—but what did they have to do to get coverage. They had to go and carry violence to an extreme. . . . But you've got to give every group accessibility. If you don't, they get it anyway by creating these pseudo-demonstrations, these pseudo-violent events.

If we stop covering the demonstrations, do they stop demonstrating or they accelerate to the point that they make a big enough bang that you can't ignore it?

I'm not sure that a newspaper or a radio station or a television station are duty bound to give large amounts of space or time to any group that comes along simply because they say they've got a grievance. The newspapers and radio and television stations, of course, are partly there for the people they talk about. But their job is far more to provide a service to their customers. These judgments are always difficult to make. When does a disadvantaged group become a legitimate news story? Is it only when it engages in some sort of violence or anti-social activity? I'm not sure that's true.

The minorities of today wouldn't be anywhere unless the media gave them coverage. And I think that has maybe caused some problems today. The majority won't speak up and the minorities speak up and the news media react to it. We give them the coverage. A minority of people is being heard, the majority isn't.

As mentioned in other sections, the "form-content" controversy goes to the very heart of what news is and what the role of the press should be in a democratic society. Unfortunately, there was little agreement among the various media representatives interviewed as to what constitutes news and how much space should be given to a discussion of the issues. There were those who considered violence to be news and the issues to be irrelevant. Others insisted that newspapers should not allow themselves to become propaganda sheets by devoting too much attention to the issues underlying violent conflict. Furthermore, while some reporters felt that violence may be played up at the expense of issues, others suggested that while the coverage does frequently focus on the violence this is perfectly justifiable.

Violence is news.—N.E.W.S. Do I have to spell it for you!

A disturbance in society is obviously a matter of importance because we place a great deal of value on an orderly non-violent society. And so when these things happen, they develop an importance of their own which doesn't have much to do with the validity of the cause being espoused.

If you get into that (issues) and start interviewing every character who has got an axe to grind, you could spend weeks writing articles. There is no question about it. But the point is—what are you really doing? You're just giving outlets to new forms of propaganda.

> Yes, there was far too much focus on the violence. You couldn't count them. There weren't that many incidents of violence and the violence was not all that violent in Yorkville. There were beatings. I can't think of one fatality . . . I don't think there was much discussion of issues; the issues were very clouded at the time. The older reporters perhaps didn't get under the surface. The younger ones— yes, perhaps the younger ones did get under the surface and said, all right there is a demonstration on the street, this is only a symptom. It's a symptom of something else that is much more deeply rooted than appears on the surface. I think they were trying to get under it, but in general no, the issues were not clear.

> The issues I think were well-known. Basically they were not new issues. In our story there was a big description of the anti-Communist feeling and a small number of interviews that were in the story. I think the emotion that these people felt did come through to an extent. As far as the issue as such, I think it was sort of a basic assumption that people at the time knew that a large number of Eastern European immigrants to Canada were strongly anti-Communist. So there probably wasn't a basic need to go into the whole situation.

Intimately related to this question is the role that follow-up coverage might have in providing a reasoned and informed analysis of a civil disturbance. As noted (earlier) 40 per cent of all incidents receive some follow-up coverage, with an average of one article. While it seems that follow-up coverage and backgrounders can be quite helpful in allowing the reader to put an event in perspective, most of the media representatives interviewed felt there was little news interest in such endeavours.

> No, there isn't follow-up. It's not adequate because there's no news interest in it.

> It's a policy to follow-up, but following-up is frequently one of those things most difficult to do in the trade. This paper (*The Globe and Mail*) does it more than most, but you are always caught up with today's news, and following up yesterday's news sometimes takes a back seat.

> I believe the *Globe* does this. The more sensational-style newspapers haven't got the room to do it, haven't got the staff to do it, and haven't got the space to do it in the paper.

CONCLUSION

While we have been unable to determine any direct causal relationship between the media and violence, some of the evidence and testimony presented in this (section) would seem to argue that there is definitely reason for concern. A comparison of news reports of violence in three different newspapers indicated that there is both a wide variation in the coverage of such events and a general tendency to isolate the violence from its context. Most participants viewed public manifestations of discontent as a means of publicizing their grievances with the assistance of the media. The media's penchant, however, for focusing on the violent aspects, at the expense of a consideration of the issues, frequently diminishes the value and credibility of a protest and may even stimulate a cycle of escalation. Furthermore, there seem to be some obvious and fundamental problems in police-press relations, especially with respect to the presence of the media on the scene of a violent confrontation. Understandably, there is a delicate problem involved. Both the media and police have their own set of priorities, and they are frequently at odds with each other. Undeniably the primary function of the police is to maintain public order, while not infringing on the rights of the protesters to present their grievances. The media, on the other hand, also have a responsibility to the public to keep it informed of major occurrences in society. At the same time, these responsibilities are not necessarily mutually exclusive. Beyond certain obvious limitations, neither side has the right to interfere with the other's attempt to carry out its responsibilities. It is obvious, however, from the testimony presented here, that such is not the case. Police-press relations are evidently in need of considerable improvement. While it is not a primary function of the police to act as a source of news, they should recognize their value in this regard by making provisions for the dissemination of accurate and up-to-date information. This need not interfere with the police department's role at the scene of a disturbance. The media, for their part, should recognize the potential volatility of their position at the scene of a confrontation and should conduct themselves in such a manner as to avoid stimulating or aggravating a disturbance. This applies particularly to newspaper photographers and television cameramen who insist in being at the vortex of a demonstration. The inability of the police and media to reach some sort of compromise only serves to unnecessarily complicate the scenario.

NOTES

[1] Richard R. Fagen, *Politics and Communication*, Boston: Little, Brown, 1966, pp. 42-43.
[2] Walter Lippmann, *Public Opinion*. New York: Macmillan, 1954, p. 3.
[3] Canada, Parliament (Senate), *Report of the Special Committee on Mass Media*, vol. III. Ottawa: Information Canada, 1971, p. 5.
[4] T. Joseph Scanlon, "The Not So Mass Media: The Role of Individuals in Mass Communication," in *Journalism, Communication and the Law*, ed. G. Stuart Adam. Scarborough, Ontario: Prentice-Hall, 1976, p. 106.
[5] Dennis P. Forcese *et al.*, "The Methodology of a Crisis Survey." Paper presented to annual meeting of Canadian Anthropology-Sociology Association, St. John's, Nfld., June 1971, p. 4.
[6] T. Joseph Scanlon, "News Flow about Release of Kidnapped Diplomat Researched by J-students", *Journalism Educator*, 26. Spring 1971, pp. 35-38.

[7] V. O. Key, Jr., *Public Opinion and American Democracy*. New York: Knopf, 1961; Robert E. Lane, *Political Life*. Glencoe, Illinois: Free Press, 1959.

[8] For a summary of the general literature in this field, see Joseph T. Klapper, *The Effects of Mass Communication*. Glencoe, Illinois: The Free Press, 1960.

[9] This seems to be the charge of Thelma McCormack in "LaMarsh's Law and Order," *Canadian Forum*, August 1976, pp. 23-28.

[10] United States Surgeon General's Scientific Advisory Committee on Television and Social Behavior, *Television and Social Behavior: Technical Reports to the Committee*, 5 vols. Washington, D.C.: U.S. Government Printing Office, 1972. (In subsequent references this work will be referred to as *Television and Social Behavior*.)

[11] The basic, but by no means exhaustive, list of research can be found in *Television and Social Behavior*; the 13 volumes of reports from the United States National Commission on the Causes and Prevention of Violence, especially D. L. Lange, R. K. Baker, and S. J. Ball, *Mass Media and Violence: A Staff Report to the National Commission on the Causes and Prevention of Violence*, vol. 9. Washington, D.C.: U.S. Government Printing Office, 1969; U.S. National Advisory Commission on Civil Disorders, Report Washington, D.C.: U.S. Government Printing Office, 1968; Otto Larsen, ed., *Violence and the Mass Media*. New York: Harper and Row, 1968; Charles U. Daly, ed., *The Media and the Cities*. Chicago: University of Chicago Press, 1968.

[12] Benjamin D. Singer, *Communications in Canadian Society*. Toronto: Copp Clark, 1975, p. 241.

[13] Communiqué from The Royal Commission on Violence in the Communications Industry.

[14] H. L. Nieburg, *Political Violence: The Behavioral Process*. New York: St. Martin's Press, 1968, p. 5.

[15] See the discussion of political crime in Stephen Schafer, *The Political Criminal*. New York: The Free Press, 1974.

[16] Nieburg, *op. cit.*, p. 13.

[17] J. M. C. Torrance, "Cultural Factors and the Response of Government to Violence" (PhD thesis, York University, 1975).

[18] Kenneth McNaught, "Collective Violence in Canadian History: Some Problems of Definition and Research," *Proceedings of Workshop on Violence in Canadian Society*. Toronto: Centre of Criminology, University of Toronto, September 8-9, 1975, pp. 165-76.

[19] Comment about Joseph Howe by Chester Morten, as quoted in Kenneth McNaught, "Violence in Canadian History," in *Character and Circumstance: Essays in Honour of Donald G. Creighton*, ed. John S. Moir. Toronto: Macmillan, 1970, p. 4.

[20] *Ibid.*, p. 75.

[21] Stuart Jamieson, *Times of Troubles, Labour Unrest and Industrial Conflict in Canada 1900-1966*. Ottawa: Task Force on Labour Relations, 1968, p. 8.

[22] For an interesting look at some of these confrontations see William Perkins Bull, *From the Boyne to Brampton*. Toronto: George McLeod, 1930; and J. K. Johnson, "Colonel James Fitzgibbon and the Suppression of Irish Riots in Upper Canada," *Ontario History* 58. September 1966, pp. 139-55.

[23] See Kenneth McNaught, *Pelican History of Canada*. Harmondsworth, England: Penguin, 1969; and Hartwell Bowsfield, ed., *Louis Riel: Rebel of the Western Frontier or Victim of Politics and Prejudice?* Toronto: Copp Clark, 1969.

[24] See Michael S. Cross, "The Lumber Community of Upper Canada, 1815-1867," *Ontario History* 63. September 1971, pp. 177-90; and Michael S. Cross, "The Shiners War: Social Violence in the Ottawa Valley in the 1830's," *Canadian Historical Review* 54. March 1973, pp. 1-26.

[25] William Rutledge, quoted in W. Bull, *op. cit.*, p. 263.

[26] In the North Hastings by-election of 1856 in Ontario, the election expenses of one candidate were said to have included 6,000 no. 1 hickory axe handles and 60 gallons of good Canadian whiskey. The whiskey, needless to say, was for his supporters. *Ibid.*, p. 168. For examples of some of the election violence which has occurred in Canadian history, see Orlo Miller, *The Donnellys Must Die*. Toronto: Macmillan, 1962; E. C. Moulton, "Constitutional Crisis and Civil Strife in Newfoundland, February to November 1861," *Canadian Historical Review* 48. September 1967, pp. 251-72; and Brian J. Young, "The

Defeat of George Etienne Cartier in Montreal East in 1872," *Canadian Historical Review* 51. December 1970, pp. 386-406.

[27] Mason Wade, *The French Canadians* 1760-1945. Toronto: Macmillan, 1949, p. 599.

[28] W. Bull, *op. cit.*, p. 270.

[29] Robert J. Jackson, "Crisis Management and Policy Making: An Explanation of Theory and Research," in *The Dynamics of Public Policy*, ed. Richard Rose. London: Sage Publications, 1976.

[30] Daniel Latouche, "Violence, politique et crise dans la société québécoise," in *Essays On the Left: Essays in Honour of T. C. Douglas*, ed. Laurier LaPierre et al. Toronto: McClelland and Stewart, 1971, p. 181.

[31] Canadian labour history is full of incidents of the state being an active party to conflict rather than a neutral arbitrator. The 1930s are a monotonous recital of the use of local police and the RCMP by the state to serve the status quo and the vested interests of employers. This decade in Ontario was marked by the appearance of Hepburn's Hussars, a private regiment mobilized by Mitchell Hepburn, the Premier of Ontario, to break the General Motors Strike in Oshawa in 1937. Some 12 years later, Quebec witnessed a more forceful intimidation of labour when Premier Maurice Duplessis used the Quebec Provincial Police as a private Union Nationale army to destroy the strike at Asbestos. See Jamieson, *op. cit.*; and Desmond Morton, "Aid to the Civil Power, The Canadian Militia in support of Social Order," *Canadian Historical Review* 50. December 1970, pp. 407-35.

[32] McNaught, "Violence in Canadian History," *loc. cit.*, p. 99.

[33] Anthony M. Marcus, "Some Psychiatric and Sociological Aspects of Violence," *International Journal of Group Tensions*, 4. June 1974, p. 254.

[34] One of the major problems that one encounters in using most cross-national data on conflict is that they generally under-report intra-societal levels of conflict. This is due to the fact that most data is derived from such sources as the *New York Times Index*, *Keesing's Contemporary Archives*, and *Facts on File*—all of which have a tendency to concentrate only on major conflict events. For example, authoritative sources have listed 380 bombings, burnings, and depredations during the years 1961-62, and 58 incidents of FLQ terrorism. This does not compare favourably with the total above. See George Woodcock, *The Doukhobors*. Toronto: Oxford University Press, 1968, p. 350; and Marc Laurendeau, Les québécois violents: un ouvrage sur les causes et al rentabilité de la violence d'inspiration politique au Québec. Montreal: Les Editions du Boréal Express, 1974, pp. 213-22.

[35] For an interesting examination of the activities of this group, see Simma Holt, *Terror in the Name of God: The Story of the Sons of Freedom*. Toronto: McClelland and Stewart, 1964; and George Woodcock, *The Doukhobors*. Toronto: Oxford University Press, 1968.

[36] An effort was made to contact a major figure in each category for each of the seven incidents. As many of these events had taken place at least five years ago, an extensive telephone search was required.

[37] All interviews conducted in person were tape-recorded and form part of the general body of research. The limited number of interviews that were conducted by telephone were transcribed rather than tape-recorded.

[38] These narratives have been prepared using the coverage of each incident as provided by *The Globe and Mail*, *The Ottawa Citizen*, and *The Toronto Star*.

[39] *Report of the Royal Commission of Inquiry in Relation to the Conduct of the Public and the Metropolitan Toronto Police*, June 5, 1972, pp. 66-67.

[40] Communication from Cliff Lonsdale, Chief News Editor, Television, Canadian Broadcasting Corporation, November 8, 1976.

[41] Guidelines with respect to the release of information to the news media can be found in by-law no. 22, *Regulations Regarding the Government of the Metropolitan Toronto Police Force*, Section 453.

Chapter 14

VIOLENCE AND THE SOCIAL STRUCTURE AS REFLECTED IN CHILDREN'S BOOKS FROM 1850 TO 1970

Martha D. Huggins and Murray A. Straus

The relationship between violence in the media and violence in society was exam-
ined by a content analysis of five children's classics published at each five-year
interval. The analysis revealed no long-term trend.

Straus examined the manner in which violence both reflects and influences
society as a whole. He assumes what he calls a "dialectic approach" to the study
of literature, namely, children's classics and society. Literature reflects and
controls a society. In order to be accepted, it must express elements important in
the lives of the readers. Literature not only reflects our cultural heritage, it influ-
ences and to some extent directs our future. It should be noted that Straus is
American and writes of Children's Classics which are American as well. It
should also be noted that literature reviewed in this study dated from 1850 to
1970 and that children's classics read in that period were largely those of our
American neighbours. Straus points out that fictional violence increases during
wartime and decreases in times of economic depression. Contrary to reality,
fictional violence occurs outside family relationships. The message communi-
cated in the literature which children read is that physical violence is an appro-
priate act, given the motive and the script.

Of the highly industrialized nations of the world, the United States is clearly one of the most violent (Palmer, 1972:15). Many explanations have been offered for this phenomenon (Graham and Curr, 1969) and undoubtedly there are a number of factors which operate to maintain physical violence as a continuing aspect of American social structure. One of these factors which has been a subject of considerable controversy is the mass media.

There are those who argue that violence in the media reflects the violence of the society (discussed in Lynn, 1969). There are also those who argue that violence in the mass media and in sports serves as a safety valve, permitting aggressive drives to be drained off—the "drive discharge" and "catharsis" models (Bettleheim, 1967; Freud and Fenichel, 1945; Feshback and Singer, 1971; Lorenz, 1966). Both the "reflec-

---

tion" and the "catharsis" theories see violence in the media and in sports as having either a neutral or a neutralizing role. They therefore contrast sharply with theories which hold that violence in the media is part of the process of transmitting and encouraging violence. Among the latter are the "cultural pattern" theory of Sipes (1973), "social learning" theory (Bandura, 1973), and "general systems theory" (Straus, 1973).

The theoretical and methodological issues underlying this controversy are so complex that an eventual resolution will require, at the minimum, an accumulation and "triangulation" of evidence from a variety of investigations. Historical studies of a variety of cultural forms are particularly needed. A study of children's books therefore seemed desirable because: (1) Most of the available research on the mass media and violence focuses on television. Children's books, however, may be just as or more important. Our informal observation is that the impact of a book read by a child (or to a young child by a significant person such as a parent) is extremely powerful. (2) The availability of children's books going back over one hundred years enables a degree of historical depth which would not be possible if the focus had been on any of the other mass media.

THEORETICAL PERSPECTIVE

We assume what might be called a "dialectic" approach to the relation between literature and society. By this we mean that literary and other artistic productions reflect the culture and social organization of the society—especially its dominant strata—and, once in existence, serve to control and mold that culture and social structure. The artist must draw on the cultural heritage of his society and must appeal to important elements in the lives of his fellow citizens if the work is to be accepted. But at the same time, the work of an artist—once accepted—becomes a part of that cultural heritage and is one of many elements influencing and controlling what goes on in the society.

Some indication of the relationship between changes in society and changes in literary contents have been shown in previous content analysis studies. Straus and Houghton (1960), for example, found that appeals to the value of individual achievement expressed in a youth magazine declined slowly but steadily over the period 1925 to 1956. Their study helped to establish what many observers had noted, but for which there was no firm evidence at that time; namely, that society has been placing less emphasis on the value of individual achievement. Content analysis may also invalidate or question a widely held belief, as in Furstenberg's study (1966) of the presumed greater power attached to the husband-father role in 19th century America. But it is important to note that neither the studies cited nor the present study provide proof

(or even a modestly rigorous test) of our assumptions about the dialectical interplay of literature and society. This would require, for example,
time series data on *both* societal events and literary content and the use
of techniques such as lagged and cross-lagged correlation. Since we will
not be presenting such data, the present paper is not offered as a test of
these assumptions. Our aim is more modest. It is simply to present the
results of our historical analysis together with our interpretation of the
trends.

SPECIFIC OBJECTIVES

One of the purposes of the study is to determine if the level of interpersonal physical violence depicted in children's books has been increasing
or decreasing during the 120 year span from 1850 to 1970. No hypothesis
was posed about the direction of change because the available evidence
does not suggest any overall increase or decrease in the level of violence
in the United States during this period (Graham and Gurr, 1969).

The second objective is to gain information on the way society defines
and labels physical violence for its next generation. This will be done by
finding out the extent to which violence in literature is depicted as an
"expressive" act (i.e., carried out to cause pain or injury as an end in
itself) or an "instrumental" act (i.e., carried out to achieve some extrinsic
purpose). Similarly, the proportion of violent acts which are presented
by the authors as "legitimate" and "illegitimate" is an indication of how
society defines and gives evaluation labels to physical violence.

Finally, the content analysis was designed to obtain information on a
number of specific aspects of the statuses, roles, motives, and emotions
of the characters involved in violence; and the precipitating conditions,
outcomes, and consequences of violence. To the extent that violence in
literature mirrors violence in the society, then such information provides
insight into this important aspect of social structure. To the extent that
literature influences society, then such information gives important
clues to the "script" (Gagnon and Simon, 1973) for violent behavior
which is presented to children.[1]

SAMPLE AND METHOD

Sample

A three step sampling process was employed. The first step was the
identification of a universe of what, for want of a better term, can be
called "children's classics." By this is meant simply books recognized by
a literary elite of the society. We focused on this type of literature
because, as Marx suggested (1964) the ideas of the elite strata tend to be
the dominant and influential ideas in the society. From this perspective,
it is not the moral evaluations of the population at large which gives rise

to a group's definitions of reality, but mainly the evaluations of the dominant class (Parkin, 1971:42). On the basis of these assumptions, we sought out lists of recommended and esteemed children's books, for example, the "Notable Children's Books: 1965-1972" prepared by the Book Evaluation Committee of the American Library Association.[2] The universe compiled by this method consists of a chronologically ordered list of all books published between 1850 and 1970 which were included in any of the lists of recommended books.

The second step of the sampling process was designed to yield five books published in 1850, and five published every fifth year thereafter, i.e., in 1855, 1860, etc.; up to and including 1970, for a total of 125 books. For those years in which many books appeared, the sample of five was drawn by the use of random numbers. If there were less than five books in the sample year (as sometimes happened in the early years), books from the closest adjacent year were included, for example, a book published in 1856 is included in the sample for 1855. Since these are all "classic" or "recommended" books we were able to find 115 of the originally selected 125 books in nearby libraries. The missing ten books were replaced by a random selection from among the other books published during the appropriate year or years.

The third step in the sampling process consisted of using a table of random numbers to select fifteen different pages from each book. We followed this procedure to prevent longer books from disproportionately influencing the results. Our data then describe any act of interpersonal physical violence which occurred on one of the sampled pages in 125 "recommended" children's books published from 1850 through 1970.[3]

Coding Methods

The basic unit of analysis consists of an act of interpersonal violence, which we define as *the use, or threat to use, physical force for purposes of causing pain or injury to another person*. Each time such an act occurred on a sample page, a coding form was completed identifying the book in which it occurred and providing space to code the type of information identified a few paragraphs back. More specific information on each of these variables will be given when the relevant data is presented.[4]

FREQUENCY AND TRENDS IN VIOLENCE

Many observers of the American scene have suggested that America is a violent society. Palmer (1972:15), for example, contends that:

> Since its inception, the United States has been in the front ranks of violent societies. Born in revolution, wracked by civil war, involved in numerous wars, it has also the tradition of bloody rioting, homicide and unrest.

According to the statistics cited by Palmer, each year there are 15,000 criminal homicides, 35,000 suicides, 300,000 serious assaults and 50,000 forcible rapes, and these are said to be minimum estimates. Other authors (Straus, Gelles and Steinmetz, 1973) have suggested that these more extreme forms of physical force only "scratch the surface of a more widespread phenomenon of violence in the United States." For example, exploratory studies by Straus, *et al.* (1973) have brought out that physical fights between husband and wife have occurred in half to three quarters of all marriages, and physical fights between siblings are so common as to be almost universal. Is the violence that is so much a part of American life found in the literature for children?

The answer to this rhetorical question is a clear yes. More than three-quarters of the 15 page "book-segments" (75 per cent) had one or more violent episodes, with a grand total of 264 such episodes. The largest number of violent episodes in a single book was 10 (in *The Boys' King Arthur*). The mean number of violent acts per book-segment was 2.1. However, these data understate the actual incidence of violence in children's books by a considerable amount. This is because of our use of "book-segments" rather than entire books. Thus, the 75 per cent containing a violent episode might well have been close to 100 per cent if we had content analyzed every page of each book. Similarly, the figure of 2.1 violent episodes per book-segment means that a 50 page book is likely to include about seven violent acts and a 150 page book about 21 violent acts.

Modalities of Violence

The variety of methods used to cause physical pain or injury to others depicted in these stories covers most of those known to the human race. These ranged from merely shaking someone (two such incidents) to hitting and kicking (39 incidents), to torture (6 incidents), to burning a person (11 incidents), to stabbing (43 incidents), and shooting (40 incidents). The most frequent type of violence involved pouncing on someone, grabbing them forcefully or causing them to fall (66 incidents or 25 per cent of the total). However, such relatively mild forms of violence were outnumbered by about two to one by the more severe forms such as stabbing, shooting, torture, and burning.

This fact is also reflected in the results which came from classifying each act on the basis of the physical injury which resulted. It was found that 22 per cent of the 264 cases described a physical injury, and an additional 33 per cent described a violent death. It is clear then that we are not dealing with "kid stuff." The essentially adult nature of the violence portrayed in these books will be shown more clearly later.

Figure 1

Mean Number of Violent Acts Per 15 Pages by Year Published

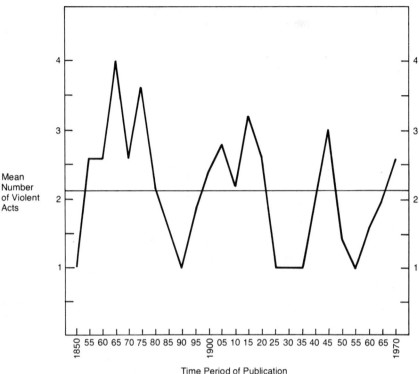

Time Period of Publication

Historical Trends

Figure 1 gives the mean number of violent acts per book-segment for each five year time period. This chart reveals no long term "secular" trend. This is consistent with the conclusions of Graham and Gurr (1969:628) concerning studies of actual rather than fictional violence. At the same time, there is a pattern to these highs and lows in fictional violence. The highs tend to occur when the society as a collectivity is engaged in violence, namely war. Thus, the highest points in Figure 1 occurred during the American Civil War (1865), World War I (1915), World War II (1945) and during the peak of the Viet Nam demonstrations in the United States (1970).[5]

The association of violence in children's books with the collective violence of the society is consistent with Henry and Short's suggestion (1954:102) that homicide rates go up during the periods of war. Also consistent with the Henry and Short study is the fact that three of the low points in Figure 1 coincide with periods of economic depression (the financial crisis of 1850, the depression of 1884, and the great depression of the 1930's). However, there were other depression periods in which violence did not decline.

FICTIONAL VIOLENCE AND SOCIAL CONTROL OF DEVIANCE

The data just presented suggests that violence is an integral part of "recommended" children's books. However, since our interest is not in children's literature *per se*, but in using children's books to gain a greater understanding of the role of violence in American society, from here on the focus will be on the nature of violence and its correlates. We have already presented one such correlate—the association of fictional violence with periods of national collective violence. This can be interpreted as a manifestation of the principle that artistic productions reflect the sociocultural matrix of the artist.

At the same time, it was suggested that fiction also serves a social molding and social control function, and it is to this issue that we now turn. Durkheim (1950) and Erickson (1966) hold that moral violations are singled out for punishment and public approbrium as a means of strengthening the commitment of the society to its moral norms. It may be that the high incidence of violence in these books occurs as a vehicle to expose and punish those who use violence. Several of our findings suggest that this is *not* the case. In fact, the implicit message is that violence is something which is effective in solving seemingly insolvable problems.

The first evidence for this interpretation is the large proportion of the violent incidents which were classified as "instrumental violence" (defined as the use of violence to force another to carry out, or to hinder carrying out, some act): Some 72 per cent were classified instrumental, compared to 28 per cent classified as "expressive violence" (defined as acts carried out to cause pain or injury as an end in itself).[6] So violence in these books is overwhelmingly portrayed as useful.

A second type of evidence against the idea that the high frequency of violence presented to children is a vehicle for conveying moral disapproval of violence is found in the outcomes for each act of instrumental violence. Of the 171 instrumental violent acts which could be coded for outcome, 60 per cent were depicted as achieving the desired outcome.

Third, we classified each violent act according to whether the author of the book portrayed it as legitimate or illegitimate. Of the 261 acts which could be coded on this dimension, 48 per cent were found to be presented in a way which indicated that they were socially legitimate acts.

Finally, additional insight is gained by cross-classifying the instrumentality and the legitimacy dimensions. This revealed that most of the acts of instrumental violence (55 per cent) were depicted as socially legitimate whereas "only" 28 per cent of the expressive acts of violence were depicted as legitimate. Thus, when violence is portrayed as a means of achievement, it tends to be given the stamp of social approval by the authors of these books. But when it is portrayed as an expression of emotion, it is depicted as illegitimate. We suggest that this relationship represents the combination of the historically important emphasis on achievement in American society coming together with the national heritage of violence.

Overall, in answer to the question of whether the high frequency of violence in children's books is part of the social control process restricting violence, the evidence suggests the opposite. Specifically, the violence in these stories is typically carried out to achieve some end or solve some problem, it is usually successful and, when used for such instrumental purposes, is most often depicted as socially legitimate. Thus, to the extent that children's books are a means of social control and socialization, they contribute to the institutionalization of violence.

A Vocabulary of Motives

If we accept the conclusion that these books are not part of a process by which the society exposes and labels violence as a deviant act and condemns its use, this does not rule out other social control and socialization functions in relation to violence. Just the opposite has already been suggested: that these books play an important role in labeling violence as legitimate and in teaching the socially appropriate occasions for its use.

As Bandura (1973) shows, aggression and violence are, for the most part, socially scripted behavior. Among the most important elements of the script for violence which are taught in these children's books are "motives" or reasons which communicate to the child the society's definition of the occasions on which violence may be used. Our initial analysis made use of 34 categories, some of which were pre-determined and the remainder added as we came across reasons which did not fit the categories. These 34 categories were then grouped under six major headings.

In designing the study, it was felt that violence in children's books would often be presented as a means of punishing or preventing socially disapproved behavior, especially on the part of children. To bend over backwards to allow this hunch a fair opportunity to be proved or disproved, we combined all coding categories which could be considered as violence used to enforce social norms or values. This included any indication that the violence was to enforce any legitimate authority, punishment for violating of aesthetic norms (table manners, etc.), lack of thrift, lying, stupidity, wickedness, greed, or the general triumph of good over evil. The "Social Control" category in Table 1 shows that all of these came to only eighteen per cent of the total number of violent acts.

Table 1
Most Common Reasons for Initiating Violence

Reason	% (N = 264)
Goal Blockage or Frustration	22
Emotional States	22
Social Control	18
Self-Defense	18
War	10
No Apparent Reason	7
Other	3

The low percentage of violence for purposes of social control does not come about because any other rationale dominates the portrayal of violence in these books. In fact, the two categories which share top place, "Goal Blockage or Frustration" and "Emotional States," include only about 22 per cent of the total cases each. The Goal Blockage category includes use of violence to remove an obstacle to attaining an end, for example, to remove a barrier to the satisfaction of hunger, to attack a person blocking attainment of a goal, to assert one's power in general. The other top category, "Emotional States," is violence motivated by some strong emotion such as shame or humiliation, revenge, or rage over having been insulted.

The Social Control, Self-Defense, and War categories combined come to 46 per cent of the motives or reasons for violence. Thus, the types of violence for which a moral case can be argued, are slightly less frequent than the combined frequency of violence to attain some other end, gratuitous violence, or violence as a result of an emotional state such as revenge, rage, or shame. Clearly, if these are morality tales, an important part of the moral code being communicated is that of the Old Testament. By and large, these conclusions apply over the entire period from 1850 to 1970. However, there was some tendency for the Social Control category to be more common prior to 1930. In addition, one of the sub-categories occurred only in the period 1955 to 1970: violence used to sanction the "stupidity" of others. Perhaps it is the increasing bureaucratization of modern society and the attendant demands for rationality, so well described by Weber (1964), which leads to the depiction in children's literature of "sheer stupidity" (irrationality) as one of the more serious moral transgressions of our time.

Capital Punishment

Another aspect of the vocabulary of motives contained in these books concerns violent death. The fact that someone was killed in 33 per cent of the book-segments (and could well be a higher percentage if entire books had been the unit of analysis) provides an opportunity to gain insight into the social definition of killing and death which is presented to children. An important aspect of this comes to light because the death often occurs as a result of the victim having committed some moral wrong or crime. That is, although the terms "capital punishment" and "death penalty" are not used, these books graphically describe use of the death penalty. And, as Bruno Bettleheim (1973) says about " . . . those great American folk heroes, *The Three Little Pigs*" (in which the big bad wolf is boiled alive for blowing the house down): "Children love the story . . . But the important lesson underlying the enjoyment and drama of the story equally captures their attention."[7]

We had the feeling that the books sampled contained many such examples of the implicit use of the death penalty. To check on this, the variable indicating death or other injury to the recipient of the violence was cross tabulated with the act on the part of the recipient which precipitated the violence. The results show that capital punishment (in the sense of a character who committed a moral transgression or crime being killed as a result of his or her bad actions) occurred in 22 per cent of the instances in which a character died. Since these are happenings of great dramatic intensity, what Bettleheim calls "the important lesson underlying the enjoyment and drama of the story" is likely to make a strong impression on the child's mind. It is not at all far fetched to suggest that this is part of the basis for the widespread and seemingly irrational commitment to the death penalty.

RACE, SEX, AND FAMILY

Race

The racial identification of violent characters in these books and their victims does not show any striking deviation from the composition of the U.S. population. Of the initiators of aggressive acts, 80 per cent were White, 4 per cent Black, 1 per cent Oriental, 7 per cent Indian, and 8 per cent "Other." The distribution for victims of these aggressive acts is approximately the same (79, 7, 2, 5, and 6 per cent).

Sex

Most of the violence in this sample of books took place between males. Ninety-one per cent of the aggressors were male, as were 86 per cent of the victims. So, violence in these books is overwhelmingly depicted as a male activity. At the same time, if the period covered by this study is one in which there has been a gradual movement toward sexual equality, then this should be reflected in a gradual increase in the proportion of female characters who engage in "masculine" acts of all types, including aggression. The lower line of Figure 2 indicates exactly such a trend.

Figure 2

Regression of Per Cent Adult Aggressors and Per Cent Female
Aggressors on Year of Publication

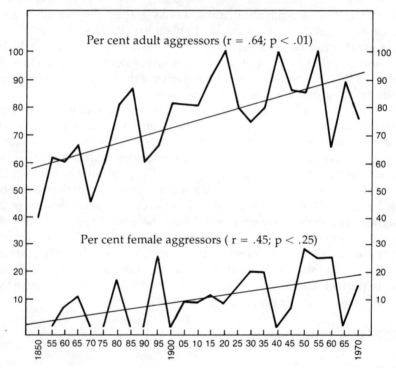

Although there is a clear upward secular trend in the proportion of women aggressors, there are also many ups and downs in Figure 2. Gecas (1972) did not find any trend over time in a study of adult magazine fiction and it may be that the observed "trend" reflects only a coincidence of random fluctuations. Arguing against this is the fact that the correlation of .45 has a probability of chance occurrence of less than .05 when based on 25 time periods. In addition, visual inspection of Figure 2 suggests a cyclical pattern within the secular trend. A spectral analysis was therefore carried out to determine if there is a dependable cyclical pattern with the time series. This revealed a cycle of four time periods (20 years) which accounts for 38 per cent of the variance.

In the absence of other information, it is difficult to interpret this 20 year cycle. One clue might be that a child reading these books at age ten will have reached maturity and perhaps be writing books of his or her own in 20 years. Authors of that generation might then tend to produce works of fiction which are influenced by the depiction of female characters in the books they had read as a child. But whatever the explanation, the fact that this cyclical pattern, in combination with the upward secular trend, accounts for 58 per cent of the variance in the proportion of female aggressors suggests that more than chance factors are shown in Figure 2. In addition, the increase in female aggressors is consistent with an increase in the proportion of women arrested for various crimes, especially violent crimes (Roberts, 1971).[8]

Adults Versus Children

On the basis of actual and potential injuriousness, and in terms of the purposes depicted, we suggested that the violent incidents in these books are not "kid stuff." The most direct evidence for this is the fact that 80 per cent of the initiators of violent acts were adults. Nor was this very frequently softened by use of an animal or other non-human characters since 80 per cent of the aggressors were human characters. So the image presented to children in these books is primarily of adults being physically violent. Moreover, the percentage of acts in which the aggressor is an adult has gradually been increasing over the 120 year span of this study, as shown by the upper line in Figure 2.

The preponderance of adult figures as physical aggressors is an instance of fiction which does *not* mirror reality. This is not because adults in our society are non-violent, but because children *are* violent. Pushing, shoving, hitting and physical fighting are more common among children than among adults, rather than the reverse as presented in these books.[9] It is possible that this reversal represents one of the myths concerning violence in middle class society, namely that violence is approved only when it is to achieve some socially worthy and valued end, such as punishment of wrongdoers, "preventative" air raids, etc.[10]

Family Violence

Another myth transmitted by these books is the notion that physical violence between family members is rare. There is a huge discrepancy between the normatively portrayed, idealized picture of the family as a group committed to non-violence between its members and what actually goes on. The available evidence suggests that violence rather than non-violence is typical of family relations (Steinmetz and Straus, 1973, 1974; Straus, Gelles and Steinmetz, 1973). In childhood, the persons most likely to strike a child are siblings and parents. In adulthood, the victim of assault or murder is more likely to be a family member than any other type of aggressor-victim relationship. There are informal norms, largely unverbalized, which make a marriage license also a hitting license (Gelles, 1973; Schultz, 1969).

The discrepancy between the idealized picture of the family as non-violent and the actual high frequency of physical violence between family members is clearly evident in these children's books. Ninety-one per cent of the violent incidents take place between persons who are *not* related. Two per cent of the violence was by fathers and two per cent by mothers. There was only a single incident of a husband hitting a wife and none in which the aggressor was a wife or grandparent. These findings are exactly parallel to those based on an informal search for instances of husband-wife violence in twenty novels for adults (Steinmetz and Straus, 1974).

The absence of husband-wife violence in adult fiction and the virtual absence of any intra-family violence in children's fiction calls for an explanation, especially since so much contemporary fiction attempts to depict reality in all its grim detail. These data do not permit an empirical answer. But we suggest that the following processes may be at work. First, is a *social control* process. The society does have a commitment to familial non-violence, even though these exist side by side with more covert norms permitting and encouraging intra-family violence (Straus, 1974). Thus, there is a tendency for the cultural representatives of the society to portray families in a way which will not encourage people to violate this norm. Second is a *social construction of reality* process. The society has an interest in having its members define the family as a place of love and gentleness rather than a place of violence because of the tremendous importance of securing commitment to the family as a social group. The myth of family non-violence is one of the many ways that the institution of the family is strengthened and supported. It helps encourage people to marry and to stay married despite the actual stresses of family interaction. Third, and most speculatively of all, the myth of family non-violence discourages probing into the aspect of the family by members of the intellectual elite, whether novelists or sociologists. We have all been brought up on this literature and read it as adults. And apparently, having accepted its basic premises, novelists avoid writing about physical violence between family members and sociologists have practiced "selective inattention" to research on this aspect of the family (Steinmetz and Straus, 1974).

SUMMARY AND CONCLUSIONS

Our study of 125 "classic" or "recommended" children's books published during the period from 1850 to 1970 revealed that not less than 75 per cent of the books described one or more actual or threatened violence. The true figure may be close to one hundred per cent because we studied only fifteen pages from each book. On the basis of these data, the typical children's book can be expected to have 2.1 violent incidents for every fifteen pages, in a third of which someone is killed. There is no tendency for this to have generally increased or decreased over the course of the 120 years studied. However, a marked tendency was found for inter-personal violence to be high during periods in which the society was engaged in the collective violence of war, and to be low during periods of economic difficulty.

It could be that the high incidence of violence in these stories occurs as a vehicle to express societal disapproval of violence. This would be indicated if violence tended to be presented as evil and if the perpetuators of violence were typically punished. The opposite seems to be the case. For example, "instrumental" violence is much more frequent than any other type and, in these stories, it most often resulted in the attainment of the aggressor's purpose.

Nevertheless, the evidence suggests that these books do have important socialization and social control functions. Assuming that aggression and violence are, for the most part, socially scripted behavior, these books provide scripts and role models through which generations of young Americans have learned how to behave violently. Among the elements of these complex scripts which must be learned are the type of motives that one can legitimately invoke to justify violence, the types of persons who can be violent and against whom violence is permissible, the level of socially acceptable injury, and the emotions which are appropriate or required on the part of the aggressor (for example, joy or remorse) and the victim (for example, rage, tears, or humiliation). All of these elements and their complex interrelations are depicted for the child in this sample of books.

Violence between family members is a major exception to the conclusion that children's books provide a script for violence. Almost no within-family violence was depicted, even though in the society generally, physical violence between family members is more common than between any other type of aggressor-victim relationship. This discrepancy was identified as reflecting the social mythology of familial non-violence. The myth of family non-violence, in turn reflects the high stake which society has in securing and maintaining commitment to the family as a social group.

266 / Violence and the Media

NOTES

This research was partly supported by NIMH grant number MH-15521 and by a summer fellowship awarded to the senior author by the University of New Hampshire Graduate School. We would like to express our appreciation to Paul Kaplan for his work on coding the 125 books, to Loren Cobb for assistance with the spectral analysis, and to Paul Drew, Arnold Linsky, Stuart Palmer, and Donna Peltz for valuable comments and criticisms on an earlier draft.

[1] Even assuming that literature does influence society, a content analysis by itself can only indicate the nature of the message. It does not provide data on either the intensity of the influence nor on the specific sectors of the population which are most, least, or not at all influenced. In a complex modern society both the intensity and the extent of influence are highly problematic for the same reasons that "functional integration" in general is problematic in such societies (Cohen, 1969: 151-156).

[2] The following supplementary material is available: (1) List of books analyzed. (2) List of book lists used to locate books for each of the five year periods. (3) Code and code sheet used in the content analysis.

[3] For 193 of the books we were able to obtain information on the approximate age-of-child range for which the book was considered suitable. We coded the midpoint of the age range for each book. These median ages ranged from five books with a recommended age of six years to one book for 16 year olds. The mean of the median ages was 10.8 years and the mode was 10 years (26 per cent of the cases).

[4] Although we coded only acts of interpersonal violence which occurred on the pages drawn in the sample, as much of the rest of the book was read as was necessary to determine such things as the social characteristics of the actors and their motives. A copy of the detailed content analysis code may be obtained from the National Auxiliary Publications Service. See footnote [2].

Two different coders carried out the content analysis. A test of the reliability of the content analysis procedure was carried out three days after the actual coding had begun. All books coded that day were done by both coders. For the 360 codings compared (10 books, 36 variables per book), there was an 87% agreement.

As a means of preventing differences between coders from influencing the trend analysis, each coder analyzed only two or three of the books for a given year. Therefore, possible "drift" or changes in coding standards which might have occurred as the coding proceeded would not bias the time series analysis.

[5] It happens that none of the books published during the peak years were "war stories". Also, as will be shown later, little of the violence portrayed in any of these books is the killing or wounding of an enemy soldier.

[6] Our coding categories were actually *primarily* expressive, versus *primarily* instrumental, since both components may be present. See Straus, Gelles and Steinmetz (1973) for a discussion of this and related issues in identifying types of violence. The coding of each act as either primarily instrumental or expressive was carried out separately from the coding of such variables as the *specific* reasons for initiating violence (see Table 1) and there is therefore a small discrepancy between the two variables. Specifically, if the two non-instrumental categories are subtracted from Table 1, this produces 71 rather than 72 per cent instrumental acts.

[7] Bettleheim was referring to teaching the work-ethic in this quotation but we feel it is equally applicable to the violence-ethic which is also presented.

[8] Of course, as those familiar with crime statistics realize, this does not necessarily mean that women have engaged in more violent acts. It is quite possible that changes in the social definition of women similar to those occurring in these children's books also characterize the perception of women by the police and public prosecutors, leading to a growth in arrest rate rather than a growth in incidence of actual violence.

[9] However, if the unit of violence is homicide and assaults which enter the official statistics, then the peak age is the middle to late 20's.

[10] Asserting that this is one way in which children's literature reflects ideal rather than actual social patterns points up the weakness of the "dialectical interplay" theory, namely that it is untestable: nothing can refute it. Correspondence can be claimed as an

instance of support of the "reflection" process and a discrepancy can be claimed as part of the "influence" process. This criticism also applies to the section which follows on "Family Violence." Nevertheless, as Cohen (1969:6) notes, untestable theories can have heuristic value. In the present case it sensitizes us to finding instances which, in our judgment, reflect one or the other of these two processes and to speculate about the underlying reasons. If these speculations point to important social processes, it can be said that the theory has heuristic value, and this would be especially so if it led to subsequent research to test these speculations.

REFERENCES

Bandura, Albert
1973   *Aggression: A Social Learning Analysis.* Englewood Cliffs: Prentice-Hall.
Bettleheim, Bruno
1973   "Bringing up children." *Ladies Home Journal* 10 (October): 32-ff.

———
1967   "Children should learn about violence." *Saturday Evening Post* 240 (March): 10-12.
Cohen, Percy S.
1969   *Modern Social Theory.* London: Heinemann Educational Books Ltd.
Durkheim, Emile
1950   *Rules of Sociological Method.* Glencoe: The Free Press.
Erikson, Kai
1966   *Wayward Puritans.* New York: John Wiley & Sons, Inc.
Fenichel, Otto
1945   *The Psychoanalytic Theory of Neurosis.* New York: Norton.
Feshback, Seymour and Robert D. Singer
1971   *Television and Aggression.* San Francisco: Jossey-Bass.
Furstenberg, Frank F., Jr.
1966   "The American family: a look backward." *American Sociological Review* 31 (June): 326-337.
Gagnon, John H. and William Simon
1973   *Sexual Conduct: The Social Sources of Human Sexuality.* Chicago: Aldine.
Gecas, Viktor
1972   "Motives and aggressive acts in popular fiction: sex and class differences." *American Journal of Sociology* 77 (January): 680-696.
Gelles, Richard J.
1974   *The Violent Home: A Study of Physical Aggression Between Husband and Wife.* Beverly Hills, California: Sage Publications.
Graham, Hugh Davis and Ted Robert Gurr (eds.)
1969   Violence in America: Historical and Comparative Perspectives. National Commission on the Causes and Prevention of Violence: Reports. Vol. I & II. Washington, D.C.: U.S. Government Printing Office.
Lorenz, Konrad
1966   *On Aggression.* New York: Harcourt, Brace Jovanovich, Inc.
Lynn, Kenneth
1969   "Violence in American literature and folk lore." Chapter 6 in Hugh D. Graham and Ted R. Gurr (eds.), Violence in America: Historical and Comparative Perspectives, Vol. I. Washington, D.C.: U.S. Government Printing Office.
Marx, Karl
1964   *The German Ideology.* Moscow: Progress Publishers.
Palmer, Stuart
1972   *The Violent Society.* New Haven, Conn.: College and University Press.

Parkin, Frank
1971   *Class Inequality and Political Order.* New York: Praeger Publishers.
Roberts, Steven V.
1971   "Crime rates of women up sharply over men's." *New York Times* (June 13):1, 72.
Sipes, Richard G.
1973   "War, sports and aggression: an empirical test of two rival theories." American Anthropologist 75(February):64-68.
Steinmetz, Suzanne K. and Murray A. Straus (eds.)
1974   *Violence in the Family.* New York: Dodd Mead & Co.
Straus, Murray A.
1973   "A general systems theory approach to a theory of violence between family members." Social Science Information, 12(June):105-125.
Straus, Murray A., Richard J. Gelles and Suzanne K. Steinmetz
1973   "Theories, methods, and controversies in the study of violence between family members." Paper read at the meeting of the American Sociological Association.
Straus, Murray A. and Lawrence J. Houghton
1960   "Achievement, affiliation, and co-operation values as clues to trends in American rural society, 1924-1958." Rural Sociology 25(December):394-403.
Weber, Max
1964   *The Theory of Social and Economic Organization.* New York: The Free Press.

Chapter 15

FROM PROFESSIONAL TO YOUTH HOCKEY VIOLENCE: THE ROLE OF THE MASS MEDIA

Michael D. Smith

The justification of a variety of injuries to children by children appears to support the position of Straus in the preceding chapter. In this chapter Smith analyzes data[1] from a population of Toronto males aged twelve to twenty-one and reports that hockey violence is learned in part through viewing professional hockey on television. Furthermore, young hockey players want to see at least as much and even more fighting in professional hockey.

There is no attempt made either to validate a theoretical premise or to demonstrate causality. Smith merely illustrates that his data appear to support observational learning theory. What is not clear in the literature on hockey violence to date is the manner in which hockey violence is learned and why it is repeated by some, yet ignored by others. In other words, theories of learning do not seem to explain the behaviour. Further research in this area, particularly among the youth of our nation, will be both a formidable and necessary task.

Violence and Canadian hockey have been synonymous since at least 1907 when a player was killed in a fight during a major league game. A court case resulted in that instance, but the accused was acquitted when it could not be proved that it was he, and not others, who had struck the fatal blow (Brent, 1975). In the following decades, violence came to be accepted as a legitimate part of the game (save for an occasional dissenting, generally unheeded voice). "Violence"—insofar as it refers to one person physically assaulting another in a manner proscribed by the official rules of hockey—was, literally, non- "violence." Most of today's players, professional and amateur, thoroughly socialized, do not consider fighting with fists "violent"; professionals claim that their games are generally not "violent." This highly charged term is reserved for only the most extreme and injurious of acts.[2]

Pressed, however, even the staunchest defenders of traditional

---

* This is a condensed version of a paper prepared for the Symposium, Contemporary Research on Youth Sports, Seattle, March, 1977. It is forthcoming in F. Smoll and R. Smith, *Contemporary Research on Youth Sports*, with the permission of Hemisphere Publishing Corporation, in which it is entitled "Social Learning of Violence in Minor Hockey."

hockey agree that fighting and all sorts of other illegal assaults are sufficiently commonplace in both professional and "professionalized" leagues as to be "normal." But, they argue, this behavior is a natural and inevitable by-product of (1) the speed, (2) the body-contact, and/or (3) the frustration inherent in the game. Besides, if fighting were not allowed, there would be more stick-work (that aggressiveness has to come out somehow). In any case, the argument goes, hockey is not for the faint of heart. It's a man's game. The transcript of the recent Ontario Government inquiry into violence in amateur hockey is replete with such testimony for the "defense" (McMurtry, 1974).

But beginning in the late 1960's, against a backdrop of public concern about violence in general, a series of dramatic events pushed hockey violence onto the front stage, making visible what for so long had been taken for granted.[3]

1969. The Green-Maki Fight. Boston's "Terrible" Ted Green and Wayne Maki of St. Louis engage in a stick duel during an exhibition game in Ottawa. Green is struck on the head by a full-swinging blow. His skull fractured, he almost dies. Both men are charged with assault causing bodily harm (the first prosecutions in Ontario since 1907); both are acquitted on grounds of self-defense. Later, naturally, Green writes a book about his experience.

1972. The First Canada-Russia Hockey Series. Amid accusations and counter-accusations of dirty play, Canada's truculent Bobby Clarke eliminates the Russian star, Kharmalov, from the remainder of the series with a blatant, two-handed stick-swipe across the ankle. Canada had exported hockey violence for years but never before quite so many millions of television viewers. Reaction in the mass media is mixed: some commentators glorify Clarke for his insatiable "desire"; others express embarrassment; a handful, shame.

1972. The Paul Smithers Case. Smithers, a seventeen-year-old black hockey player, engages an opposing player in a scuffle outside a Toronto arena following a raucous midget hockey game. Kicked in the groin, the other boy collapses, chokes on his own vomit, dies. Smithers is convicted of manslaughter and sentenced to six months in jail, a decision causing bitter and prolonged public controversy.

1974. The Hamilton-Bramalea Game. Players, officials, and spectators brawl throughout this Ontario Junior B playoff game in which 189 penalty minutes are assessed and five players and one team official are injured. Fourteen policemen finally quell the fighting. The Bramalea team withdraws from the playoffs and is promptly suspended by the Ontario Hockey Association, which finds no justification for the team's refusal to play "because the game was not as violent as many others in recent years" (McMurtry, 1974, p. 17).

1974. The Ontario Government Inquiry and Investigation into Violence in Amateur Hockey. Toronto lawyer, Bill McMurtry, is commissioned by the Province to inquire into the Hamilton-Bramalea debacle. In an extensive investigation, culminating in five days of public hearings and producing a 1,256 page transcript, McMurtry concludes that professional hockey is the number one cause of amateur hockey violence. His report is widely circulated and hotly debated.

1975. The Forbes-Boucha Case. Boston's Dave Forbes and Minnesota's Henry Boucha engage in a minor altercation for which both are penalized. Forbes threatens Boucha from the penalty box; then, leaving the box, lunges at Boucha, striking him near the right eye with the butt-end of his stick. Boucha falls to his knees, hands over face; Forbes jumps on his back, punching, until pulled off by another player. Boucha is taken to the hospital, where he receives twenty-five stitches and the first of what turns out to be several eye operations. Forbes is indicted for aggravated assault in Minnesota, but a hung jury results in his acquittal.

1975. The Maloney-Glennie Fight. Toronto Maple Leaf, Brian Glennie, bodychecks a Detroit player. In retaliation, Detroit's quick-fisted Dan Maloney knocks Glennie down with a forearm blow, punches him repeatedly, and allegedly bounces his head on the ice. Glennie goes to the hospital with a concussion and other injuries. Maloney is charged with assault causing bodily harm. Hung jury—charges dropped.

1976. The Jozdio-Tardiff Beating. In a World Hockey Association playoff game, Calgary Cowboys' Rick Jozdio administers a devastating beating to top scorer Marc Tadiff of the Quebec Nordique. Both benches empty, and a wild, half-hour melee ensues. Tardiff, unconscious, with a severe concussion and other injuries, is finished for the season. Quebec threatens to withdraw from the series unless (1) Jozdio is suspended for life, (2) the Calgary coach is suspended for the rest of the playoffs, (3) the League President (the official observer at this game) is fired or resigns. The demands are met in part, and the series continues. Jozdio is charged in Quebec with assault with intent to injure.

1976. The Philadelphia-Toronto Playoff. In a brawl-filled playoff contest in Toronto (resulting in a new Philadelphia penalty record) Toronto's Borje Salming, a Swedish non-fighter, is badly beaten by Philadelphia's Mel Bridgeman. Further brouhahas involving players, fans, and a policeman result in three Philadelphia players being charged—on orders of Ontario's Attorney General Roy McMurtry—with criminal offenses, from possession of a dangerous weapon (a hockey stick) to assaulting a police officer. The hockey establishment, insisting it can look after its own affairs, accuses McMurtry of headline-seeking. But considerable support for his actions is registered from other quarters.

A myriad other less sensational happenings have combined with the foregoing to keep hockey violence in the public consciousness: criminal indictments and convictions—of players, coaches, fans—at the minor level; refusals of teams to play against certain other teams for fear of serious injuries; revelation that professional organizations have deliberately merchandised violence; denunciations by a few highly respected players and coaches (Bobby Hull, Jacques Lapierriere) of what has come to be known as "goon" hockey. Even a Member of Parliament has urged the Canadian Government to condemn the NHL's "encouragement of excessive violence" (*Toronto Star*, 1976, Dec. 17:c3). Rule changes in professional and amateur hockey have occurred.

Yet reduction in overall levels of violence are not apparent, claims to the contrary notwithstanding. And despite increasingly perceptive and responsible commentary in the mass media, professional hockey's "cheerleaders" continue to fawn over the fighters and tough guys. The ethos of the professional game—the nullification of skill and ability by physical intimidation—remains entrenched from at least the midget level (age fifteen) up (Smith, 1977).

Professional hockey's influence on youth hockey seems to operate in two main ways. The first has to do with the structure of the "system." The fifty or so professional teams in North America depend upon junior leagues for a steady outflow of "talent." Most of the ablest amateur players are strongly motivated to advance through minor hockey to junior professional and thence to professional ranks. But en route, the number of available positions progressively diminishes, and competition for spots becomes increasingly intense. Professional standards determine who moves up and who does not. These include the willingness and ability to employ, and withstand, illegal physical coercion. Some performers with marginal playing skills are upwardly mobile— even as young as fourteen—primarily because they meet this criterion.[4]

Secondly, North Americans have been socialized into acceptance of professional hockey's values, chiefly through the communications media. Small wonder that minor hockey is the professional game in miniature when consumption of the latter has for decades been nothing short of voracious. Violence has been purveyed by an almost bewildering variety of means, blatantly, artfully, often no doubt unconsciously: attention-getting pictures of fights (sometimes without accompanying stories); radio and television "hot stove league" commentary (chuckles about Gordie Howe's legendary elbows or the hundreds of stitches in Ted Lindsay's face, a breathless report that a new penalty record has been set); the sheer amount of attention given "enforcers" and tough guys (Dave Schultz was a virtual media "star" in his Philadelphia heyday); newspaper and magazine pieces ("Detroit's Murderer's Row,"

"Hit Man"). In American cities full-page newspaper advertisements show Neanderthal-like, cartoon characters belaboring one another with hockey sticks. "Crunching No Nos are slashing, hooking, charging and high-sticking," one legend informs, "Don't let this happen to you; buy a season ticket to the Robins' 74-75 season. Watch it happen to others." The *Atlanta Flames' Yearbook* cover of a few years ago, sold in NHL arenas everywhere, featured an eye-catching scene of multi-player brawl. Highway billboards: San Diego's "Mad, Mean, Menacing, Major League Mariners." At least two feature movies whose major themes turn on hockey violence are currently in the making. "Blades and Brass," the award-winning National Film Board of Canada short, highlights body-thumping and bloody faces. The Better T Shirt Company manufactures shirts emblazoned with pictures of cartoon players gleefully engaging in various dirty-work ("Hooking," "Charging," the captions read). Even the Topps Chewing Gum people are in the violence business. Consider the following, not atypical bubble gum card biography: "André is one of the roughest players in the NHL. Opponents have learned to keep their heads up when he is on the ice. André won't score many goals, but he's a handy guy to have around when the going gets tough." Whatever their form, the media messages are clear: violence and hockey go together.

Young performers, also, may learn specific behaviors from professional hockey, directly and through the mass media. The conditions for observational learning and modelling (i.e., Bandura's social learning) via TV are almost laboratory-perfect: models who get money and attention for aggressive acts, observers' expectations of rewards for the same behavior, close similarity between the social situations portrayed on the screen and subsequently encountered directly by observers.[5]

Yet the association between violence in sport as portrayed by the communications industry and violence in youth sport has gone virtually unexamined by researchers. It receives to my knowledge no mention in the voluminous outpourings of the U.S. Violence and Media Task Force Report of the National Commission on the Causes and Prevention of Violence (Baker and Ball, 1969) or in the Surgeon General's Report on Television and Social Behavior (1972). The Interim Report of the Ontario Royal Commission on Violence in the Communications Industry (1976, p. 16) manages a seven line statement on the current state of knowledge—and a plea for research.

In the remainder of this paper, some mainly descriptive data are presented on the relationship between professional and minor hockey violence, particularly as mediated by television. The theoretical perspective is that of observational learning. Young players and non-players are compared on the extent of their consumption of the professional game and the amount and kinds of violence they claim to have learned—and for the players, practised. Attitudes regarding the role of violence in professional hockey are examined.

METHOD

The data are from a 1976 survey of amateur hockey violence. Subjects came from three populations of Toronto males, aged twelve to twenty-one: (1) "select" or "allstar" hockey players, (2) house-league hockey players, (3) non-hockey players. From the first two populations, eight hockey organizations were selected (six select and two house-league); the organizations were then stratified by age-graded playing division. Including the non-players, who were not subdivided, thirty-four strata were thus constructed.

The sampling frame consisted of all registered players in the organizations. Using simple random sampling without replacement, 740 selections were made, proportionately from each strata. Selection probabilities ranged from .33 to .45. Removing non-respondents and foreign elements (goaltenders, players released, traded, injured, or for some other reason not playing at least half a season) resulted in a response rate of 88 per cent; the actual number of players successfully interviewed was 551, a 74 per cent completion rate. Weighting, to correct for unequal selection probabilities, resulted in a final weighted sample of 604. One hundred and eighty non-players, from six schools, were sampled with certainty, yielding response and completion rates of 96 and 84 per cent, and 153 interviews.

Following a pretest in late 1975, the survey was carried out during April, 1976, immediately after the hockey season. Professionals employed by York University's Survey Research Centre conducted the interviews, which averaged one hour in length and took place, in most cases, in the interviewees' homes.

DATA

The pattern of data regarding players' and non-players' consumption of professional hockey, directly and via the mass media, is briefly as follows. Tickets to major professional hockey in Toronto are both scarce and expensive first of all; as one might predict attendance was infrequent. The majority of players (65 per cent) and non-players (88 per cent) saw games live only two or three times a year, at best. Professional hockey is consumed chiefly through the newspaper, it seems. Table 1 shows that approximately 53 per cent of the players and 39 per cent of the non-players did so on a daily basis; and over 80 per cent and 70 per cent at least once a week. TV was the next most popular medium, almost 70 per cent of the players and 60 per cent of the non-players watching once a week or more. Magazines and books ranked third. In each case, players clearly out-consumed their non-playing counterparts. Consumption also increased slightly in the player sample among older and select (as opposed to house-league) boys.

When respondents were asked if they had ever "learned anything" from watching professional hockey, almost 90 per cent of the players and almost 80 per cent of the non-players replied affirmatively. As for the learning of violence, specifically, over half of each group responded yes to the question: "Have you ever learned how to hit another player illegally in any way from watching professional hockey?" A selection of descriptions of what was learned appears in Table 2. But learning is not necessarily doing. Table 3 shows frequency of performance, among players, of the illegal tactics acquired.

Table 1
How Often Do You Read About Professional Hockey in the Newspaper (in per cent)?

	Frequency						
Respondents	*Daily*	*2-3 week*	*Once week*	*2-3 month*	*Once month*	*2-3 year*	*Never*
Players	53.4	18.5	11.6	5.7	4.5	1.7	4.7
Non-players	39.5	17.8	13.8	6.6	5.9	3.3	13.2
Totals %	50.6	18.3	12.1	5.8	4.8	2.0	6.4
N	381	138	91	44	36	15	48

$X^2 = 21.21$ Significance = .002

How Often Do You Watch Professional Hockey on TV (in per cent)?

	Frequency					
Respondents	*2-3 week*	*Once week*	*2-3 month*	*Once month*	*2-3 year*	*Never*
Players	39.6	30.6	17.5	7.2	3.3	1.8
Non-players	43.4	17.1	17.1	12.5	7.9	2.0
Totals %	40.4	27.9	17.4	8.2	4.2	1.9
N	304	210	131	62	32	14

$X^2 = 18.57$ Significance = .002

Table 2
Descriptions of Illegal Hitting Learned from Watching Professional Hockey

I learned spearing and butt-ending.

You sort of go on your side like turning a corner and trip him with a skate.

Charging. You skate towards another guy who doesn't have the puck and knock him down. Or coming up from behind and knocking him down.

Sneaky elbows, little choppy slashes Bobby Clarke style.

Hitting at weak points with the stick, say at the back of the legs.

Getting a guy from behind. Getting a guy in the corner and giving him an elbow.

Coming up from behind and using your stick to hit the back of his skates and trip him.

Butt-end, spearing, slashing, high sticking, elbow in the head.

Put the elbow just a bit up and get him in the gut with your stick.

Wrap your arms over his shoulder from the back and tear his arms and stick. Step forward and stick your foot in front of his foot.

Along the boards, if a player is coming along you angle him off by starting with your shoulder then bring up your elbow.

The way you "bug" in front of the net.

Clipping. Taking the guy's feet out by sliding underneath.

Sticking the stick between their legs. Tripping as they go into the boards.

I've seen it and use it: when you check a guy, elbow him. If you get in a corner you can hook or spear him without getting caught.

Giving him a shot in the face as he is coming up to you. The ref can't see the butt-ends.

Dirty tricks—butt-ending, spearing—without the referee seeing them.

How to trip properly.

Like Gordie Howe, butt-ends when the ref isn't looking.

To what degree do consumers accept the "goon" or "enforcer" in professional hockey? The great majority of players (76%) and non-players (88%) felt that a performer "who gets paid to beat up the other guys" does not deserve his high salary. At least two reasons could account for this: respondents' disapproval of the role on moral, aesthetic, or like grounds; and/or their belief that it is more hindrance than help in a team's ultimate goal: winning games. The data suggest the former reason probably figured strongly, because almost half the respondents stated that a player of this type probably does help his team to win.

The majority view aside, a significant number of players—close to one-fifth—expressed support for so-called "goon hockey" at the professional level. These advocates tend to be found at the older and select levels where boys are probably more completely socialized into the culture of the game.

Table 4 has to do with the general issue of fighting in professional hockey. Most respondents wanted less; yes 36.1 per cent of the players wanted about the same amount (which is to say, a lot). Again this support varied positively, though not dramatically, with age and select hockey background.[6]

Table 3
How Many Times This Season Have You Actually Hit Another Player
in This Way (in per cent)?

5 or more		3-4		1-2		Never		DK		Inapp.	
%	N	%	N	%	N	%	N	%	N	%	N
15.0	90	6.0	36	15.9	96	20.5	124	0.21	1	42.5	257

Table 4
Regarding the Amount of Fighting in Professional Hockey This Year,
Would You Like to See More, About the Same Amount, or Less Fighting
(in per cent)?

	Amount of Fighting				
Respondents	More	About same	Less		
Players	2.9	36.1	61.0		
Non-players	0.7	8.2	86.8		
Totals %	2.4	31.3	66.3		
N	18	233	493		

$X^2 = 35.65$ Significance $= .000$ Missing Observations $= 9$

House-league	4.3	28.6	67.1	54.3	322
Select	1.1	45.0	53.9	45.7	271
Totals %	2.9	36.1	61.0	100.0	
N	17	214	362		593

$X^2 = 20.63$ Significance $= .000$ Missing Observations $= 11$

12-13 yrs.	2.4	23.8	73.8	27.7	206
14-15 yrs.	0.9	29.3	69.8	31.2	232
16-17 yrs.	5.6	37.6	56.7	23.9	178
18-21 yrs.	0.8	38.3	60.9	17.2	128
Totals %	2.4	31.3	66.3	100.0	
N	18	233	493		744

$X^2 = 24.74$ Significance $= .000$ Missing Observations $= 9$
Gamma $= -0.19$

SUMMARY AND CONCLUSION

1. A majority of the 704 youth interviewed consumed professional hockey once a week or more through newspaper and TV. Live attendance and consumption via books and magazines were considerably less frequent. Players were generally greater consumers than non-players.

2. Most respondents reported learning various skills and orientations from viewing professional hockey, including methods of illegal hitting, some of which were described in colorful detail. A greater percentage of players than non-players reported general learning; approximately equal percentages learned illegal hitting. No differences by age or level of competition were found in the player samples.

3. Among players who learned illegal tactics, 60 per cent stated that they had used one or more of the tactics at least once or twice during the season.

4. Only a small minority of respondents (but more players than non-players) apparently supported the enforcer role in professional hockey, being of the opinion that those who filled it deserved their high salaries.

5. A larger minority of both groups, again more players than non-players, wanted about the same amount or more fighting in the professional game.

6. Affirmation of the enforcer role and of fighting in general was strongest among older and select team players.

I have argued that mass media portrayals of violence in professional hockey have contributed to the spread of a social climate in youth hockey conducive to violence. The findings indicate also that specific acts of assault are learned via observation of professional hockey, and subsequently performed. Survey research methods, of course, do not unravel causality, and the present data can be taken as supportive of more than one explanation of media effects; but the data seem to make most sense in the light of observational learning theory. My guess is that media presentations of professional hockey provide observers with blueprints for violent behavior in their own games.

NOTES

[1] This research was funded by Canada Council Grant S-74-1693.
[2] Subjective meanings imputed to the term vary widely, of course (see Blumenthal *et al.*, 1972, pp. 72-95, for example). The statements regarding players' usage were derived from interviews with approximately 100 NHL performers and dozens of amateurs conducted during a field work phase of the present research.

[3] An issue generating much popular attention is whether violence in sport has increased, decreased, or remained constant over the decades. Certainly it is not a recent phenomenon. There were public outcries and official reform actions in boxing, wrestling, football, and hockey early in the century. The question becomes somewhat irrelevant, however, in light of two considerations. First, the transformation of sport to industry and its attendant exposure via the electronic media gives rise to different implications for the different eras (Hallowell and Meshbesher, 1976). Second, the emergent character of social problems renders comparative data on incidence spurious (even provided such data were available); social problems are what people say and think they are at any given point in time; indeed, they tend to have a three-stage career as Hubbard, DeFleur and DeFleur, (1975, p. 23) point out. Initially, there is an "emergent" stage. Persons or groups perceiving a social condition as problematic lobby for attention and support from politicians, agencies, the media, and others. Public awareness grows, and shared definitions about the condition begin to emerge. Judgements are made that corrective steps should be taken; ameliorative action is urged. Given enough recognition, the problem becomes legitimized. During the "legitimization" stage widespread consensus is reached that people ought to be concerned about the condition. If official social machinery comes into being for long term alleviation of the problem, then the "institutionalization" stage has been reached. At this point, bureaucratic interests, whose careers depend upon continuance of the problem, may generate information that it is indeed still present. In this way, social problems become more or less embedded in a culture.

[4] For sociological studies of violence in professional hockey see Faulkner (1973, 1974); on minor hockey, Smith (1974a, 1974b, 1975, 1977) and Vaz (1976; Vaz and Thomas, 1974). See Smith (1978) regarding the linkage between individual and collective violence in hockey and other sports.

[5] Reviews of this theory and the research it has generated can be found in Bandura (1973), Bandura and Walters (1964), and in the Surgeon General's Report (1972; especially volume 2). In a critique, Ellis (1977) argues that this and the other principal social psychological paradigms of the effects of media violence on violence in society are of limited utility because they are designed to explain impulsive rather than instrumental violence, and it is the latter that citizens are likely to experience. More than this, the dominance of these paradigms has diverted attention from the connection between media violence and instrumental violence in society.

It appears that most hockey violence is of the instrumental type (Smith, 1974b). It can be accommodated within the observational learning paradigm, however, by shifting the latter's emphasis from learning to performing. That learning of aggressive acts from live or media-mediated models occurs appears solidly established. What remains unclear are the variables that determine whether or not aggressive behavior in the observer follows. Bandura states that this varies with the observer's perceptions of the rewards and punishments given to the model and/or likely to be given his own matching behavior, but then pays very little attention to these response consequences for the observer. Ellis maintains that the "pay-off structure" for the observer is crucial in coming to understand instrumental aggression: "What happens to us after we behave aggressively is a critical influence on the likelihood that we will behave aggressively in the future." The present research does not deal directly with this notion, but previous work reveals the existence in hockey of a social climate in which violence is rewarded increasingly as boys get older and in select as opposed to house-leagues (Smith, 1975; Vaz, 1976). The point is: observational learning theory is capable of handling some kinds of instrumental aggression.

The theory becomes sociological when it includes what DeFleur and Rokeach (1975, pp. 226-227) call the social categories and/or social relations perspectives. The latter might consider, for instance, the extent to which observers encounter real interactional situations similar to those presented on TV (thereby increasing the likelihood that they will behave aggressively). The social categories perspective might focus on why boys, say, behave more aggressively than girls, even though girls learn as much aggression from watching violent TV programs. This would be explained by reference to sex differences in conduct norms (see also Goranson, 1969, pp. 395-413).

[6] See the original version of this paper for detailed tabular data on the foregoing findings.

REFERENCES

Baker, R. and Ball, S. J.
1969   *Violence and the Media*. Washington, D.C.: United States Government
            Printing Office.
Bandura, A.
1973   *Aggression: A Social Learning Analysis*. Englewood Cliffs, New Jersey: Pren-
            tice-Hall.
Bandura, A. and Walters, R. M.
1964   *Social Learning and Personality Development*. New York: Holt Rhinehart and
            Winston.
Blumenthal, M. D., Kahn, R. L., Andrews, F. M. and Head, K. B.
1972   *Justifying Violence: Attitudes of American Men*. University of Michigan: Insti-
            tute for Social Research.
Brent, A. S.
1975   "The criminal code governs the hockey rink too!" *Crown's Newsletter*,
            June, 8-13.
DeFleur, M. L. and Ball-Rokeach, S. J.
1975   *Theories of Mass Communication*. New York: David McKay.
Ellis, D.
1977   Mass Media effects on violence in society. Unpublished paper. Depart-
            ment of Sociology, York University.
Faulkner, R. R.
1974   "Making violence by doing work: selves, situations, and the world of
            professional hockey." *Sociology of Work and Occupations*, 1, 288-312.

1973   "On respect and retribution: toward an ethnography of violence." *Sociolo-
            gical Symposium*, 9, 19-36.
Goranson, R.
1969   A review of the recent literature. Pp. 395-413 in R. Baker and S. J. Ball
            (eds.), *Violence and the Media*. Washington, D.C. United States Govern-
            ment Printing Office.
Hallowell, L. and Meshbesher, R. I.
1976   "Sport violence and the criminal law: a socio-legal viewpoint," *Trial*.
            American Trial Lawyers Association.
Hubbard, J. C., DeFleur, M. L. and DeFleur, L. B.
1975   Mass media influences on public conceptions of social problems. *Social
            Problems*, 23, 23-24.
La Marsh, J., Beaulieu, L. and Young, S.
1976   Interim Report of the Royal Commission on Violence in the Communica-
            tions Industry. Ontario Government Printing Office.
McMurtry, W. R.
1974   Inquiry and Investigation into Violence in Amateur Hockey. Report to the
            Honourable R. Brunelle, Ontario Minister of Community and Social
            Services. Toronto: Ontario Government Bookstore.
Smith, M. D.
1978   (Forthcoming). "Precipitants of Crowd Outbursts." *Sociological Inquiry*.

1977   "Hockey Violence: a test of the subculture of violence thesis." Paper
            prepared for presentation at the Southern Sociological Association
            Annual Meetings, Atlanta, March.

1975   "The legitimation of violence: hockey players' perceptions of their refer-
            ence groups' sanctions for assault." *Canadian Review of Sociology and
            Anthropology*, 12, 72-80.

1974a.   "Significant others' influence on the assaultive behaviour of young
            hockey players." *International Review of Sport Sociology*, 3-4, 45-56.

1974b.   "Violence in sport: a sociological perspective." *Sportwissenschaft*, 4, 164-173.

Television and Growing Up: The impact of Televised Violence
    1972   Report to the Surgeon General, United States Public Health Service, from the Surgeon General's Scientific Advisory Committee on Television and Social Behavior. Washington, D.C.: Government Printing Office.

Vaz, E.
    1972   "The culture of young hockey players: some initial observations." P. 211-215 in A. Yiannakis, T. D. McIntyre, M. J. Mclnick, and D. P. Hart, (eds), *Sport Sociology: Contemporary Themes*. Dubuque, Iowa: Kendall-Hunt.

Vaz, E. and Thomas, D.
    1974   "What price victory? an analysis of minor hockey league players' attitudes towards winning." *International Review of Sport Sociology*, 2, 33-53.

SUBJECT INDEX

Aggression
   as irrational conduct, 14
   as natural political behaviour, 221
   as protection, 14
   as release of tension, 26
   frustration-agression hypothesis, 106, 109
Anger, as moral indignation, 56
Assault
   Criminal Code of Canada definition, 171
Attributions of violence, 55-56

Battered children
   and Canadian law, 97-100
   a case history, 112-126
   detection of injuries, 94
   historical perspective, 95-7
   Ontario rates, 94
   pro-physical norms, 83, 103-4
Battering parents
   and the lay therapist, 112-126
   and Parents Anonymous, 104
   and social deprivation, 102
   as emotionally handicapped, 105-107
   identification of, 124
Battered wives
   commitment to marriage, 84-5
   education and occupation, 84
   external constraint, 87
   previous experience with, 82-3
   severity and frequency, 81
Biology and criminality, 42
Biological theories of violence, 5-7

Capital punishment
   social definition presented to children, 261
Children
   expressions of fear and loneliness, 130
   expressions of violence, 130, 263
   rejection and physical abuse, 130